HD6058 .B65
Convers

P9-ARY-628

DATE DUE

HIGHSMITH 45-220

CONVE

CONVERSATIONS

Working Women Talk About Doing a "Man's Job"

edited by

Terry Wetherby

Les Femmes
Millbrae, California

Cover design and illustration by Betsy Bruno

Published by LES FEMMES PUBLISHING, 231 Adrian Road,
Millbrae, California 94030

First printing: June, 1977
Manufactured in the United States of America

3 4 5 6 7 8 - 84 83 82 81 80 79

Library of Congress Cataloging in Publication Data

Main entry under title:
Conversations

    1.   Women—Employment—United   States.   I.   Wetherby,
Terry.
HD6058.B65   331.4'0973   76-53343
ISBN 0-89087-922-2

Table of Contents

These conversations were held in 1976 with real flesh and blood women working in the United States. The interviews were tape recorded face-to-face or by telephone. Although portions have been deleted and sections juggled for transition, each woman represented in this book speaks for herself.

Susan Borger, Judith McKelvey, and Patricia Ann Straat chose to edit and rewrite sections of their interviews; as a result, their words in this book must not be regarded as totally spontaneous. In the remaining cases, the interviews of CONVERSATIONS are in keeping with the original dialogues as much as punctuation, readability, a few negligible interviewee changes, publisher's dictates, and the human ear allow.

photo credits:

Susan Borger, Thelma Carthen, Mary Ewing, Nancy Johnsen, and Sophie Maxwell by Mario Castillo;
Donna Garrett by Columbia Pictures Industries, Inc. © 1976;
Shirley Muldowney by Shirley Muldowney Enterprises;
Kay Holloway by *Fresno Bee;*
Marcia Carsey by American Broadcasting Company, © 1976;
Judy Jensen by George Laycock;
Doris Tarrant by Cress Studios.

Acknowledgments

A special acknowledgment of gratitude to those women who so generously granted interviews, including those absent from these pages due to space limitations and publisher decisions.

The following persons have been of particular help along the way:

Phyllis Butler, former editor of Les Femmes, who originated and encouraged the concept of BLOCKBUSTERS, the original title of CONVERSATIONS;

Mario Castillo, photographer;

Studs Terkel, for his book WORKING;

Evelyn Wetherby, Middletown, Kentucky;

Mike Guthrie, Middletown, Kentucky;

Bill Svabek, John O'Connell Community College;

Elyse Mayberry, Twentieth Century Fox;

Jayne Townsend, San Francisco Chapter, National Organization for Women;

Hildur Ashby, Shelton, Washington;

Laurie Malmstrom, KTVX-tv, Salt Lake City;

Tom Gannon, *Western Banker;*

Mike Delaney, American Bankers Association.

To these and all persons who aided through letters, clippings, introductions, and chance remarks, I extend my sincere thanks.

Introduction

One of this society's most destructive systems of inequities has been predicated on the belief that women are fit only for narrow, stereotypic roles. Institutions reinforce and sustain this belief. Some religions' "sacred" writs declare it so. Schools flood the brains of the nation's young with sex-biased teachings, instructional materials, and counseling. In the meantime, physical education programs "develop" young women into weaklings. Almost everywhere—for females—the same limited, sex-appropriate behavior is prescribed by parents, peers, norms.

One major (and obvious) result of this system is that career options of adult women in the United States are sorely restricted. Socially, religiously, educationally, and—most important—psychologically, the vast majority of women are not free to establish goals and develop careers outside accepted "female roles." Few tradition-breaking female role-models are to be found.

This book, being about women engaged in traditionally male occupations, is about rugged individualism and self-determination. The collective consciousness of the nation creeps toward change; women, like those presented in the following pages, pioneer the way.

These 22 interviews, chosen from more than 30, provide information about the existence and the absence of discrimination, and about discouragement and encouragement in often unlikely places. Although the accounts, personalities, backgrounds, motivations, and goals of these women vary radically, their common denominators are a strong self-image, hard work, and a culture which casts them as oddities.

Who these trailblazers really are, how their lives have led them to knock at the doors of traditionally male workplaces, and to enter, what they experience once inside: these are the areas into which this book sheds light.

In my own experience, with a masters degree in creative writing and no satisfactory source of income, I opted to learn a trade. I wanted a skill which paid well and had no destructive impact on the primary pursuit of my life—my writing. After attending a public technical school sporadically for more than a year, I am now employed as a welder at Triple A Shipyard in San Francisco. On the job and in my union, Boilermakers Local 6, I have enjoyed total equality and a heartening sense of camaraderie with my peers; there has not been a hint of discrimination.

Some of the women of *Conversations* have not been so fortunate; others have been greatly encouraged by men along the way. Whatever their experience, these female individuals have made inroads. Behind them, employment doors are a little more open; around them, attitudes are more positive toward sexual desegregation of occupations.

Ingrained attitudes toward sex-appropriate roles in the workplace have done inestimable harm to millions of lifetimes. It is my hope that *Conversations* will serve to eradicate some of the fears, myths, and ignorance still prevalent in our age.

Terry Wetherby
San Francisco

CONVERSATIONS

Nancy Kaye Andersen

To handle a knife is like learning to write. Cutting's an art, definitely.

After only a month as an Alpha Beta supermarket bagger, Nancy Andersen was selected to be a butcher. Andersen, then nineteen, took the opportunity and "didn't know what" she was getting into. She entered a world of razor-sharp knives, slicers, and hamburger mixers as big as stoves—a world where the temperature is constantly fixed at 51 degrees Farenheit and *all* her peers are men.

At the time of this interview, Andersen lived at home with her parents in Penngrove, California, a town of 300 people, "one gas station, two bars, and one grocery." Andersen had been with Alpha Beta a little more than a year.

I'm a journeyman meatcutter at Alpha Beta in Santa Rosa. I break and process meat—pork, veal, lamb, beef, fish and poultry—breaking it down from whole carcass into steaks and roasts. Processing is just breaking into certain cuts of beef— your rounds, your chucks, and the different varieties. Then you're steaking things into counter form.

If I had been a butcher ten or twenty years ago, I would have to do everything. But nowadays, Alpha Beta, for example, has a main breaking plant in Colorado. We receive the meat in cryovac [broken down] form. It's brought in by train and then to our store by truck. We get whole rounds, chucks, all your short ribs.

All of the meat is fresh. The unions haven't allowed the meat to come in frozen yet, so we can keep our jobs. Everything now has to be in fresh form for fresh meat case. If it were frozen,

1

the meat-cutting would all be done in a centralized place. They think that will come within five years. It will cut down on a *lot* of jobs. Some people think that our jobs can't last too long.

Physically, your work must be hard.

Yeah, it's hard. But no harder for me than it is for a lot of the guys. Your lifting is hard mainly. Your boxes of pork rinds weigh about 75, sometimes 80 pounds. And you're expected to lift.

Did you find this difficult at first?

Oh yeah! [Laughs.] But eventually you just get so you can handle it. You learn how to pick things up. Most of the guys are really cooperative and everybody works together. You're never working alone, except at night.

How did you become a meatcutter?

I worked in Alpha Beta first as a courtesy clerk—a bagger. Then the store supervisor asked me if I'd be interested in taking the job; there was an opening.

Why did they ask you?

They felt that I was qualified for the job. I worked a little harder and had a little more initiative than other people did, I guess. I was willing.

There are fields opening. And companies are under pressure to get women into these kind of jobs. Some women haven't been successful. I think a lot of the guys have made it hard for them. A lot of guys feel that women are taking jobs away from men that have families. I'm single and I'm making as much as guys that support families with four kids. [Andersen's first job was part-time work in a real estate office during high school; her salary was minimum wage. She next worked at Beneficial Finance doing "secretarial work." Her beginning salary: minimum wage. Because Andersen wanted a "different kind of work," she applied at Alpha Beta.]

Was there opposition to your becoming a meatcutter?

When Gregg, the store supervisor, said he wanted me to be a meatcutter, everybody said, "Oh. *No way!*" They said it was really crazy and that sort of thing. But it wasn't.

I went to Alpha Beta's main plant and took tests—a math

test, a coordination test and that sort of thing. And then the following week I started working.

You get familiar with all of the machinery at first . . . the saws, the grinding machines, the weights. You learn to wrap meat. A lot of the meatcutters today were wrappers. I had had no experience at all. So it was kind of rough when I started out.

Did you like meatcutting at first?

I've *always* liked it. I like physical work. I've been raised around horses all my life, so I've been outdoors and I've never enjoyed working in an office.

During the first month, I made hamburger and wrapped and did very little cutting. You have to get used to the saws and that sort of thing. It takes a long time. You're afraid . . . [Laughs.] Meat's slick! And the saws are *fast*.

You were afraid?

Oh *yeah!* The knives are sharp. You have to learn to sharpen your own knives, to use a steel. You get knicks and cuts.

What are the occupational hazards?

Losing your *fingers*. I've known people who have lost fingers. The year that I went to school, there were two guys who lost fingers out of about 20 or 25 people.

A lot of it doesn't happen while you're an apprentice, though. It's after you turn journeyman. When you're an apprentice you're pretty careful. [Laughs.] You're not as fast as a journeyman. But after you get going, accidents happen. You just always have to be on your toes.

What was the most difficult adjustment for you when you began meatcutting?

I *never* thought I'd get used to the cold. The shop is kept at 51 or 52 degrees all the time. Some butchers never get used to it, and they've been in the business for 30 years. Now I'm used to it and I love it.

When I first worked I wore long underwear every day. [Laughs.] I wore my gloves in the cooler, my coat and everything. Now it isn't anything for me to go in there, because I guess your body adjusts to that.

Butchers get arthritis. A lot of them get frost-bite too. You take inventory in the freezer, and sometimes it's pretty cold. The health department wants your grinder in the cooler which is really cold. [Laughs.] The cooler is where your meat is kept at a certain temperature in the 30s or 40s. You really get cold—that hamburger's *cold!* [Laughs.] And you lift your luggers which weigh about 35 pounds. Those luggers are heavy and you have to lift them up and throw them in the grinder. I was freezing to death [laughs], until I got used to the cold.

I've had two fingers get *pretty cold*, and I went to the hospital. They finally started coming around. But I know guys who'll go in that cooler when we're taking inventory, and they'll just have to get out of there every five minutes because they can't stand it. And I can stay in there.

Men have problems with jobs too, just like women do. If women only knew that, I think it would help them succeed, if they really want to do it.

How did you become a member of the butcher's union?

You had a thirty-day period. You worked in the shop, and they saw how you could get along and how you liked it. I got along *fine*.

What is your attitude toward the union?

I think it's good for me. I believe in the union, and I attend the meetings. It's a good thing.

They keep everybody in line. We've had problems in our shop, and certain members haven't been able to work in the shop because of the *rules* of the union. And it is a strong union. It's by the book, and that's *good*. The members *are* kept in line.

We *do* get a lot of money, and I think most of us work for it. [Her union initiation fee was 166 dollars. Dues are sixteen dollars a month.]

What is your salary?

I make $286 a week. That's for a forty-hour week. You make two dollars night premium. That's two dollars more for the evening if you work after seven o'clock at night or before seven in the morning. [Andersen works from 2 to 11 p.m. and from 8 a.m. to 5 p.m. on alternating days. When she began training as a meatcutter, she made "about 150" dollars a week.]

You are a journeyman?

I've worked with Alpha Beta for over a year. And they felt that I was ready to be turned journeyman so I could be of value in their shops as a journeyman cutter, not as an apprentice. Now I have an apprentice training under me.

In the union hall, I am still an apprentice. I serve a two-year apprenticeship with the union.

What training do you receive?

Alpha Beta sends you down, every two months, to their main plant in Milpitas for training. You run cutting tests, watch movies, and that sort of thing.

When you first start working you learn to wrap, you work on your slicer. Then you make the grind—your hamburger, ground lamb, and your ground veal.

Then through the union, you go to classes every Tuesday night for a year. This is with a junior college program. You learn book work, strictly book work.

Do you know of other female journey"men" butchers?

No. *Not one girl* went through the union school with me. I don't know of any.

What is your typical day?

One day you work 2 to 11 and the next day you work 8 to 5. I wear a smock, an apron over that, and then a hardhat.

Usually you'll just start right in on the block. You'll start boning, cutting steaks, cutting up chickens, bagging chickens. The head of the shop would be telling me what to do, or if he's not there then the second man would be running the shop. Everybody else is journeyman cutter.

You just cut till you go home. You help people at the counter, you load the counter, and you set up displays. We have contests throughout the company for our displays.

In Santa Rosa, I bone twelve or thirteen (beef) rounds a night. They weigh about 65 pounds a piece. And that's a *lot* of boning.

What are the physical results?

Your arms really have to get in shape. And *especially* your hands. Your hands are grasping that knife all the time. Your knives have to be sharp, and you have to learn how to sharpen them yourself. I use a six-inch boning knife. You can use up to a twelve-inch steak knife—that's individual. We buy our own knives and scabbards ourselves. They cost almost 60 bucks.

Boning is what you use your hands for the most. It just takes time and experience to learn how to hang onto the knife. When you wake up in the morning, your hands are curled up like you're *still* hanging onto that knife!

Other tools?

Once in a while I use a hand saw. It's a regular hand saw like carpenters use.

Then you have your boneless saw which you use to cut all boneless meat. Then your boning saw. These are power saws and band saws. They're fixed on a table.

These are dangerous?

Oh *definitely!* [Laughs.] They'll take off your finger pretty quick.

But these saws don't move, only *you* move. When I went to work I was first taught that that saw doesn't jump around. It stays in one place, and *you* stay to one side of it.

Are you stronger than most women?

That's where I have an advantage over a lot of girls. I'm just built a little bigger. I'm about five feet five and weigh about 135 pounds. I'm built strong.

Most guys can just pick things up and throw things around, and they never really hesitate, where me . . . I would draw back. The guy I worked with first and learned a lot from weighed about 200 pounds and was about five foot nine inches tall. [Laughs.] And it was easy for *him* to say, "Well! Do it this way!" It didn't matter how he lifted it anyway, because he was so *big!* [Laughs.] It wasn't so easy for me. Eventually I learned to lift so it was easy and didn't hurt my back. Lift with your knees and not with your back.

Your speed is really important. I think this is a drawback for women, because when I lifted things, I wasn't as fast. You always have to push. Competition—there *is* competition.

Were there times when you thought about quitting?

Oh yeah. When I thought I was never going to *learn*. To handle a knife is like learning to write. Cutting's an art, definitely. And the lifting was hard to learn, even though my father was a carpenter and we worked with him a lot.

What made you stick with it?

I've always been raised with the idea that if you want something bad enough, you can do it, no matter what it is.

Whenever I'd come home, I'd have my parents and my boyfriend, who are behind me *all the time.* They'd say, "You're into it now. *Go!* Don't give up now because times are getting tough.''

What is your family background?

We've always lived in the country and had four or five acres. My father's a general contractor and my mom is a registered nurse, but she hasn't worked in twenty years. She really is a housewife.

My Dad's built homes and apartments, and we've always helped him out and worked together. I have two older brothers and a younger sister. [Andersen was born February 22, 1956.]

I'm still living at home [laughs], but I'm getting married. My boyfriend's a butcher too. He's an apprentice now—he's just starting out.

How is that, to be more advanced in the trade than your boyfriend?

It's created *no* problem. I've helped him out a lot, and he helped me when I was an apprentice too. He gave me support and that's really *super.*

Do you regard meatcutting as a fulfilling occupation?

Many times I go home and know that I *really* did the job well and that I'm doing what I've wanted to do for so long. It doesn't pay off all the time. I might go home really tired with my hands all cramped up from boning, but I love it.

What attitudes have you *had* to change to be effective in the job?

I think it's really hard for a woman in any job like this to get self-confidence. That's one of the biggest problems I've had.

In gaining confidence, it might help if there were another woman I could talk to and say, "Hey, do you ever have problems with this or that?" There's just no one I can really talk to like that because there are no women butchers in this area.

I always had a tendency at first to let things bother me because of the job. I'd go home and I'd think, "I'm just not *fast* enough! I've got to work *harder!*" And that's on your mind *all the time.* But you can't let that bother you constantly, or you'll spend more time worrying than concentrating on the work.

You work with men all day. Do you feel like an outsider or loner?

Not at all. They treat you like one of the guys. I work with five men and one woman wrapper.

Some of the guys *do* try to push you around. I've been left in charge of the shop before and guys will just kind of go their own way. I've been left with things to do and they're supposed to help me. They'll say, "Well, we can't do that now!" And I'll say, "Well, look! I'm the one in charge and we'll do it this way, because this is the way we're supposed to do it."

Do they cooperate then?

Yeah. [She hesitates.] But I think it's a little hard for them to swallow the first time. Eventually I'll have my own shop, and you have to be able to talk to these sort of guys.

What is the best way to talk to them?

Just tell them where it's at, that's all . . . in a nice way. You can't go screaming and hollering at the top of your lungs. When I eventually have the task of running my own shop, it's going to be kind of hard for me, because I've always looked at a man as the one who ran the shop. I have to change my own thinking and get with it! [Laughs.]

Male meatcutters have been positive in general?

I've never had any hardships from anybody feeling that I don't do my job.

Most of the guys I work with are really super. We *do* have a lot of union help that comes into the shop one or two days a week. They see you cutting with a knife and they think I'm a wrapper. They say, "You can get thrown out of the union for that!" I'll say, "What for?" And they'll say, "*Wrappers* aren't supposed to pick up a knife!" Then I tell them, and it blows their mind. [Laughs.] Once I work with the guys for a while, they don't think there's anything funny about me being there in the job.

Have you had *any* problems with co-workers because you're a woman?

The people I worked with never made it a woman in a man's job. I was expected to do the things that a man did. And I *did*. I'm in a shop now where the situation isn't quite the same. Before, I was working for a guy that expected me to do *everything* everybody else did. The work was the work. My boss never thought I can do it, but I had the drive. I took it upon myself to say every night when I went home, "That's alright! I'll be there one day and you may be working for *me!*" And it helped.

If you really want to do anything, I've always felt that you can do it. I've had a great opportunity and I intend to make a future of my work.

Now in the shop I'm in, the guys just treat you like you're a woman. The main thing is lifting. When I went to work in this shop, the manager said that he looks at me as a woman meat-cutter and he doesn't expect me to lift as much as the other guys. He said, "If I ever tell you to go into the cooler to get something and if it's too heavy, have one of the guys help you. I don't object." He said that *he* asks for help a lot of times too.

Do you regard his approach as more humane?

I do. But I think that there's no reason that a woman should be a burden to males working in the same shop. If she *can't* pull the weight, I think she should get out.

The work is hard, and you can't make anybody else's job any harder than yours is. It's important for a woman who doesn't feel she can handle it to get out—in *any* job.

Is meatcutting a good field for women?

Certain *types* of women. I guess I'm in a position now where I look at it from a guy's standpoint. I wouldn't want any girl in there that didn't want to hang loads. You hang the meat that comes in on rails. It's hard work.

And you have to learn how to get along with the guys. If a girl had never had brothers or boyfriends and didn't like to work with guys, it'd be *tough!* Because of the language. [Laughs.]

I've worked in a lot of shops, just one day or two days when they needed a cutter, and I've always gotten along. But I don't say that's because of the people, it's because I've *wanted* it that way.

A lot of girls tease guys and stuff like that, but you can't do that because you work with them eight hours a day. [Laughs.] You can't be running after each other in the meat department. You always get guys who will ask you out, but it's just like working in an office as a secretary. You don't want things to start up, because that makes it hard on everybody else. Besides, they know I'm getting married.

But as far as the job, I never really say, "Gee! I'm doing something that very few women are doing." I never really think of it that way. Most of the guys say, "You're *good* at the work, so we don't have to worry about it."

It *does* take a certain kind of girl to do the work. You have to really like it and be a part of it. There's too many people who just go to work and then go home.

Are you competitive?

I always want to be better than the guys.

What are your opportunites?

The opportunities are endless. If I should ever decide that I want to go into something else in the grocery, I could. There are people who started out as janitors at Alpha Beta who are head men now. It's really great.

It's good for *me*. If I ever get tired of going to the shop and just cutting meat, I could sit at a desk and order their meat from Colorado. I could go into sales . . .

Alpha Beta is quite open to women?

They really are. And in the union, too, there really aren't too many that have made me feel like an oddball.

Some of these guys do feel that you're taking jobs away from men, as I said, but generally they have been okay. And you always find somebody who really helps you out.

What men have really helped you in the trade?

One of the guys I worked for when I first started. Since we don't get our beef in whole carcass, you learn what each piece is and not what part of the cow it comes from. This man worked for another place one or two days a week breaking beef. I went with him and learned to cut whole carcass beef, which a lot of butchers nowadays don't know how to do. Now I know how to do it.

He was a journeyman cutter and a super teacher. He had a whole lot of patience. It was *really* an opportunity.

How do female customers react to you?

Most of the women say, "I'd like to talk to one of the butchers" or one of the cutters. Then by the time they find out I'm a cutter, they've forgotten what they wanted to ask me! Women are *really* surprised, *more* so than men.

Do women have confidence in your ability?

Oh, definitely! That's the main reason the store wants women butchers, because women do most of the shopping.

I've had women ask me things about cooking and I can be more helpful to them than most men, because I do a lot of cooking myself. I always try something new. Women will tell me at the store, "Well, gee, I cook it *this* way." I'll go home that night and I'll try it because that's the way you learn things. [Andersen also sews, does "some needlework," and goes trailriding with her Dad.]

When you marry, will you expect your husband to help with the housework?

Oh yeah! Because we're both working. My boyfriend and I have that kind of relationship anyway. I wash, he dries—that sort of thing. [Laughs.]

Alice Bertemes

It will be hard for me to just stay home because I'm used to being with the public and just shooting the breeze with the boys...

Because she was always good at "figuring," Alice Bertemes was hired in 1946 as a bookkeeper for the Farmers Cooperative Grain Elevator in Taunton, Minnesota. In 1956 she was named manager. At the time of this interview, Bertemes was, as far as she knew, one of two lone women managing grain elevators in the entire United States. Those two women have never met.

Bertemes stands out as an influential figure in agrarian Minnesota, as an example of the rugged individualism that built rural America, *and* as a woman of great will and determination.

Widowed more than a decade ago, Bertemes lives in Taunton, population 220. She was born on a farm fourteen miles away, in 1918. Because her family was so poor that she was unable to buy clothing, Bertemes did not finish high school. The Depressions' hard times forced her into restaurant work for $3.50 a week. Her business sense has brought her a long way since then.

Using her intelligence and ability to relate to men as cornerstones, Bertemes has built a viable operation from a grain elevator that was failing when she took over. The Farmers Cooperative Grain Elevator today serves 1,500 shareholders, farmers who have learned to put their faith and the fruits of their labors into the hands of one woman—Alice Bertemes.

Well, I tell you, my husband years ago ran a shoe shop and I fixed the binder canvas, which is what the farmers used to cut the grain. I used to help him down at the shop once in a while, and I knew the farmers pretty well from working with him. And the board of directors went up to the high school where I went to talk with the superintendent and asked what my background was as far as figures. And the superintendent, of course, gave me a very good recommendation because this was always my hobby—I loved to figure. When I went to school it was *so easy* for me. So, then they came and approached me up at the house, and they wanted to know if I would be interested in coming over to the elevator as a bookkeeper. So this is the way I started way back in 1946.

How did you work your way up?

Well, when I started as a bookkeeper the elevator was very obsolete. I worked at an old table and it was really *terrible!* In fact, I was going to quit the day I started because there were so many mice in the office. [Laughs.] But my husband kept encouraging me; he said, "You better stick around. We'll just trap those mice!" So I kept on. I got these market papers, and I started reading them. The manager we had at that time was very poor. He just didn't seem to know *anything!* He got me kind of discouraged because I'd tell him, I'd say, "Well, you bought all that grain yesterday, you'd better sell it!" And he would just go around and chew his tobacco and spit on the floor. And I used to get *very angry.* [Laughs.] I thought there must be *some* way we can *do* this! So I just started reading and got to thinking. I was so *determined!*

In the meantime, this man that I worked for embezzled some money from the elevator. So it was really quite a mess when I started. They were in the hole *real bad.* We came a long way up.

This manager went so far as to try to set the elevator on fire one morning—tried to burn the evidence. I was right there at the time.

He was actually going to burn the elevator?

Yes, he *was, including* all the records. But we got everything out. The firemen went up above and found that he had soaked a bunch of rags and set them on fire. So of course he was canned right there—he was let go.

So then the second man that was there, they put him in as manager and put me in as assistant manager. That was in 1953. [Her salary as assistant manager was "about $250 a month."]

I was assistant manager until 1956. Then the other man quit and I took her over. [Bertemes' starting salary as manager was $350 a month.]

How large an operation was that when you started?

Well, when I started, all the bushel capacity we had was about 30 thousand bushels. And all the stockholders we had were about 150. And now, today, we have right around 1,500 shareholders.

We do in the neighborhood of a million and a half to two million dollars worth of business a year. There are some larger, but for this area it's pretty good. We're one of the largest co-ops in Minnesota.

We get grain from about 22 miles around. We get a lot of farmers in the area.

Describe the structure and operation of the elevator.

A cooperative elevator consists of a group of farmers who own the elevator and elect seven board of directors who, in turn, elect the manager.

The grain elevator takes in grain from the farmers who raise it. And then we, in turn, handle this grain and ship it to a commission firm for the farmers. The commission firm takes this grain and mills it, processes it, or otherwise sells it for export.

The elevator we have is a new building, built in 1959. It's concrete. It has six large concrete tanks which hold on the average of 22 thousand bushels each. Plus it has fourteen smaller bins, up above, that average around four to five thousand bushels apiece.

We take this grain over a scale, and we have a hoist which hoists up the trucks, and the grain—in turn—goes in these bins.

If the farmer wishes to store it and not sell it on the day he brings it in, he can just leave the grain with us, and we will store it until the day he wants to sell it.

The grains that we handle are corn and oats, soy beans, flax, rye, barley, and wheat.

The major product is feed. We make our own feed. It's the only thing we make from the bottom up. But then we handle fertilizer and all chemicals, feed, twine.

The stockholders have a share in the elevator. At the end of the year the money that the cooperative makes goes back to the stockholders. We pay back a certain amount of cash and the rest is kept as what you call stock credits on the stockholder's books. Then when he retires, or in case he would pass away, this money all goes to him or his family.

What do you do on a daily basis?

My job consists of buying and selling grain, buying feed, selling feed, fertilizer, chemicals, and the hedging of grain. By hedging grain, I'm talking about selling grain on the futures.

The first thing when I come in in the morning, I get what they call a "market report" in the mail, which gives me the market from the day before. So I go over the paper to look at the market so I can get some idea of what the market is probably going to do today. I think whether I should sell or hold on. You have to do a *lot of reading* in this business.

Futures?

Say for instance you could sell soybeans on the November future. This means that when you bring in your new crop, you could sell it on the November future and deliver it in November. That way you protect yourself. In case the market goes down, you've *already* got it sold.

It's not really a risky business, because your price is locked in. The only thing is that when you do this, you want to be sure you have the grain to cover it. Because when the time comes, you *have* to deliver.

Have you ever lost on the market?

Well, yes. A few years ago when the soybeans dropped so *terrifically*. They were up to twelve dollars and then, just like that, they started dropping a dollar a day. And you just *couldn't* even get in the market because they were going down the limit. You couldn't buy and you couldn't sell. So I got stuck with a few of those. I took a little licking, but it's one of those things you have to do.

How many stockholders are women?

I'd say there are about 50 women that are really stockholders. When the husband is a stockholder, the wife usually comes in too and attends the annual meetings with him.

How many women bring grain to the elevator?

Oh, we have a *lot*. I'd say right now that there are probably 300 or more. We have more women come into this elevator because I'm a lady running it. They're not afraid to come in, as they might be if it was run by a man.

Do any of these women actually own their own farms?

No. We don't have any of those at all.

You work with men all day?

That's right. I spend a *lot* of time with patrons. They come in and this is half of the business; you *have* to communicate with your patrons. It takes a *lot* of time. You have to explain markets to them. They want to know what the market is doing, so you have to talk with them.

They'll come in and maybe they'll want to know if I can get some winter wheat seeds for them. Well, then I'm on the telephone looking for this. You have to be of service to your patrons.

This is what I do. And then of course I have a good bookkeeper. This is *important*. [Bertemes supervises five employees.]

You must deal with a lot of farmers' problems?

I had a farmer come in the other day, just to *show* you what I really have to go through. We've had a really dry year and hay is *so* short this year (76). So I had a farmer come up to the elevator and he said, "Say Alice, you've *got* to help me."

He had a problem over his wildlife ground. Wildlife ground is where they let the grass grow up so the birds can build their nests in it. But this year was so dry that they gave the farmers permission to cut this for their livestock. This farmer had some of this ground on his farm. His neighbor came in and started cutting it. And he says, "Now *what* am I going to do, Alice? You are going to *have* to help me!" And I told him, "I don't know what I'm going to do, but I'm going to sure *try!* But in the meantime," I said, "don't let that man go in there on that ground!"

So I called up Congressman Knowland and got ahold of his assistant, and we did get the thing straightened out. I put a stop to it. The other farmer that was doing it, I called him up, and he came in and actually thanked me. He said, "I didn't *know* that the man wanted the *hay!* If he had told me, I wouldn't have taken it." This is just one of these things that happen. I guess I was what you call the "peace maker."

Does dealing with men all the time take special ability?

Well, yes it *does*. I'll say this, you learn to talk a *man's lan-*

guage. Which I suppose is not so good, because I find that I can't go to Ladies Aid parties anymore because I can't communicate very good, if you know what I mean. [Laughs.]

What do you mean by a "man's language?"

Well, they come in, and they give me a pretty rough time once in a while. They'll tell me this and that, and they'll say, "Well *damn it,* you know that you said that!" And I have to stand up and answer them back the *same way* they talk to me! Otherwise they'll walk right over you. This is the way I've done it. And I have got them trained so they know when I *say* something, I definitely *mean* it. I have to have authority. [Her tone is very strong and determined.]

Perhaps being a woman has *helped* you deal with men?

I think so. When it comes to dealing with the commission firms, with the railroad men and people like that, I *will* talk to them like a man, but yet they don't *dare* talk back to me because I'm a *woman!* [Laughs.]

What do the women in the community think of you?

Well, right now it's all good. I had a few problems, years ago. I'd call up to their home and I'd ask for a woman's husband, and she'd say, "*Well!* Now *who* is this calling?" [Imitates insulted tone of voice.]

She'd think, "Well, my *gosh!* A *woman!*" [Laughs.]

Has your job affected your image as a woman?

Well, I really think that me doing the job that I am doing has really made the women in this community feel much more important. There are very few other elevators that *ever* have a woman come to a stockholders meeting. But at *this* elevator, practically every husband brings his wife along.

When I put my notice in the paper for the annual meeting, I *always* put in: "This Includes Your *Wives.*" They *are* important!

You must be well respected?

I would say that the whole community and stockholders do respect me a lot. This is one reason that I've stayed as long as I have. They have told me they'll hate to see me leave. They come in and they ask me this and they ask me that, and they say that if it hadn't been for me they don't know *how* they would have even gotten started. Maybe their sons got started farming because I've helped them all. It's been fun to watch the younger generation grow up. These men are *terrific* friends. When one of them passes away, it's like one of the family.

You represent the elevator at the stockholders meetings?

That's right.

Usually each month, unless I'm too busy, but for *sure* quarterly, I make up my own report, which is a report on how the elevator is doing. Then I call a board of directors meeting and I go over all this material with them—*how* we're doing in each commodity and *what* we're doing.

At the end of the year, we have a stockholders' meeting where we invite all the stockholders to come in. This year I served a smorgasbord, and it went over *real big!* [Laughs.] Then I get up and read the audit to the stockholders, and I go through it and explain everything just as it is. Most elevators have the auditors come out and do this. But they say they like to have me explain it, that they get more out of it.

What is your major accomplishment at the elevator?

There *is* one thing they all give me so much credit for. In 1959 we had a stockholders meeting about adding on some space to store grain in. And at that meeting, they just *couldn't* figure it out. Then the question was brought up of why we couldn't build a *new* elevator. A new one and a *big one!* And I said, "Well, we'll *try!*"

So I went with the board of directors to the Bank for Cooperatives in Minneapolis and met with those people. And I had *no trouble at all* in getting the money to build it! I asked for 150,000 dollars and they said they'd give it to me right away. And I thought this was pretty nice! This is one thing that people really admire me for around here, because they said there wouldn't be *anybody* who would have the *guts* to do it!

Why was the Bank for Cooperatives so willing to lend that much money?

The reason was because of my working at the elevator. By looking at my financial statement, they saw what I had been doing and that I had been making money for them *every year*. And I told them that if they would give me that money, I said, "I'll *guarantee* you that within five or six years at the most I'll have you paid off." And I did too.

Are there any occupational hazards?

Well, yes. We're dealing with chemicals and fertilizers. I was going out to the fertilizer spreader once and this is where I got arthritis in my knee. I stumbled in a rut and fell down and twisted my knee. This is one thing which has been bothering me. You're going out in all kinds of weather.

What are the hazards in the elevator itself?

I'll tell you what's bad is the *dust*. I have an allergy and I take shots once a month up at the clinic. Otherwise I couldn't take it. It's really dusty in the elevator. [This allergy developed after she was employed at the elevator.]

Is this a very enjoyable occupation for you?

Yes, I would say so. If I didn't enjoy it, I guess I wouldn't be there!

You feel that your job is worthwhile?

This is *right!* The job that I have got, you *have* to put your heart and soul into. You have to operate as if you are operating your *own household.* You just can't go up there and sit and watch the clock!

What is your salary?

Just lately my salary has gone up. First I started out at 100 dollars a month. Today I'm getting 600 a month, *plus* I get a commission on the profit. It usually runs around 10,000 dollars a year. They usually give me five percent of my net local earnings.

How many more years do you think you will manage the elevator?

I tell you, for the last two years I've been wanting to retire and quit. I've been here so long, and I really don't have to work this hard. It's *hard work!* But the board of directors wants me to sort of semi-retire and just go up to the elevator probably two or three days out of the week, until they can get somebody broken in to take my place. So I'm thinking about doing this for another year or two. It will be hard for me to just sit *home* because I'm so used to being with the public and just shooting the breeze with the boys, you know what I mean. [Bertemes works from 8 or 9 a.m. to 5:30 or 6 p.m.—the longer hours and on Saturdays, if the elevator is particularly busy.]

How have you handled competitors?

Well, first when I started, to give you an example, there was another elevator in town. This of course was when I had *just started.* I was only assistant manager and all the grain was going there. We just couldn't get any grain to come our way. I noticed what the guy was doing—he'd go out and he'd take the farmer to a little bar downtown; he'd buy him a shot, and pat him on the shoulder. And I thought, "*Well!* If *this* is what it takes . . .!"

One day I went outside and there was a farmer in line at the other elevator, and I said to him, "Why don't you come over *here?* I don't have to take you to the bar, but I've got a little shot in there." So he came over to our elevator, and as he came over I said to the guy that was manager then, "Now! We're going to treat him *real good,* because then he'll go out of here and he'll tell his neighbors and then *they'll* start coming." And this is the way we did it.

Do you know of other women managing grain elevators?

I hear that there is one. I think that it's either in North Dakota or South Dakota, where her husband passed away and she took over.

You graduated from high school?

Well, you know, I never really did get my certificate of graduation. My folks were *very* hard up. We were on the farm and it was in the thirties—in the Depression. My folks were very poor. They had no money. And I had a brother who had clymatoid rheumatism and he was in bed. So I left school and stayed home to take care of him for a while, then I went back to school.

Of course I had *no problem* with my grades. I'm not bragging, but I *was* pretty sharp! I kept on going to school until finally I could see that it was just *impossible* for me to even get money to buy clothes to keep on going. So I decided I had to quit. The superintendent talked to me, and he wanted me to stay *so bad!* And I could have gone back, and I know I would have graduated, but six months before graduation, I took a job in a restaurant in Marshall, Minnesota. I helped out in the kitchen.

That was my first job. I started out at $3.50 a week. I worked until I got married in 1938. After that I worked down at the egg produce, breaking eggs. [At age twenty, she married and moved to Taunton, seventeen miles from Marshall.]

Why were you breaking eggs?

Well, in those days they had this big egg processing plant going in Marshall—Weiners did. So I worked there for three or four years. We broke eggs, and powdered eggs were made from them.

I enjoyed that job! I got 85 cents an hour. In those days, that was pretty good pay!

Why did you quit?

I was helping my husband also. Then it got to be too much—he had so much work—so I kind of quit the egg processing. I'd just help them out when they really got busy, and they'd call me, because they liked me so well.

When I started working at the elevator, they still called me and wanted me to come back to the egg processing plant.

What is your home like?

I have a nice five-room home here in Taunton. I have a real nice garden that I raise. I have three lots, 150 x 150. And I have a lot of shrubbery that I trim. My biggest hobby is gardening and taking care of my flowers—I have a *lot* of flowers.

Your life is very connected with the land.

Yes, that's right! It makes me feel good. I just feel that *everything* comes from the earth, and this is the way I like to have it.

Karate School Director

Susan Borger

> *When I was a child—like all children—I had an idealistic picture of what the future was going to be. Most people lose that around their college years, if not sooner. When I started studying martial art, I found it again. And I still have it.*

Shakuhachi (Zen-style flute) music fills the room where Susan Borger and I sit drinking tea. This is the cheerful studio-kitchen of the dojo she heads. It is Saturday and, although there are no formal classes on weekends, students work out in adjoining rooms of the dojo—a beautiful place, sunlit, with hardwood floors and songs of caged birds.

Students come into the room occasionally. They are respectful. They call Susan Borger "Sensei" [teacher]. They are all male, predominantly caucasian.

Born in 1942 in the suburbs of New York, Borger obtained her bachelor's degree, with concentration in art, from Sarah Lawrence "one of the most expensive colleges in the world." Her parents struggled to give her every advantage, including trips to Europe and art studies in Italy. In New York she worked in various secretarial type positions. "Jobs," she says, "are a miserable subject!"

She was never athletically inclined until—at age 25—she began the traditional Matsubayashi-Ryu Karate training in New York. In 1971 she was the first woman to live and train for a long period of time at the headquarters dojo in Naha, Okinawa. There she tested for Sho Dan, first degree black belt, and there she reached a major turning point in her life: recognition of her "real teacher" Chotoku Omine, head instructor of all Matsubayashi-Ryu schools in the United States. Borger assisted Omine in establishing a U.S. headquarters in San Bruno, California. Then, suddenly, the Master died, and Borger experienced a role crisis which est training resolved.

Borger's way of life is "Karate." "Everything I do," she says, "I do for Karate." She immerses herself in the Japanese arts which will strengthen understanding of herself and aid in the polishing of her character. Her hands are calloused from punching the makiwaras—the flexible upright boards in the dojo's training room. She "sits" zazen [meditation] every day. She studies Japanese tea ceremony, calligraphy, sumi-e (ink painting), Zen-style archery, sword, *and* practices the Okinawan weapons of sai and bo, as part of kobujitsu, the art of weapons. She does not dance or "date." On Friday nights, after the last classes of the week, Borger might share beer and a spirit of camaraderie with the more advanced students. She might go to a samurai movie.

Despite the fact that she teaches Karate classes and heads the dojo, Borger stresses her continually evolving understanding of Karate and the "Way," emphasizing that she is a student, constantly learning. She is the first woman in the world to achieve the rank of San Dan, or third degree black belt, in Matsubayashi-Ryu Karate.

A unique product of the West, Borger holds a position traditionally reserved for Japanese and Okinawan men. She schools herself in the art of control, extending it as far as this interview which presents her—in the words she carefully chose and personally edited—to the world. "Karate" is capitalized throughout the interview at her request.

In this dojo we practice Shorin-Ryu or Matsubayashi-Ryu Karate, a very traditional system. I provide space for people to find themselves through self-development and training. At the same time, they become fantastically strong physically!

Karate is the art of empty-handedness. And self-defense is not force against force. If it were, the stronger would always win! Self-defense has to do with judgment, wisdom and timing, gained through concentrated physical and self training.

What is the purpose of Karate for you?

The purpose of this great art is for people to study themselves. My purpose in Karate training is to train myself to become a better human being, to be wiser, stronger, clearer, and more able to serve others. In actual practice the students are training me, not the other way around! I am here because I wish to be trained.

Oh, God! It's really rough sometimes! [Laughs, shakes her head.]

This training is at the core of my life, but I never take it for granted. I have to renew my commitment to it every day, every class. I can never rest on what I did yesterday. As a Karate student, training is an agreement with life to do my best.

The class is set up so that you can put yourself out 100 percent. You know what it means to commit yourself completely, and you know when you don't. Sweating purifies you.

When you enter the dojo, you leave all of your problems, your opinions, outside. You come to the dojo with only yourself in order to experience Karate totally.

Define dojo.

Dojo literally means "place of the Way" or "hall of spiritual training." It usually refers to a martial arts school, but a school of tea ceremony, Zen meditation, or flower arrangement might also be called dojo.

There are fifty Karate dojos in the United States connected with Master Shoshin Nagamine. Of these fifty, only one other dojo—in Illinois—is headed by a woman, together with her husband, although she may not be active any more.

This dojo has over 5,000 square feet. There are eight areas, the largest of which are the main dojo area and the training room. In the main dojo area we hold Karate classes. The training room has all kinds of equipment, most of which Sensei Omine designed and built himself. [Omine is her Master or "Sensei," now deceased.] He designed it specifically for Americans, because they're not in good shape! There is weight training equipment, wooden racks, balance beams, ladders on the ceiling, Okinawan-style weights, and six makiwaras for punching. The makiwara is a flexible upright board with a curved back and straight front wrapped with rice rope. The rice rope is for building callouses. One makiwara is leather-wrapped for people who don't want calloused hands.

We have a zendo here, a room with cushions devoted entirely to zazen [meditation]. We have a shrine in the zendo with pictures of our Sensei. The students can use the zendo any time, light incense, and "sit" [meditate]. Regular meditation practice is a part of each class. We don't teach any religion, but the advanced students are required to "sit."

Our tea ceremony room is set up Japanese style with mats and tokonoma (alcove) which serves also as a quiet place where a student can read a book, sit quietly by himself, or have visitors. We have a library of Zen books which the students can take out.

Then there's the large kitchen-studio where I do my brush painting.

Describe Matsubayashi-Ryu Karate classes.

We have a very traditional class. It has a form. And I feel that it's a work of art in itself. The exercises follow a beautiful order that takes on more meaning the more I practice. We practice the traditional blocks, punches, strikes, and kicks to build strength, flexibility, agility, and health. And we strive for focus, timing, speed, power, balance, coordination and spirit. It is not only that these exercises work for the best self-defense and health, but that they come down to us from olden times. Therefore, in perfecting the movements, the wisdom of those people before us comes to us, too.

Karate practice is doing without thinking. It's direct experience not put through a second verbal process. People feel satisfaction from having lived each class.

Master Shoshin Nagamine opened the first Karate dojo ever opened to the public. Before that, people who were fortunate enough to learn Karate—usually only the first son of a samurai-class family—had to learn in a teacher's backyard.

After World War II, Okinawa was completely devastated. Many young people had lost hope. Master Nagamine's experience and love of Karate, which had been cut off by the war, inspired him to reopen a dojo. He strove to provide young men with the means to recapture their spirit through self-improvement, so that through Karate they could regain control over life and destiny.

We cherish this spirit today and want to share it with people. In Karate, by your own will and your own willingness, you conquer your own weakness and improve yourself and the quality of your life. This training is tremendously satisfying, and it *never* ends.

What is your background in Karate? In athletics?

When I first began studying Karate, I didn't know it was "training." I took it originally for self-defense and to get healthy. My brother encouraged me. [He is three years older than she and her only sibling.]

My mother was a very good athlete and they wanted her to train for the Olympics. But I was artistic and not athletic at all! In school when they would pick the teams, I was never picked first. I thought then, "Well, why bother!" I felt that I could never be really good like my mother.

I started studying Karate in New York in 1968 and trained there for three years. We used to run in the snow—through Central Park—barefoot at night. I never asked what the reason was. You can *make* a reason not to do anything! We don't teach that way here.

When I was ready to test for Sho Dan, which is first degree black belt, I went to the headquarters dojo in Naha, Okinawa, where I trained under Master Nagamine, the founder of our style. That was in 1971. Master Nagamine was 65 years old then.

I trained there for four months. I lived in the school and worked out twice a day. And I was fortunate to be able to eat my meals with the Master.

Were other women active at the headquarters dojo?

Occasionally young women join the dojo. But no one has made it a long-term practice. I believe I am the first woman ever to live at that dojo and get black belt there. Okinawan girls have other opportunities for training in traditional things such as tea ceremony and Okinawan dance. And they leave Karate to the men.

How were you chosen to be the first woman?

Master Chotoku Omine, 6-Dan Renshi [chief instructor] black belt, was Head Instructor of all Matsubayashi-Ryu schools in the United States. He was returning to Okinawa for a visit and invited some higher ranking students to go with him and train at the headquarters dojo. Two men and I were invited.

What is the rank system and your rank?

Everyone starts out in seventh "kyu." Kyu means "class." They progress up to First Kyu, testing every four to eight months, depending on ability, attendance and attitude. A student is required to train at least three times a week for at least three years before he is able to test for "Sho Dan." "Sho Dan" means first step or first degree. And there are ten degrees or ranks, with the latter four reserved for older people who have been training for many years.

Sho Dan is the first black belt rank and does not mean you have "graduated," but only that you are pretty good at the basics. In Okinawa, shrines often have gates called "torii" at the bottom of steps, with the shrine standing at the top of the hill.

Sensei Omine used to say that at Sho Dan you are standing under the gate looking up at all the steps. There are ten steps to climb in Karate. It's a life-long struggle.

Master Nagamine is 9-Dan (Ninth Degree Black Belt) at 70 years old. He still practices every day. He told me, with a laugh, that his body feels like an "old junk car." But it certainly doesn't look that way to us! It's just inspiring to see him.

I am San Dan or third degree black belt.

Why should women study Karate?

Oh, this is important! I want to encourage women to study this great art. It's hard to say it in just a few words because there is so much depth to it. But briefly, Karate promotes a strong, healthy, graceful body and peaceful and wise mind. It creates confidence and poise that is so beautiful, once experienced, no person would want to live without it.

What prejudice have you encountered as a woman in Karate training?

During my first three years of training in New York, I felt there was prejudice against women because, physically, we cannot do as much as men. I always had the feeling that they wanted me *out!* Their point of view seemed to be that women are physically inferior and *spiritually* inferior!

So my experience in my first dojo in the United States took confidence away from me instead of adding it. Of course, real confidence comes from true inner certainty about the way things are. It has nothing to do with the way other people act toward you. But I didn't understand that at the time.

When I got to Okinawa, I expected the Okinawan men to be more condescending than the American Karate men. But I found just the opposite. In Okinawa the men were all like big brothers. They treated me wonderfully. They encouraged me constantly and made me feel that they respected me and were proud of my being there. They respect women more than American men do.

There is an attitude on the part of most men that women can't do things. But the real problem is that women listen to it.

The more I learn, the more I know that I am the one responsible for what happens in my life. I used to blame problems on being a woman, but I've learned that I'm creating my life. I'm responsible. When I'm coming from a positive place, I make space for other people to participate positively.

What did you experience as the only woman in the Okinawan dojo?

I was fairly lonely. I lived at the dojo and no one there spoke English. I spent my free time going around the island doing water color paintings and playing with Master Nagamine's grandchildren and their friends. Training at that dojo was truly one of the great experiences of my life.

Master Nagamine's family and all the students were so good to me. And the unpretentious, peaceful spirituality of the Okinawans deeply impressed me. I got to know Sensei Omine better. I experienced that he had a deep, deep trust in human nature and in the god-like essence basic to all people, women equally with men. That god-like essence can be brought to shine forth through training. He didn't tell me all this in exact words; I just felt it. And I knew I had found my real teacher.

When I returned to the states I went to study at the school where Sensei Omine was teaching in New York. And a year later, in November, 1972, I went to San Francisco to help him found a Headquarters dojo for the United States. He chose San Francisco because of the large Japanese community and the closeness to Japan in feeling and distance. In 1973 I went back to Okinawa to assist his family's move to the U.S.

What was your exact role in the dojo and with Master Omine?

I was called "Jokyoshi" meaning assistant instructor. I led many classes. But there is a big difference between *leading* the class and "teaching." Teaching means taking total responsibility for assisting people's lives. Sensei was the *only* teacher. And as Jokyoshi, I served Sensei by handling all the mechanics and logistics of running the dojo and the business.

It was a perfect situation in that Sensei was teaching Karate and adding tremendously to people's lives. Although he took responsibility for everything that went on in the dojo and I discussed all business matters with him, he supported me totally in handling those matters for him.

Was this dojo a money-making venture?

We did not commercialize the dojo, that is, do anything in the dojo for the sake of "making money." We never allowed monetary needs to interfere with our purpose of teaching people, so we also started a small photography business. Sensei Omine had been a professional photographer in Okinawa, and he enjoyed it.

As Jokyoshi, were you happy with your life?

I saw my life as always heading here. I was very fulfilled and happy. I felt we were really contributing to the world through Sensei's teaching. And I was proud of my part.

I was grateful to my parents that I had the background and education to assist him.

I loved being Jokyoshi, and I had *no* desire to be the teacher. Then Sensei died suddenly, and I *had* to become the teacher or give up the whole dojo.

What was your reaction to Master Omine's death?

At first I completely drowned myself in intensive training. My mother died the same week as Sensei, and only the intensive workouts gave me relief from unremitting grief over the double loss. But mostly it was the students that helped me. Their love and support were incredible, truly inspiring. I wanted desperately not to let them down. But it is impossible to fill the shoes of a master. Sensei Omine was not only a great Karate man but a human being of enormous wisdom, compassion, and strength; whereas I found myself to be weak, greedy, selfish and ignorant, in comparison. [Laughs.]

After considerable prodding, my brother got me to take the est training [Erhard Seminars Training]. Then things started to clear up for me.

How did the est training help you resolve your conflicts?

In the est training I experienced myself to be whole and complete as I am. I experienced my life to be a process unfolding before me, so that I have all these things to do and to grow into and become. And yet I am okay right now, with all of my faults.

Karate is a self-study. You are continually becoming more and more aware of your shortcomings so you can polish your character. As you train, you get to handle more and more of your own weaknesses or faults.

So after the est training, I was able to say: this is where I am and I don't like it, I would like to be better than this. And I could still get the job done. I learned that my former misgivings must not stop me from accepting the role of teacher because there was no one else better qualified in the dojo. I also got clear about what the role of the teacher was. When I thought it meant to be like Sensei Omine, I would be completely confused and in a state of despair, since no one can even imitate a master. But when I saw that to be the teacher meant to serve people, I could handle it. I will continue to do my best as long as people want to come here and train.

I am grateful to Werner Erhard, the founder of est, for est enabled me to share with others—through my own participation in life—what I experienced from our great Master Omine.

I do not mean to intimate that I am even remotely qualified to propagate Sensei Omine's teachings in the world. But since his teaching is the guiding force in my life and because of the est training, I am no longer afraid to share my own experience in Karate with others. The most important thing, for me, is that I am a Karate *student,* and I am just acting the role of the teacher.

What is your work history?

I had many jobs in the business world, and I continued to work until shortly before Sensei Omine died. I had good secretarial skills, but I was never able to find any job that allowed me to use my creativity and talent for a long period of time. I did sell my paintings [watercolors] with my mother acting as agent. But as far as jobs are concerned, I'd prefer not to go into detail.

Your family background and education?

We were upper middle class people, but my parents had been very poor as children and struggled for everything they had. My parents were crazy about me and gave me every advantage. For example they sent me to study in Europe at a beautiful Renaissance villa in Italy and to Sarah Lawrence. They really struggled to send me there, despite the fact that it's one of the most expensive colleges in the world.

I chose Sarah Lawrence because of its unique educational system. The classes were small and we only had to take three subjects a year which we studied very deeply. My parents were thrilled that I wanted to go there and that I was accepted.

My mother wanted me to be a successful artist. They hoped I would make a good career in the art world. She paid for my first Karate classes for self-defense. [When Susan was 25 years old.]

My brother was the one who got me interested in Karate.

How has your brother influenced you?

When I think of my brother, the idea that most comes to mind is "You can do it!" He has always supported me and encouraged me to do things in life. I try to encourage my students to be that kind of brother to their sisters. In fact we should all give that kind of support to people in our lives.

Who were your role models?

I never really had any until I met Master Omine. I want to be the kind of person he was.

I do enjoy samurai movies. Many of those characters inspire me to work out harder.

What is your personal life outside Karate?

Karate is my personal life. I spend my free time with the students and friends we meet through our studies. And I spend a lot of time alone painting and practicing.

My only purpose really is to train, to serve the students, and the true art of Karate by hard practice. I am continually discovering what Karate is. I want to serve Sensei Omine by striving to keep the Way that he transmitted to us. It's done so much for me that I want to help offer Karate and the Way to other people so they can benefit from it too.

Are you a liberated woman?

Liberation means freedom. And freedom to me is a state of mind of being clear. It comes from being responsible and honest and, therefore, confident. One achieves this by training. Karate and Zen training are the Way for me.

What is your salary?

Just enough for the basic necessities.

What Japanese arts do you study other than Karate?

I'm studying kyudo, sumi-e (ink) painting, and—more recently—tea ceremony, calligraphy, and Japanese sword. I also practice sai and bo, Okinawan weapons which are part of our advanced Karate practice called Kobujitsu [art of weapons].

What is the purpose of Kyudo?

I started Japanese Archery or "Kyudo" which means "way of the bow" about 1970. The purpose of Kyudo is to perfect the character of the person who practices it. This is the objective of Karate training, also. Kyudo is very slow moving and outwardly the feeling is completely different from Karate. But inwardly the spirit is the same for me. Kyudo is called "moving Zen" or "standing Zen."

I go to classes twice a week at the Kurumi-An dojo or "Walnut Tree Hermitage." It is a beautiful outdoor dojo with a 28 meter Kyudo range. The bow is eight feet long.

In the Karate dojo I have a short range straw target. We call it "makiwara," but it's not anything like a Karate makiwara. In daily practice I shoot only four to ten arrows. It is the spirit of each shot, not the quantity of arrows, that counts.

What dichotomies do you experience between your Western background and Eastern disciplines?

Before I started Karate training I was very interested in Western art. I spent a couple of years in Europe looking at art, and I painted all the time. I used to go to the museums in New York three or four times a week, sometimes every day. I searched and searched for some personal realization through art, and I couldn't find it.

After I had practiced Karate for about three years, I had the occasion to take Sensei Omine and my Zen teacher, Reverend Sogen Sakiyama, to visit the Metropolitan Museum in New York City. We walked through room after room of the paintings that I had loved so much in previous years. And what I experienced was *shame.* I felt ashamed of all those heavy, worked-on paintings.

Shortly before that I had seen a show of Zen painting and calligraphy. I had been deeply impressed by the immediate freshness and aliveness of that art.

That day in the Metropolitan Museum I resolved to devote myself to the study of Japanese brush painting. And I gave up Western style painting.

As I see it now, in Western art the emphasis is not on the person who practices it, but on the results. I noticed that in Western culture so many great artists went crazy or committed suicide; whereas in the East, artists changed their names continually to avoid fame and also gained spiritual peace as their years advanced. I realized that it is the doing, the experiencing, that matters.

Marcia Carsey

> *Just work and* do! *I think the worst*
> *thing you can possibly do is program*
> *yourself into thinking it's difficult.*

In the plush offices of ABC in Century City, California, Marcey Carsey—because of her buoyance and vivaciousness—somehow comes as a surprise. One would tend to expect a harder facade. Carsey is more like an amiable cousin who has made it, losing none of her *joie de vivre* and friendliness in the process. Indeed, in the television industry, she *has* made it in terms of both position and salary. At age 33, she is paid "over $50,000 a year" as ABC's vice president in charge of comedy development.

Carsey adores her work. "It's *me!*" she says. *"It's* all *me!"* The apparently innate instinct she has for good television comedy has gone into development of such shows as "Barney Miller," "Kotter," and those ABC comedy series which began airing in January 1977, after this interview.

Carsey's rapid climb to one of the highest positions ever achieved on television networks by a woman began with tour guiding at NBC and a "schlep" job on the "Tonight Show." She moved on to portray the "bouncey" housewife on television commercials, and in 1971 landed a job as story editor on the now-defunct Tomorrow Entertainment. Carsey was on her way. The doors opened to ABC and, after less than two years with the network, in 1976, she was named to her new position.

Married to a comedy writer 23 years her senior, Carsey has a young daughter and lives in Los Angeles.

The goal of my job is to get good comedy programming on the air. That can happen in a number of ways. Most of the time producers and writers come in to suggest ideas to me. Sometimes we go on the basis of that. My background is reading and story editing. I know from the words on the page what is good and what isn't.

I don't care if the writer is known or unknown, as long as I can read something in script form, preferably in comedy, that he has written before.

If I feel a concept is unique and fresh and can work for us, and the writer has enough going for him that I want to work with him on a script, then we'll buy it. And it's as fly-by-the-seat-of-the-pants as *that!* [Laughs.] They really don't have to have a track record. I can tell. I'm in the curious position now where I have two choices and only two. I can say "No" or I can say "Yes." And when I say "Yes," it generally means laying out a goodly sum of money according to Writers Guild minimums for a pilot script. If I have faith in the writer, I do it.

Sometimes we *internally* come up with a concept that can work for us—that's new, that's fresh. Or we come up with a personality that we want to create a show for, as frequently as we can, because it's so much easier for a writer or producer to construct a show for a personality than it is to try to cast at the last minute and hope to *God* that magic happens! [Laughs.]

I've been developing comedy series at ABC for a year now. I've been with ABC for two years. The first year I spent not strictly in development. It was a strange job where I was handed a show to be the network liaison person—approvals of casting and stuff. But the show had already been decided when I was handed it. The second year I was moved strictly into comedy programming development.

How rare are women vice presidents in television networks?

It's relatively rare to find women vice presidents in the networks, but not as rare as one would think. As far as (ABC) west coast programming is concerned, there are two of us. There's one next door here, Pam Dixon. Diane Barkley was vice president here three, four years ago. She was in charge of Movie of the Week and was, if not the first, then *one* of the first women vice presidents.

It's not that common, but I must say that the feeling about ABC—even when I was on the outside—is that they have been very receptive to women, for *years* now. In fact they hired me three months pregnant! [Laughs.] And I gave them the choice. I was very happy in the job I was in. I said, "Why don't we talk after I have the baby. If this is a little inconvenient for you, why don't we talk later?" And they said, "No, no! It's *not* a factor!" which I thought was lovely of them.

What discrimination against women exists in the television industry?

I've encountered *no* discrimination whatsoever. I've found it nothing but an advantage to be a lady. There *are* a lot more guys out there than there are ladies in every position. But that's changing. Not that many women have presented themselves. Not that many are trying. But this business is wide open to ladies, especially now.

Recently, in the last five years or so, the business of television is more and more aware that the viewers are mostly women *and* that women control most of the dials. And a lot of the programming is done from that point of view. Also, just for general purposes, they're anxious to give women a break. But mostly it's that philosophical awareness—a pragmatic awareness—that the audience is women.

There aren't that many women screen writers, although I must say organizations like MTM (Mary Tyler Moore Productions) and Norman Lear, to some extent, have nurtured women writers, also women associate producers and women producers.

Describe your typical day.

A network job is very seasonal because there are certain times of the year when you push very strongly to put lots of projects into development, and there are certain times when that levels off and the primary job then is to make those projects you've put into development *work* [laughs] . . . following them through. We are trying to do away with that seasonal aspect of the network process so that there is not a development blitz and then a pilot season. For this past season (1976), we made something like seventeen comedy pilots in about a month and a half period. And it's just *crazy* because the other networks and producers are scrambling for the *same good talent*, the same writers. It's just unbelievable. So what we're working toward is to try to make maybe two pilots a month and spread it out over the year.

But this month [July], during a typical day, I usually try to reserve the mornings for meetings. Maybe four or five meetings a day with producers, writers who have ideas. The afternoons I try to reserve, although it doesn't always work out—the best laid plans of mice and ladies [laughs]—for the stuff that is my job, really. And that is thinking where we're lacking in shows, thinking how we can make the development scheme better—whatever.

How intense is the pressure and competition?

What creates good comedy?

This is what I meant by a kind of fly-by-the-seat-of-the-pants thing. At ABC I find that *nobody* looks at tv cues which is a strange list of personalities viewers are attracted to—a private thing. [Survey or poll.] We don't ever get those. We don't believe they mean much. I'm glad for this because I wasn't sure when I took a job with a network whether I was going to be regimented to death. But ABC has a very healthy mix between the research, the numbers, the *science* of programming, and the instinct of programming. But mostly we all agree it's an instinctive process. The whole business of movies and television is a business of *magic!* You *can't* program by computer. It's as horribly intangible as an idea or a writer, a combination of a personality and an idea or *something* that just lights up the room! [Laughs.] There certainly is no formula.

How intense is the pressure and competition?

I don't mind pressure, so sometimes I don't recognize it when it's upon me in full force. [Laughs.] There are *many* deadlines. Year by year, the competition between the three networks has been increasing greatly so that you'll notice that shows get ripped off the air now much quicker than they have in the past.

The whole Nielsen system, as well as some other factors, has stepped up the competition among the networks terribly. The effect of it has been mostly healthy, very good, although it is frustrating. You *do* take the chance of a good program that one could nurture getting ripped off the air early. But by and large, I think that the ones that are taken off the air deserve to be taken off. [Laughs.] Once in a while you make a mistake, but because of the stepped-up competition we really are forced to find fresh ways to bring people to the television set. You can't go with the same old stuff any more. This, of course, makes my job more *fun*. It's more fun to try new things.

What is your background?

I was born [1944] and brought up in Weymouth, Massachusetts. I lived in the same house all my life until I went to college. My father was a draftsman at a shipyard. He was on strike a lot. We never had *no* money and we never had any extra money. Middle—nice middle. Apple pie mommy. Super kind of nice childhood. Trees to climb in the backyard.

Older brother. He's five years older. We're both a little *crazy*. I don't know how we came to be. But he runs his own company. He's an adventurer of the first order. [Laughs.] He's *terrific!*

I went to the University of New Hampshire. Graduated with a degree in English Lit, qualifying me for absolutely nothing. Then I opted not to accept some sort of teaching assistantship thing and instead go out into the real world.

So after a season of summerstock—I always loved to act—I went to New York City because one *has* to go to a city after having gone to the University of New Hampshire! [Laughs.] And the most fun thing that appeared to be going on there was television.

So I got a job as a tour guide at NBC. Gravitated toward the "Tonight Show" which was the most action that was happening at NBC. Some kind of schlep job—I was answering fan mail for Johnny Carson. About three months later I became a production assistant on the show.

How did that transpire so quickly?

It's quite *easy*. You just jump with both feet into what seems *exciting* to you. If you're bright and eager to do whatever's to be done, you just do it, that's all. It just seemed always kind of easy. Just work and *do!* I think the worst thing you can possibly do is program yourself into thinking it's difficult.

I was only production assistant by virtue of the fact that I was working for the producer at the time. His name is Jack Carsey, whom I later married. It was funny . . . It was toward the tail end of my working at the "Tonight Show" that we even thought of dating each other.

My job on the "Tonight Show" really consisted of everything. Finding out who was in town to book, sometimes helping him with the interviews of the "crazies" that he specialized in, *whatever* had to be done. It was just a job that was everything.

You found the work exciting?

Tremendously! It was tremendously exciting. Even tour guiding and answering fan mail was exciting. I *love* television. I was working in an area that I adored. I don't mean just television, I mean *theater. Everything* to do with entertainment.

Why do you love television and theater?

Why, I just *do!* It's *me! It's all me!* It's not that I feel something about the rest of the world. When I was in college I got my first taste of being on stage which thrilled me to no end. But I also adored the backstage thing. I was good at it too, which always helps. I was good at the on-stage stuff and I was good at the off-stage stuff. And I knew always what was *good* and what was *bad.* I love not only making it happen on stage but feeling it happen inside me when I'm watching a good thing.

I don't know where it came from or why, but I just love it. I think it's the most exciting thing in the world!

Why did you leave the "Tonight Show"?

After about two years I got a job at an ad agency, because I was as far as I would go on the "Tonight Show." It was fun and I learned a lot. *Time to leave!*

I worked for William S.D. Advertising in New York as a program supervisor which was one of those flukey jobs that's wonderful to get because it sounds important and—in fact—*is* important and *pays nothing!* [Laughs.] For 117 dollars a week I was recommending to Winston [cigarettes] what shows they should and should not buy into. I was kind of being a network spy. I would find out what the networks had in the works, sneak looks at them when I could and make sure that R.J. Reynolds was buying into the good stuff. Always I just kind of know what's good and what isn't, as much as anybody can. I'm kind of good at that.

How do you explain this sense of "what's good and what isn't"?

You either *do* or you *don't* have a feeling for that, I think. And I don't think you can learn it. Maybe it's just that my tastes kind of run with the people out there or something. I don't know what it is, but I always go by what I feel about something, not by what I think they will like!

[Here Carsey explains that she and her husband decided to marry when he "landed a job on Laugh-In" as a writer and relocated to southern California. "So I married him," she says, "and came out with him."]

What other west coast jobs led to ABC?

I did several things for a couple of years. I acted in commercials for several years. Usually I'm cast as a funny housewife or something with energy in it, bouncing around with a bottle of Boonesfarm wine in my hand or something! [Laughs.] It's *fun!* And a commercial usually takes only one day.

The first solid nine to fiver I landed here was after a year and a half. It was with Roger Gimbel at Tomorrow Entertainment, a subsidiary of GE. They produced "The Autobiography of Miss Jane Pittman," "Birds of Prey," "The Glass House"—a lot of *good* stuff. Long form television things . . . very nice things.

My function was story editor for the television wing. My major job was finding good material and suggesting ways that material could turn into a good movie for television, the writers that could make it work, the producers, whatever. It was essentially what I'm doing here, only it wasn't out and around so much.

Especially because we were starting a new company, we had to kind of generate the stuff from scratch. I was in touch with publishers a lot for new books coming out, going through writers' materials, original material, anything! Part of my job was kind of research, I guess you'd call it. I had to read as much material by as many people as I could just to see who was doing good stuff.

Didn't you get tired of reading?

I *never* get tired of reading. I could sit in the closet and just read things *all day*. It never bothered me. I loved it!

It got better and better. As Tomorrow Entertainment made its name in the community, the material I was reading got better and better because suddenly they were coming to *us*. So the last year I spent there was the best year.

I was with Tomorrow Entertainment for its entire life from 1971 to 1974—from when it first began when Roger Gimbel was looking for an office until it went under when GE decided it wasn't making a profit soon enough or big enough. That was shortly after I came to ABC, although I didn't know it [was folding] when I left.

You had great responsibility as story editor?

Being story editor carried a lot of, I guess, responsibility. It's fun, kind of. And I tend not to think of it as responsibility or as pressure. If you like what you're doing, it's more *exciting* than anything.

One thing I learned and Roger taught me is to trust my own

opinion wholly. It's a hard thing to do [laughs], especially when you're at the beginning of that kind of job. I was reading material written by people who had been in the business a lot longer than I had and were sometimes names that I had heard buzzing around inside my head—writers who are kind of household words. I was a little bit snowed by it. It took me six months to a year with Roger telling me to "say yes or no," and then to tell him why. You have to go with how you *feel* about something. It's the most important thing I learned at that job.

How were you hired by ABC?

I must say I always have loved ABC. They seem to be the most experimental of the three networks. At the time, being with an independent company that was selling to the networks, I got the feeling that ABC was more *innovative*, that they were *more receptive* to women in specific, that theirs was a fresher, younger approach to programming.

I had the feeling that a network is a good place to be at some point in a career in this business, an exciting place, and that ABC would be the network I would choose. That was floating around in my head somewhere, although I was so happy in Tomorrow Entertainment.

I'm undriven, if that's the word. I have never been good at making plans for my career. I think I choose not to. I had no definite plans as to what to do next because things tend to fall into place without your planning down the road.

There came a point at Tomorrow Entertainment where I was restless. I think I had been there two years. I had done for the company and for Roger, and it had done for me. I came to the point where I was repeating myself. So I told, I think, maybe two people. [Laughs.] One was my husband and one was a team of producers, Christensen and Roosenberg. I just mentioned to them that I was getting a little crazy, a little restless. A couple of months later, they got a call from Steve Gentry at ABC. Steve was, and is, in charge of dramatic program series here. He was looking for somebody to hire. Rick and Bob mentioned me, so I went to see Steve. We went to lunch together. We liked each other, and he offered me the job. I gave Roger Gimbel my notice, and he counter-offered so strongly that I couldn't say no. It was not only money, but increased responsibility—being handed projects that were my very *own* and seeing them from start to finish—that I could *not* refuse. I put that much time in Tomorrow Entertainment and that much energy and that much—believe me—*work*, so I couldn't turn him down. So I stayed with Tomorrow for another year.

Out of the blue, after a year, Andy Siegel who was then in charge of comedy programs at ABC called me and just said, "I'd like to meet you. I'm looking for somebody." And I said, "I'm sorry. I went around with Steve about that last season, and I don't think I want to leave Tomorrow Entertainment. I don't think I want the job you're offering, *and* I don't think you can meet the money." But I said, "Why don't we meet each other . . .?"

So we met, and we liked each other and he said, "I would like to hire you." And I said, "Well, there are several reasons that it's not right. (A) I know the range of salary you pay and I think I'm a little past it, and I don't want to get into a thing where you have to stretch, and ABC feels that they're putting themselves out. (B) I'm happy where I am. And (C) I'm pregnant." So I said, "Maybe we can talk later. I *do* want to work at ABC at some point in my career, but I guess this is not the right time."

Andy went back to Michael Isner, who is his boss, and they came back to me again. They brought me in to talk to Barry Diller who was Michael's boss at the time. And you know, part of the psychological thing when you say, "No," you become more attractive to somebody. It's only human nature. [Laughs.] And part of it was that they knew me from my reputation at Tomorrow—that I was good at what I did—and they needed creative people.

ABC's motivation at that time was to hire creative people. My story editing background appealed to them and the fact that writers thought well of me. They wanted to reverse the network image of kind of being salesmen and accountants, or whatever, and of network executives being non-creative. So, the combination . . . And finally I said, "Well, I might as well do it." I talked to Roger and he said he couldn't do anything [to compete salary-wise]. That was in 1974.

Your first responsibilities at ABC?

First I was a program executive. I was handed three shows, for which the deals were made, the concepts of the stars and the producers and writers were set.

They were difficult shows. None of them succeeded. It was a difficult first year.

So a great deal of energy and money might be spent on shows that are never aired?

Shows generally are aired. It's very seldom that they aren't. Even the pilots that we do that don't sell are played off usually, because they're good programs. They just, for some reason, don't fit into the schedule or whatever, or something is just a bit off, and that doesn't put it over the top.

Isn't this frustrating?

I don't find this terribly frustrating. My ego isn't at stake. I am perfectly aware that it is not primarily my creative input that is going to make or break a good show. I can help or I can hurt, sometimes. But I can't make or break the show. If it fails, I am disappointed, but the responsibility lies in *many* different areas. Mine is one of them. [Laughs.]

How did you become vice president?

When I had been at ABC a year [in 1975] Fred Silverman was hired as programming chief. He restructured slightly the network. The job I had no longer existed. I was either going to fall into current programming or into development. Since my background and my love is development, I was put into development, reporting to Andy Siegel who was then in charge of comedy programs. That was a very nice year I spent, developing comedy series along with Andy. Although I was reporting to him, he is a gentleman and secure enough to give me responsibility that approximated his. It was a nice learning period without being dumped upon with a full load of responsibility—a good year of *solid* training.

Then a strange shift happened. Andy Siegel, my boss, was moved up and over. He was made a vice president, which he had wanted for a long time, and was moved over into current programming. And I was put in his job. He was dissatisfied with his new position and, after about a month, he took a job at CBS in charge of comedy program development.

That same day I was made vice president in charge of comedy program development here, for whatever reasons I can't tell you. I mean it just *stunned* me. I moved directly into the position. It was strange, and I was pleased and delighted.

You must have real ability?

I'm good at the job, yes. I knew from the beginning what I had to do. It's an overwhelmingly big job, I must say. It's [laughs] sometimes *overpowering!*

Overpowering?

The mere fact of having to put, or wanting to put, 25 or so pilot scripts into work in, say, a month and a half time. There's no one else that has a comparable position to mine. We do have a New York development arm, but generally *I'm it.* This is not to say that Michael and Fred don't initiate things from time to time. But I do the bulk of it—25 or 30 scripts. That's where we are at the moment. The fact is that whatever is good we'll put into work, and we'll find the budget to do it somehow. Hopefully some of these pilots become series.

Based on the scripts, we'll go to pilots on some and not on others. The scripts in general you can predict. If you know the writer and the quality of his work and the producer involved, then you know that the script will come in—if not in perfect shape—at least in fixable shape. But the next step is the hard one, going from script to pilot, because many factors come into play.

The casting is *monumentally* important in a comedy show. If the nation can't fall in love with the star, it is not going to be a hit. That's it! And there are *not that many* performers available to us that can guarantee that. We often cast people that we don't know, that nobody knows, that we've seen at the Comedy Store, which is like an improvisational nightclub where they try out their material. If a writer or producer says to me, "There's a guy or a lady appearing at the Comedy Store tonight at 11:30—terrific for a comedy series—go and see them," I'll go. We're desperate for new people that are funny and likeable. Television eats up a lot of people per season.

What do you mean "eats up"?

There are a lot of comedy series going on the air, and all those comedy series have maybe five—at least five—regular recurring characters who are locked to that series. In other words, they're *off* the market. You figure that we have four new series on the air [in July 1976] and we plan two more, at least, in January 1977.

Are you the only decision-maker as far as which scripts go to pilot?

It's not only my decision. It's Michael's and Freddy's, their management and mine. When I took a network job, I had fears that it would be very corporate and bureaucratic. But I find it very—how can I say it—*informal,* easy, nice! If I like a script or if I want to develop a concept, *or* if I like a writer, personality or something, I go to Michael and say, "I'm excited about this. Let's *do it!*" And he says, "Tell me about it." More than likely he'll say, "Go ahead!" Fred is the same way. They listen. Essentially they understand the value of instinct and the creative process. It's *terribly* pleasant.

You have only two "bosses"?

Yes, which is a lovely thing. Michael, my boss, is kind of in charge of everything on the west coast. He reports to Fred, and that's *it.*

How do you respond to all of this work?

I'm used to working—the syndrome. Partly because of my middle class hard-working background and partly because I'm a lady, I'm *used* to working all the time. I have always assumed that whatever job I have, I'm going to be working my *ass* off! Weekends, nights, whatever.

Your husband understands the demands of your work?

Sometimes. I think one of the reasons I married my husband, although I wasn't aware of it at the time, is that he's terribly *good* for me. He's terribly supportive and encourages me to be everything I can be. And he's terrific! He's 23 years older than I am. That's part of what makes him secure. He *knows* who he is. [Laughs.] [Jack Carsey still works in the television industry as a comedy writer.]

Which is your first priority, work or family?

I have a baby. She's a year and a half. I understand *exactly* what's important and the priorities in my life as I have established them. *She's* first. *She and Johnny* [her husband] are first. And this [job] is second because I think that's the way it should be in anybody's life. I would be disappointed if my husband's priorities weren't those.

I think that we're people and, by the nature of people, life has a whole *lot* to do with *love.* That's where it is. It's your soul that you have to take care of first. Although this job does nurture my soul too, it's got to be second.

I work long hours, but whenever my daughter needs something or is sick or whatever, *that's* first. The job gets dropped.

Thelma Carthen

*I will suggest that working in a shipyard
is* not *play* . . .

Born in Arkansas in 1923, the youngest of five children and the
daughter of a carpenter, Thelma Carthen was reared in Shawnee,
Oklahoma. Thanks to the Great Depression, she learned early that
"if you wanted to work, you worked *hard*, because if you didn't, they
could just walk out on the sidewalk and get someone to take your
place." In 1943, with her husband about to enter the service and a
new-born baby, Carthen began her welding career. She was nineteen years old.

Carthen was there when war opened employment doors for women, and she was there when those same doors slammed shut,
leaving women jobless at the end of both World War II and the Korean "conflict." "The government is really worse than anyone else,
as far as kicking the women around," she says. As a ship welder,
she has had three employers: Kaiser Shipyard, Mare Island Naval
Shipyard, and—since 1953—Bethlehem Steel Corporation's Ship
Building Division in San Francisco. She has watched the role of
women change radically in this society and—in the front ranks of
women who stick with traditionally male occupations—Carthen has
made waves.

In the course of her career, she has worked on troop landing
barges, Liberty ships, Victory ships, submarines, destroyer escorts,
an underwater subway tunnel, oil tankers, wine tankers, and pas-
senger ships. At the shipyard where she has worked for more than
two decades, Carthen still walks "one to two miles" to the one and
only women's restroom.

She is a member of the Boilermakers Union, married to a carpenter, and the mother of three grown children.

I hadn't done an awful lot before I became a welder. I grew up during the Great Depression. I married young, as a teenager. Like most of the young people, I worked. In Woolworths, Kresses. I decorated windows in Woolworths for a while in 1942.

Then they started hiring women welders, which was *unheard* of. I didn't even know what welding was, but they were advertising on the radio about the time I had my first child. So I had to wait until after he was *born!* And I went to work at Kaiser Shipyard in February of 1943.

I really started welding because, since it was during the war, I knew my husband would probably be going into the service. I knew I was going to have to make a living. And I *had* to have a job. I didn't want to go back to Woolworths; that didn't *pay* anything. Welding paid quite a lot more than anything else I knew how to do.

As I recall, I started at $1.20 an hour. I only worked three months before I passed my journeyman's test.

I ended up on graveyard shift. That paid $1.56 an hour. I remember *that!*

Women welders were a minority?

Women were very much a minority in Kaiser Shipyards (Richmond, California) where I first worked. There were *plenty* of women in the yards doing everything else. They were operating cranes, burning (cutting metal with oxy-acetylene equipment), *but* on the welding crew, there was just myself and maybe one or two other women sometimes. There were 14 or 15 people on the crew.

When I started welding, it was just something else to learn. In the Depression, if you wanted to work, you worked *hard*, because if you didn't, they could just walk out on the sidewalk and get someone to take your place. So hard work didn't bother me.

My training was strictly on the job. When they hired me they sent me to welding school for *five days!* They didn't have enough machines for the students in the welding school. I *did* learn what a welding rod was, how to put it in my stinger, and how to strike an arc with that rod. That's about *all* I learned in that five days, because I never had a machine. Just once in a while when someone took a break. Then I could try *their* machine.

Really the only place to learn how to weld is right out there on the job. I don't care how long you go to welding school, it doesn't mean you know how to do a job when you get it.

What was your first welding job?

I was sent out as a trainee to the outfitting dock. Once the ship is basically built, it is tied up to the dock for finishing the interior. Part of the leaderman's responsibility was to teach the trainees. So the first thing he did was put me on a job. He burned a few rods and let me watch him. Then I started. It was flat welding on the ship. When I got that down pretty good, then he had me doing different jobs that were vertical and overhead.

First thing I knew, the leaderman came around and said, "I think you're ready to go over and take your test so that you can get journeyman's pay." It took him over a month to talk me into it.

I was the only woman they had on graveyard shift (11:30 p.m. to 7:00 a.m.) who would climb right out over the *side of the ships* to work. [Laughs.] A lot of the men wouldn't, as far as *that* goes. I don't see anything dangerous about it. They had staging, which is similar to scaffolding. They had a little ladder you could get out there on. That's what you call hanging staging. But of course if you fell it *was* a long way down. I climbed smoke stacks in the rain, that sort of thing.

I suppose I must have been a tom-boy when I was growing up, because I wasn't afraid of heights. I can go any distance up in the air I suppose, *if* I have something to hang onto once I get up there. But I won't go *six feet* up in the air if they expect me to walk out in space on a *plank!*

What happened to women welders after the war?

First off, at the end of the war, Kaiser laid all the women off. *Period. Right down the line.* It didn't make any difference how good they were or anything.

At the time I didn't know any better. I still had a living to make. Uncle Sam still had my husband tied up, and I had a baby to support. The allotment in those days for a wife and a child was 80 dollars a month. That was *hardly* enough to live on!

[Carthen worked as a waitress until her husband was discharged from the service. They returned to her hometown of Shawnee, Oklahoma where they started the first Veteran's Cab

Company in the country. She was "dispatching and doing all the bookkeeping" until they "were fixing to" go broke. They returned to California where she worked at two assembly line jobs. At Cutter Laboratory, a typical "woman's factory job," she put "penicillin into little boxes." Later, employed by a glass company, she "inspected and packed different types of bottles, canning jars, baby food jars." This was a "good factory job for women at that time," she says. The pay scale was $1.20 an hour, with an incentive plan. The more she produced, the more money she made. Carthen was "a pretty fast worker."

Here she updates the story of her welding career, mincing no words about the discrimination she—as a woman with a trade—has experienced during three decades.]

The government is really worse than anyone else, as far as kicking the women around. During the Korean War, they started a heavier ship building program. Mare Island [Vallejo, California] had had women welders during World War II, and when the Korean War started, they opened up to women again. The Navy was the employer.

When women were hired at Mare Island in 1950, they hired us only as temporary employees. Any of us who had not been there before weren't even put under the civil service program. We were under social security rather than civil service retirement benefits. The women who had worked there in World War II did have a choice, but the rest of the women didn't.

I never did think that this was right, but there was not one single thing I could do about it. It always bugged me that they didn't include sex in that first anti-discrimination law to begin with. They had race, creed and color. We could have any *religion,* be any *color,* but they *didn't* put sex in there. They finally did put sex in the law, but it hasn't done an *awful* lot of good!

In 1953 when the war was winding down, Mare Island laid off pretty well down the seniority line. They went far enough to get all the women, except two. And these two women had to make a fight through Washington. They were given lay-off notices. They stayed because they had been there during World War II and were in the federal government's seniority system. The rest of us didn't have any seniority to make a fight with anyway.

Mare Island was hiring again in the mid '50s. Most of the

men that had worked there before and had been laid off went back to work. The foreman did talk to me. He said, [she imitates a masculine authoritative tone] "I would *not* let my *wife* come out here and do this kind of work!" And I said, "I'm not asking you to let your *wife* come out here and do it. But *I'd* like for you to let *me* come back and do it!" Women didn't have a *chance!*

Why did you apply at Bethlehem Shipyard?

In 1953, when I was about to be laid off by Mare Island, my leaderman suggested I apply at Bethlehem. I said, "Oh, they won't hire women." But he encouraged me to try. So I called the personnel office. The personnel man said he hadn't even thought about hiring women, but he would talk to the foreman about it. One of the other gals, who was a pretty good welder, and I went to Bethlehem.

How did the men react at Bethlehem? The men there really thought it was a *big joke.* But I talked to the welding foreman. I showed him my card from Mare Island showing what welding tests I had passed. The foreman sent us over to take Bethlehem's welding test. And I think by that time everyone in the *shipyard* had been alerted, because I never *saw* so many people around! There was a big crowd of men.

My friend and I actually were a couple of smart alecks. We knew we could weld. We knew good and well we could *pass that test!* [Laughs.] There wasn't any question about it!

We took the test. And sure enough we *really knew* what to do with the welding rod!

Were other women welding there?

Bethlehem had been strictly a man's world since the end of World War II. There had been some women there during the war, but there hadn't been any women working there since. We were the first two.

After we were hired, Bethlehem gave tests to other women. They hired a total of 27 women.

How long have you been in the union?

When I got my first welding job in 1943, I had to join the Boilermakers Union in 30 days. Being a member of the union is required. No one works at Bethlehem Steel or Kaiser if they don't join or belong to the union.

Have the Boilermakers discriminated against women?

The same laws that govern companies, as far as discriminating against women, govern the unions. In 1963 Bethlehem Steel and the Boilermakers signed a contract which included seniority. Before that, if they didn't like the color of your eyes, they could lay you off. After the seniority system was signed into the labor contract, the unions still did *nothing* to help us women, until we made a fight. And we did have to *fight!*

We took a few of the lay-offs out of seniority. They were laying *women* off primarily. The union wasn't helping us. My friend Leota, a welder, told the union that if they didn't back us up in our job fight we would *sue the union*. I backed her up.

[In addition to their threat to sue the Boilermaker's Union, Carthen and her friend Leota Williams presented the local union's business agent with a letter outlining their grievances and salient features of their work history with Bethlehem Steel Corporation's Ship Building Division. The letter, combined with the suit suggestion, according to Carthen who is still employed by Bethlehem, "substantially ended lay-offs of women welders at Bethlehem, out of seniority, in so far as equal qualifications are concerned." Carthen's dual grievance—against her union and her employer—was resolved less than a week after her last illegal lay-off on New Year's Eve, 1971.

How have men treated you on the job?

I had leadermen and supervisors at Mare Island who gave me a chance to learn different metals and welding techniques. The men I worked with were very helpful if I ran into trouble. Of course, that was a small group on that submarine job. Individuals as a whole didn't discriminate but the *government did*.

At Mare Island, I worked strictly on submarines. My experience there taught me a great deal. When I went to Bethlehem, I was one of the very few welders who knew how to run low-hydrogen and stainless steel rods.

At Bethlehem they were very leery of the idea of hiring women, but they didn't hold it against us. They gave all of the women flat work so we wouldn't get *hurt!* They had guards walking up and down the first two or three days to make sure nobody got fresh. [Laughs.] I was *younger* then!

Have you ever had a problem with men getting "fresh"?

Not for a few years, *damn it!* [Laughs.]

How do you command respect?

Although I have worked in shipyards most of my life, I have
found that if you demand respect, you *get it* for the most part. I
think attitude is the key. I have a job to do and *I do it.* Generally the men are very nice. They're as nice to women on the job as
they are to other men. I haven't had to put up with any problems from men at Bethlehem Steel. If there ever had been any
difficulties, the supervisors would have backed us up.

Do you enjoy welding?

Actually, I like welding. There's no comparison between shipyard welding and assembly line, because I'll have a *different
job* every day. Some days I have a lot of different jobs, which
can make it rough. You can spend as much time running to
your machine and setting it as you do working.

I do flat. I do vertical. Overhead. I weld collars [similar to
brackets] down in the top of a tank. You do something different all the time, as opposed to assembly line work where you do
the same jobs day in and day out.

Sometimes I get welding jobs that I hate like poison. And
there isn't *anything* interesting about it! [Laughs.] For example
if I have to crawl in the double bottoms on all fours.

From one section to the next, I crawl through a 14-inch hole.
Once you get into the section, maybe you can sit up and maybe
you *can't.* I've worked lots of places where the only position
you can get into is to crawl like a snake and lay down, and raise
up on one elbow to try to change rod. *That* is the kind of job I
hate! But it doesn't come every day.

I get sort of wound up in my work. I'm interested in how
much I can do. We have an incentive program and are paid by
the amount of work we do.

Is ship welding very hard work?

I don't know of many things that are harder than pulling or
carrying your welding lines and cables. That part of working in
a shipyard and building ships is physically difficult. But once
you are on the job, the welding itself is not physically hard.

Is the work dangerous?

Being a welder is no more hazardous than being a carpenter or a lineman climbing poles. You do a *lot of climbing*, climb a lot of ladders. Of course you have to carry your rods but I don't think it's any more dangerous than most any other kind of work that a man might do.

But there are *all kinds* of dangers in a shipyard for someone who has never worked in heavy industry. All *sorts* of hazards. You have to be prepared to climb ladders and work off of staging, the same thing as scaffolding. You *stand* on those boards! You *don't* fall off of them!

You have to be very careful. If someone's working up over you, you either ask him to move or you move, if you've got any *sense.* Anyone working above you is likely to drop something. The hard hats, which we are required to wear, will help a *little* bit. But if 50 pounds falls from 50 feet up, it can go all the way through you. Hard hats won't save you from a heavy load. There's no way.

Like anything else, you learn by *doing, observing.* I've worked in three different shipyards during my career. All of them have held safety meetings, particularly with the new hires. They tell them what to watch for. For instance if 100 people are welding on a ship, maybe half of them have welding lines strung around. So you watch where you walk.

Are there many deaths?

I've always been completely amazed that there are so few fatalities in shipyards. I've been with Bethlehem Shipyard for 23 years, and I can count the fatalities on the fingers of one hand.

I don't know of any welders that have been killed out there. On the *Petri,* a wine tanker, I did know a welder who was very badly burned. That fire was caused by an acetylene leak.

What is the greatest danger?

The greatest danger around a shipyard is fire or explosion. The burning equipment is acetylene and oxygen. If the person handling the burning line doesn't know what he's doing, if he's not *very careful*, he can cause a backlash. As far as I know, burning lines have been the only cause of fires at Bethlehem.

Have you been burned?

I have little scars and little burns all over me. That's after a good many years. I don't care if you wear your leathers and shirts buttoned tight—those little sparks have a way of getting in and burning you. But it's just a little burn. It's nothing serious.

In all this time, I've only had one burn that was bad. It had to be dressed a few times because of infection.

How are you protected?

The type of protective clothing a welder wears may vary somewhat from job to job. Some welders, for example, may never be required to wear leathers to keep from getting burned.

In a shipyard, where you're in all kinds of positions, welding a lot of overhead, all kinds of metals, and right under your work, you wear leather overalls. They're just like farmers' overalls except they're made out of leather. And you wear a leather jacket, buttoned up tightly. Leather gloves. And boots. They like for you to wear safety-toes, which are steel-plated toes.

You always wear safety glasses. *Absolutely!* It's required, but I wouldn't think of working without glasses for the simple reason that you have to knock slag off of your weld. And even with your glasses on, you can *still* get slag in your eyes. Glasses also cut down the possibility of getting flashes, I'd say, by 80 or 90 percent.

If you look at a welder's arc with your bare eyes or even through glasses, you can get a flash. The ultra-violet rays burn your eyes and dry the fluid out. It may not do permanent damage to your eyes, but it's *very* painful. You don't know you have it until several hours later. You may wake up with a flash. And it's just like your eyes are full of sand. It's just like a real bad sunburn but it's on your eyes.

In the welding helmet, you have a dark lense to protect the eyes. But glasses will help, if you raise your hood and someone's welding around you.

Is welding unhealthy?

I do not think that welding hurts anyone, health-wise. There are certain kinds of metals that could be detrimental, but you just have to use the proper safeguards.

Stainless steel and some other metals, I have found, I'm allergic to. If I weld them, I'd *better* wear a respirator.

For my age, I'm a very healthy person. When I'm working, I don't do much of anything else. Except a very little bit of cooking and a few dishes. Now that my kids are raised there's only the two of us. And my husband is very good at helping me. [At the time of this interview, Carthen appeared quite fit. She weighs 120 pounds and is 5 feet 6 inches tall. She had just experienced her first accident.]

How many accidents have you had at work?

I have just had my *first* and *only* accident on the job. It was one of those freak accidents. Some planks had been piled up for staging. When I started across them to get my welding line, the planks went down. And *I* went down with them. It was a very short distance but those planks hit my leg and my arm. Fluid has formed on the knee. I had a badly sprained wrist. And my knee started twisting, *that's all*.

But, for *crying out loud*, I broke a foot a few years ago! Fell down on my *own kitchen* floor!

[Several months later, she was still laid off due to this fall.]

What is your salary?

My salary varies tremendously, depending on how much time I work and the work load. In 1975 I made a little over $22,000. That was a good year as far as salary was concerned. I worked some overtime, but not a lot. The year before that, I made a little under $16,000. [Carthen explains that in her marriage, "money is always a joint effort" and never "an issue." "It has never made a bit of difference to us who makes the money," she says.]

Is welding a good field for women?

I think it's a *marvelous opportunity* for women. I wish I had had the rights, when I was young, that women have now.

I have seen two or three young women who were hired right out of school by Bethlehem. They hire young men right out of welding school too, but the young women don't stay.

Welding in a shipyard is a lot different from what is experienced in welding school. They *don't know* what they're getting into. The women will just stay two or three weeks, then they quit. Maybe they go to work in shops where they take it a little easier.

One thing that makes it hard at Bethlehem is that the work is outside. You're out in *all kinds of weather*. Even if you're on a dry job, you're going to get wet when it rains, because you have to get outside to get your line. You might have to walk ten minutes to get to your machine.

I *will* suggest that working in a shipyard is *not* play like it is in welding school, where your [steel] plates are there in a booth right in front of you.

When a place like Bethlehem hires you right out of welding school, they *know* you don't have any job experience. If you pass an appearance test [appearance of the weld] they will give you a chance, but you have to be willing to work for it.

They start you out at union scale. Bethlehem hires you at journeyman pay, even though you come right out of school. I think it's about $7.40 an hour. [Hourly pay for members of the Boilermakers Union is $7.57]

Has welding interfered with your sense of femininity?

Doing a dirty job doesn't mean you're any less of a woman. I've heard a lot of women say, "Oh, I would *never* be a welder! It's such a *dirty* job!" It *is* a dirty job, of course. You get awfully dirty. But I found from the first day I welded that all you have to do when you go home is get in the bathtub. You use some good old soap and water and that dirt comes *right off!*

Some people think welding is hard on your skin. Some of the women I work with are 60 years old. And they have *beautiful* skin. Not even any wrinkles.

What is your attitude toward women's rights?

I go along with *all* the women's rights we can possibly get. But I think one thing that younger women tend to forget is that the women in this country didn't even get the vote until 1918. I was born in 1923. Women couldn't even vote in an election until five years before I was born. I grew up in an era where married women *certainly* didn't work at all. Even up to 1940, if a woman got married, she was *automatically fired* from most jobs. School teaching was a little safer than most.

In 1939, my supervisor at Kresses got married. She lost her job immediately. When a woman got married she supposedly stayed at home and took care of the house, and the husband earned the living.

When the war came along, changes *did* come about. When the government drafted your husband, the allotments were too small to live on. This was one of the things that started the women moving into the job market. There was a manpower shortage, so there were employment opportunities for women where there had never been before. They would *never* have tried to use women in those areas if the men had been *at home*.

As soon as the war was over and the men started coming home, everything closed *right back down* for women. There was no such thing as women's rights!

Before sex was added to the law, an employer could not discriminate because of race, creed, or religion, but an employer *could* discriminate legally on the basis of sex. Finally they added sex.

Ginger-Lei Collins

How could I quit? It wouldn't do any good for the next woman who came along.

Ginger-Lei Collins' biography is a mixture of startling facts, not the least of which is that at age 20 she worked an average of 86 hours a week on the Alaska Pipeline and earned a whopping $38,000 in 1976 for the toil she adores. In 1975 she went to Alaska largely because of her childhood friend Paula "Dodie" Burdick, a pipeline surveyor.

When Ginger Collins was fifteen, she quit school, married, worked as an under-age cocktail waitress in Florida, dug ditches, and eventually—when a driver didn't show up for work one day—drove dump trucks. Collins has been driving trucks—the bigger, the better—ever since, proving in the United States' last frontier that a woman can do just as well as a man behind the wheel and often-times better. Collins' skill, in fact, has proved embarrassing to and frequently unmatchable by her male co-workers.

Surprisingly enough, Collins experienced no discrimination as a female truck driver in Florida; the men were respectful and helpful, bearing with her while she learned the trade and tore up a $900 transmission in the process. In Alaska, however, Collins' extensive work-related difficulties stemmed directly from the fact that she is an extremely attractive young woman who is highly competent at her job. She describes those experiences in painful detail. "You've got to be careful of hurting the men's egos," she says.

When she's not working as a Teamster—chauffering boulders in huge semi-end dump trucks, hauling riprap in end-dumps, leading wide-loads down Alaska roads—Collins makes her home in Mill Valley, across the Golden Gate Bridge from San Francisco. Her step-father—whom she calls "Father"—is Al Collins, well-known veteran broadcaster of San Francisco radio station KGO.

My first job on the pipeline was in 1975 driving a ten-wheel end-dump at Old Man Camp. For three months I hauled backfill, or crushed rock, for the pipe.

I came to Alaska in January of 1975, and I joined the Teamsters in Juneau. I became a doby member, which is someone who hasn't worked under the union and pays ten dollars a month dues until you get a job. I went to the hall for call twice a day and just waited for jobs to come down to the doby list.

I waited for six months, going to the union hall every day, and waitressing in different places.

When I first got to Juneau, I worked for the City, running a 966 Cat front-end loader on snow removal. A front-end loader has four wheels and a big bucket in the front of it to pick up things, to move things. I was moving snow, loading trucks with snow, scraping five, six, seven inches of ice off the streets.

I didn't have any money, and I was staying in a hotel. The city would only pay you once a month, and the hotel was costing me 80 dollars a week. It had a restaurant and bar, so I was working there at night-time to pay my rent and just to have food money. I lived off of my tips for a month while waiting for my check from the city. I had just maybe a 100 dollars when I arrived, and that was it.

What possessed you to go there?

An old friend, Dodie [Paula Burdick] was up there in Fairbanks, but I only had enough money to get to Juneau.

I had to work two eight-hour jobs for two months. I quit both of those jobs when I got enough money to go to San Francisco to get my pickup truck. I drove back up to Juneau and got a job working at the Hilton as head cocktail waitress for three weeks. Then I went to Fairbanks and worked for about a month waitressing, and there were no union calls at all. So I went to Anchorage and worked for a month as a cocktail waitress. Then I went back to Fairbanks and worked as a waitress. I would go to work at nine o'clock at night and get home at six o'clock in the morning. I'd go to union call at nine o'clock, go back and go to sleep, and go back to the union hall at two o'clock in the afternoon, go back and go to sleep and then go to work waitressing at nine that night. I did that for a month until I finally got a truck driving job that came down to the doby list in Fairbanks.

How do you bid for a job?

You have A, B, C, and D card members. The D is the doby list. When they have a call, say for a fifteen-yard end-dump which is the ten-wheel end-dump, they give A card members first chance at the job, because they've been there the longest. If no A card members want the job, it goes down to the B list. If the B list doesn't want it, it goes down to Anchorage, and if Anchorage A and B list members don't take it, then they bring it back to Fairbanks to give A and B card members another chance. Then they bring it down to C. Eventually it might get down to the doby list.

If other people on the same list want the job, they'll give it to whoever's been out of work the longest. You just put your card in the window.

I was sent to Old Man Camp which sits inside the Arctic Circle, about 100 miles north of the Yukon River. I was driving a 15-yard end-dump for Associated Green Construction.

How many women were in that camp?

The camp had 900 men, 65 women, and eight married couples, but there weren't any other women truck drivers. There were women that were in the Teamsters—warehouse drivers and bus drivers—but there weren't any on the trucks.

When I first went to that job, the guys on the crew had never worked with a woman before. When you first get there, you're being tested. They were very polite. They didn't have anything to say until they got to know me by working with me for awhile, and I showed them I could drive.

When I first got there, they thought I was a trainee. So the foreman put me in a truck with another driver; he was showing me how to drive a truck, and I never said anything. Then, after lunch, it was my turn to drive; I was going to go for my lesson. Well, I got in the truck and I drove it, and I knew what I was doing. He was *shocked!* I had hauled asphalt in Florida.

People, especially construction people, talk. So he went and told everybody that I had driven before. Then they started testing me, like putting me on a hard haul, a hard place to back up and dump. I proved to them that I knew what I was doing.

What problems have you had on the job?

There's all kinds of problems on the job. You do have to prove yourself when you first get there. They assume you cannot do the job because you are a woman. So they put you on really *hard* jobs. They're seeing how much you can do. And at the same time, the other people that are driving are competing with you, 'cause they want to be better than you.

When I was on the semi-end dump trucks, we had a hill called Hog's Back Hill that was really hard to get up. We were empty getting up the hill. The road was loose, and, having no weight in the back of our trucks, you could spin out on the hill. You had no traction unless you sort of idled it and didn't give any acceleration and strain on your tires. Well, for three or four months, I was the only one getting up the hill.

The thing that they didn't like about it was that one of the drivers would say to another driver, "How come *you* can't get up that hill and *she* can?" They were competing with each other to make sure they could do what I could. And it got really bad, to where if I was comin' down the hill and I'd see somebody stuck on the hill, I wouldn't look at them. They really cared about what the other drivers said to them about it.

One time my foreman came up to me and said, "Would you do me a favor? I hate to ask you, but when you see one of the other drivers around, would you spin out on the hill?" I said, "No! If I can make it up that hill, I'm *going* to make it up that hill!"

What makes men accept a female co-worker?

They all say the same thing, "If a woman can do the job, then she should have it. If she can't, then she shouldn't be here."

At first they're going to see what kind of person you are, why you're there, why you're doing this. If they don't like it, then they're going to make it hard for you. If they like it, then they're going to help you.

Men get their first ideas about a woman on the job from the first woman they work with. I know of this one woman who, when it came time to put her chains on in the snow, was standing out there holding her chains, waiting for a man to come by and put them on for her. If somebody works with a woman for the first time and she's got that attitude toward driving a truck, then they're going to have a bad attitude toward every woman truck driver they see. If they first work with a woman who gets out there and takes care of her truck, that asks questions and wants to learn and shows interest, then they're going to have a better feeling for the next woman.

Goin' into a traditionally man's job, I have got to prove myself to them and show them that I can do it. I'm not always pushin' it. I just go and do my job, because I *know* I can do it.

One time I had to take the boom truck to Delta Camp, about fifteen miles from Isabel. The superintendent saw me drivin' a loaded low-boy once before that, and then he saw me on the boom-truck. He just didn't think that a woman could do it. And he went into the Teamster shop and told the dispatcher that no women are allowed on boom-trucks or low-boys, only on little flat beds and dirt trucks. Well, you can't *say* something like that!

I went in there and, in front of my foreman, I told the Teamster steward, "You can't *do* that! That's discrimination! That's *prejudice!*" They let me take the truck to Delta. If I didn't say anything, the next woman would not be able to get on a boom-truck or low-boy.

I had a laborer that was with me on the boom-truck and did all the little labor stuff. He told me that he wouldn't have said anything; he would have just quit and gone and tried to get money for it. You know if they lay you off on a discrimination deal, then you can go get money for it. But I wouldn't quit. How could I quit? It wouldn't do any good for the *next woman* who came along. I want the next woman who comes along to have a better chance.

How many women truck drivers are on the pipeline?

On my first job at Old Man Camp I was the only woman driving trucks. In 1976 there was one other woman, Greta, who was on the end-dumps at Isabel Camp. Then there was the woman with the chain situation . . . they learned on the pipeline. I know of one other woman, Sue, whose father has a logging company in Oregon. She's been driving all her life. She was hauling the 80-foot sections of pipe up North. I only know of these four, though there may be a few more. I was the only woman on the semi-end dumps. There were seven end-dumps on that crew at Old Man.

Does it ever pay off to be a woman?

It does pay off to be a woman! My boss let me have a chance to learn how to drive the semi-ends. He didn't do that for any of the men who wanted to learn. And the only reason I think he did that for me was because I was a woman, and he liked me.

Why did he like you?

Because I worked hard, and, well, later on he fell in love with me. Which is maybe why he let me learn how to back up the tractor-trailers. He was the same person that asked me if I would do him a favor and spin out on Hog's Back Hill.

It got to the point where if I had lunch with one of the drivers too many times, he would either transfer that driver or not speak to me. I went to a bar in Paxton with one of the drivers one night and he [the foreman] didn't speak to me for four days. Paxton is about twenty miles south of the Camp. It's lodge-like with a gas station, a restaurant, and bar.

Did you have a relationship with this boss?

I had *no* relationship with him, and I never gave him any cause to be the way he was.

I was doin' my best. I was tryin' all the time. He told me one time, "If you can get up that hill, you can have a truck." Well, I made it up that hill all the time—maybe it was because I was determined.

When I went home at night, for the three weeks before the trucks ever came, I used to think how to back those up, which way to turn the steering wheel. I'd get up in the morning and my roommate would say, "What are you *doin'?*" I'd be layin' on the side of the bed, pretending like I was backin' a truck 'n' trailer. [The foreman eventually had Collins transferred to another crew and to another location, Isabel Camp.]

How did you react to this transfer?

I couldn't see at that time exactly what was happenin'. I couldn't see that he just couldn't stand me bein' around there anymore because he was in love. At that point I felt like here I was tryin' my *best!* It was like bein' kicked, like it wasn't any good doing your best.

I just couldn't believe it. He gave me the chance to learn to back up the trailers in the first place, and I was hurt! I was *really* hurt.

I felt like it was sort of degrading to go from the semi-end dumps to the end-dumps, because everyone on the end-dump crew at Isabel knew that I was driving the semi-end dumps. So I told him when he was driving me from Pump Station 10 to

Isabel that I wanted to go on my two weeks R and R, and he said, "Well, when you come back and you're back for a week and you think you can work, you come and talk to me and I'll see about getting you back."

He told everybody a different reason why I transferred. After I was back on the end-dumps for one week, the foreman of the end-dump crew quit, and this same guy came up to my truck and said, "Now that Dick's gone, I think I can get you back." [Laughs.] Something was *really* wrong! After all this stuff, it finally came into my head why I was transferred. It was because *he* could not handle it!

After that, every time I saw him he would always ask me to come back. I would *never* go back. I finally got over havin' all the hate for him.

What other difficulties did you have on the job?

There's a training program in Anchorage; after you go to it, you're sent to one of the camps. About 25 percent of the truck drivers on the pipeline come out of that program. They gave me a woman trainee once when I was drivin' end-dumps.

The training program was ten days. When you have a trainee, you get 75 cents more an hour for nine hours of the workday. This woman was nineteen, and she learned really fast. She *loved* it, and she learned how to down-shift which is one of the hardest things.

Then they gave me another trainee. And *this* woman trainee, she didn't want to drive a truck! You'd tell her to back up or somethin' and she'd say, "No, I *don't* want to do it!" She fell in love with one of the drivers out there and she wanted to always ride with him. Everytime I'd tell her something, she'd say, "I know. I know." And *then* she wouldn't do it.

I couldn't stand it anymore, so I went to my foreman and said, "Mike, can I trade trainees with somebody? *Please!*" He said, "Talk to me tomorrow about it." He just didn't really want to listen to me about it at all. The next morning I tried to talk to him, and he didn't want to listen then either. So that night I talked to the head of the training program; he went to the foreman (Mike) and told him to put her on another truck. Well, that deflated the foreman's ego, when somebody had to come and tell him what to do on his crew.

One day another driver didn't show up. So his trainee came to my truck. There were just four of us that had trainees. The trainee got in my truck, and he was with me the whole day. I went up to my foreman and I said, "Did you pay me for that trainee?" He says, "No, I didn't assign that trainee to you." I said, "Well, *why* didn't you take him off my truck earlier?" He says, "Who was it, before, that went and talked to the head of the training program?" I said, "I did. You wouldn't *listen* to me!" I was pissed. He says, "I ain't payin' you for that trainee, and I *guarantee* you I'm not!" I said, "Why don't you just pay me? You'll get in trouble, man." He just didn't like me!

About three days later I got paid. I had the Teamster steward after him and I got the pay. [Collins also cited several other incidents created by foremen's biased attitudes toward her.]

How many women were in Isabel camp?

At that time there was 1,700 people living in that camp, and about 300 women.

About half to three-quarters of the women that come to a pipeline camp move in with somebody within three days to a week.

Three days to a week?

Most women there have a boyfriend immediately. Some women feel that if they have a boyfriend, they won't have any hassles with the other men, that it makes it easier.

What was your typical day driving semi-end dumps?

You get on the bus with everyone else and go to the job site. You start your truck up, and you go to the pit or the quarry—to wherever you pick up your rock. It was about seven miles away. You get loaded up, and you come back to the dike; we were building the dike. You dump and you go back and get another load.

You carry about ten loads a day, with about a half an hour lunch. Every day is completely different. There's never two days that I can remember that are alike.

People think you go around in the same circles all the time. But the circles are not the same all the time. Different things happen every day—you may go to different places.

Do you enjoy the work?

Oh, I have so *much* fun! 'Cause I *love* drivin' trucks. I do! [Laughs.]

What do you like about it?

I just like it. When I was a kid, I used to love to drive, too. I used to always bug my parents to let me drive. I've always liked drivin' and I like goin' on trips.

One thing I really like is drivin' a *big* truck. The steerin' wheel's *this* big. [Holds out her hands.] And you have a *huge* engine, a huge hood in front of you. And I just like sittin' up there, up high, sayin', "Look at me!"

You get a sense of power from it?

Sort of. It makes me feel good because I say to myself, "Look at what I'm doing. I can *do* it!" And I have *fun* doing it too, which makes it even better.

Another thing is that this year [1976] I have learned so much. I learned so many mechanical things.

How have you learned?

When something goes wrong with the truck and the mechanic's working, I watch him and I ask him what that part is, how to adjust my brakes . . .

I want to know more about the trade. I want to be a better truck driver. In truck drivin' there's not only drivin' the vehicle, but in a lot of jobs you have to work on them yourself. Sometimes they won't hire a woman because she doesn't know mechanics. I'm thinkin' of takin' a beginner's mechanics course this winter. I *want* to know more about it.

What does it take to be a good truck driver?

To be a good driver, you have to have common sense. You've got to have lots of courtesy with other drivers. You've got to know *who* has the right of way. A loaded truck always has the right of way. A truck comin' up hill always has the right of way. Don't *ever* stop a truck comin' up hill, especially if they're loaded, because it'll burn the clutch out tryin' to start up again. They'll have to back all the way down the hill.

A lot of drivers don't know that, but they learn it after they've been there for a while and they get cussed out. A lot of foremen don't know it either. They'll stop their truck on a hill, loaded, and *boy,* they get told!

Have you found that many foremen or bosses on the pipeline are incompetent?

Very inexperienced! Qualifications for being a foreman are being able to give orders, give directions, yell, and wave your hands! [Laughs]. A lot of people get in a lot of trouble.

You have good mechanical ability?

I do learn really fast. There's a lot of things that I do learn fast. I love to sew . . . and cooking too.

Truck driving can be dangerous?

Yeah. I've seen two people killed. A lot of times, it's running out of brakes. You've got to know what to do if you do lose your brakes. I've been in some bad situations a lot of times, without havin' any brakes.

One time was when I was at Old Man [Camp], and I was goin' down Fish Creek Hill loaded. My brakes hadn't been adjusted in a long time. On the pipeline, they won't let you adjust your brakes; the mechanics have to do it.

I'm goin' down this hill, and I have plenty of air but no application to my brakes. It was muddy. There was a skid truck in front of me, which is a flat-bed, that had a bunch of pieces of wood on it. And then there was a tractor-trailer comin' up the hill. *And* there was a twelve-foot drop. I've got my air horn on full blast, and I had the choice of goin' off the twelve-foot drop, runnin' into the skid truck and having all the skids come into the window, runnin' head-on into the other truck, or waiting patiently for it to get up the hill, which is what I finally did.

There's just so many different kinds of things that can happen. When I was at Old Man, they had nothing but dirt roads, so we had blow-outs all the time. I've had 'em going 50 miles an hour, loaded, downhill.

Is there a high mortality rate on the pipeline?

There is a high death rate. I know of three people that were killed in trucks on the pipeline.

Doesn't this make you nervous?

A lot of people get killed drivin' trucks because they're careless. I'm careful, *really* careful. You do have to be on the alert, especially for the other drivers. I have seen some *bad* drivers on this pipeline! They do some things that scare you sometimes. Some of them just like to ride a center line; they're afraid they'll go in the ditch. I'd rather go in the ditch than head-on! The other drivers are a *big hazard!*

I'd say three-quarters of the truck drivers on the pipeline

never drove before. They employ about 20,000 people on the pipeline. And it's such a big job you can't get all professional people.

What physical strength is required of you?

One of the things is chaining down the heavy equipment on the low-boys. I've found an easy way to remedy that. You use these long bars called cheater bars. I had a four and a half foot bar made for me, and I can tighten any binder the men can tighten, just with the leverage. That *was* a problem at first, but I fixed that. [Collins is 5'9" and weighs 134 pounds.]

How did you get into truck driving?

Well, I was in Florida, and I was waitressing. I was in Florida from age fifteen to eighteen. I had many waitress jobs. The reason I had so many jobs was because I was serving cocktails to make some money. I was too young; I'd tell them I was of age and they'd find out later.

I got tired of that work. The last restaurant job I had in Florida, I was assistant manager of a steak house in Tallahassee. I was sixteen, almost seventeen. They thought I was nineteen. And all the women underneath me that I would hire and fire and train, teach to wipe down a table fast, they had all graduated from college.

I was tired of it, *really tired* of it. I saw some women diggin' ditches along the side of the road one day. I stopped and asked one of them where do I go to get a job, and she told me. I went there and they hired me. This was for Archie Davis Construction Company; they did all the contract work for the telephone company, which was digging ditches, laying underground telephone cable. For about three weeks I had a shovel in my hand all the time, digging ditches.

It was *real* hard work, the hardest work I ever did. It got to the point sometimes in the day when you just didn't want to lift another shovel. If you didn't have that shovel in your hand, they'd fire you! And I was makin' $2.25 an hour! But that's Florida. It's a non-union state. And waitressing is 80 cents an hour.

How did you move from ditch digging to truck driving?

On our crew we had a six-wheel dump truck, a gas-burner with a four-speed transmission and a dump on the back. Our driver didn't show up one day, and I said, "Oh, I can do it. Show me how to dump it—I can do it."

So they said okay and let me drive the dump truck. And that was the *first big truck* that I ever drove besides pickups.

How many women were employed with you?

Oh, there was a *lot* of women. There was as many women laborers as there was men. And a lot of the women were drivin' those flat-beds and six-wheel end-dumps.

I got tired of all the manual labor. So one day when I went to Roberts Sand Company to get another load of sand, I asked the guy if he needed any drivers. They had *bigger* trucks there. And he said, "No. Mr. Roberts won't hire any women."

The next day, I was sittin' in the six-wheel dump truck at lunch time, and this guy comes up to me—his name is C.W.—and he offers me the job drivin' the ten-wheel end-dump, hauling asphalt and making $2.75 an hour.

Did you know C.W.?

No, I never saw him before in my life! I was just sittin' there eating lunch, being really upset because Roberts Sand Company said they didn't hire any women.

I told this guy, "Well, I don't know how to drive 'em." He says, "We'll teach you how." He was about 55 years old.

He said, "When can you start?" And I said, "Right now!" He says, "No, wait 'til tomorrow morning. What time can you come in?" *He's* askin' me what time *I* can come in! I said, "Well, what time do you start?" [Laughs.]

This was with Peavy and Son Construction Company, haulin' asphalt. I was drivin' a ten-wheel end-dump. They didn't really *teach* me how to drive it. They put me in the truck with this guy who was about 25 years old, a show-off sort of person. We drove around one block, *maybe*. It was a five-and-three transmission, five gears on one and three on the other. I'd *never* been in a truck like that before, and he says this gauge is that and that one's that and that one's that—and it was my truck! That was it; that was my training. And the first few months that I was there, I tore up a lot of things. [Laughs.]

Were other women driving trucks for that firm?

No. I was the first woman they ever had in that company. When I started there was fourteen trucks at the asphalt plant that Peavy owned.

After I was there for about three weeks, I tore up my transmission. I put it in gear and I didn't put it in all the way, and it popped out and broke a tooth on the second gear. I'd get flat tires—maybe run over something. And I got my mirror caught on a sign and I tore it off. Things like that.

You weren't fired?

The reason he kept me after I tore up the transmission was that I wanted to know *everything* before that. And they *knew* I did. I showed a *lot* of interest.

The first week I was there they played an awful joke on me that made me realize I had a lot to learn. The asphalt plant had broken down and everybody was getting fuel filters put in their truck. If you get little particles in the fuel filter you have no power at all. So they were showing me how to put the fuel filter in. And I told them, "This thing goes up the hills really *slow!* They said, "Well, why don't you just go ask C.W. to order you some spark plugs and condensers." I said, "Okay." So I went to C.W. and asked him. He said, "Sure! But where you gonna put 'em?" And I turn around and everybody's laughin' like crazy, and they said, "Diesel engines don't have spark plugs and condensers!" And that's how much I knew when I first started.

It was a rotten joke—and I'd *love* to find somebody to play it on [Laughs.]—but it showed me that there was a lot to learn. So I always asked questions and asked them to show me how to do things. They saw that and that's why I stayed after I tore up the transmission which cost them 900 dollars. That's a lot of money in Florida.

I worked there for about a year. I got up to $3.50 an hour. I took home about $175 a week which is *good* money in Florida. I worked 50-some hours a week. We were haulin' asphalt on the week days. We also paved the main runway at Tallahassee International Airport; we did that at night. On Saturdays and Sundays we hauled the stuff to make the asphalt.

Did you have difficulties with your co-workers?

No. The co-workers I had in Florida were all from the south, and the southern people are very hospitable people. If they like you, they're gonna help you in every way they can, which is the way they were toward me.

But don't they still have an idea of southern womanhood?

Yes, they do.

Then how do you explain their cordiality to you as a truck driver?

Well, maybe one reason is that they came to me and asked *me* to go to work for 'em. And the other drivers that were there helped me in learning anything. They really do show respect in every way. [Collins still corresponds with C.W.]

How does the behavior of male co-workers in Florida compare to that in Alaska?

I never had any problems with the men that I worked with drivin' trucks in Florida. I did have real problems in Alaska.

The only time I had problems was with those two foremen, when one was emotionally involved and the other one felt threatened. The end-dump foreman felt threatened because I knew as much as I did. You've got to be careful of hurting the men's egos.

In Florida they liked me as a person, and I got along with them *really* good.

Describe your self-image.

I'm very sure of myself. Even when I was little, I was so hardheaded that I *knew* what I wanted to do. I had my own thoughts, and I wouldn't listen to a lot of people.

If I want to do something, I'm gonna do it. If someone says "no," it won't do any good.

If you're sure of yourself and feel good about yourself, you can feel good about other people and respect them.

What is your education?

My father [Al Collins, her stepfather] was just set on me graduating from high school. And I couldn't find anything that I wanted to *do* in high school. If I was ever good in anything, it was Art and P.E. I barely made it through school; it was always C's and D's. That could be because I was moved around so much. My father is a disc jockey, and I went to eleven schools, mainly in California and one school in Pittsburgh. I went to tenth grade for three months in Pittsburgh and I never knew where *any* of my classes were except for Art!

And now, here I am—I went up to the ninth grade, and I'm making more money than the average American! I'm almost making more money than my father is. That's one thing that makes him feel really good, that I'm doing so well for *myself*.

He is so *proud* of me. He is *so proud!* I really wanted to prove to them that quitting school was okay.

Everybody wants their parents to be proud of them. If you have any feeling about your parents, you want them to feel good about you.

If they don't give you support, it's gonna be really hard, but if you do somethin' and they say, "Go *do* it! That's really *good!*" It makes you feel a lot better.

Did you quit school to get married?

No, I quit school and *then* I got married. I didn't even know the guy when I was goin' to school.

I quit school because I was goin' to Mt. Tam in California and I had African culture, history of jazz—*good* classes, and I was *interested* in them. And when I was in eighth grade I had wood shop and I really liked it. So when I went to Pittsburgh, I asked them if I could have wood shop. They said, "Wood shop! Wood shop is only for boys! And *don't* you come to school with *pants* on anymore!" I had to have biology, typing, math, English, just the same thing over and over. And that's why I only went to my art class, and that's why I quit school, because I *didn't like that school!*

That affected me so *much* when they told me that I couldn't have wood shop because I'm a girl. That was the *first* time that anything had happened to me where there was really a *line* drawn! I was only fifteen—fourteen or fifteen years old—but it hit me *really hard.* That's maybe now why I think, "They can't *do* that!" [Collins evidenced great anger in discussing her educational experience, more than she displayed at any other point in the interview.]

How do you respond to working on the pipeline?

I'm so glad that I've been given the chance. It's something to really take advantage of. It's never gonna happen to me again. When the pipeline's over, I'll make good money, but I won't make half as much as I make now. I think all the time how lucky I am. How many people 20 years old are able to make this kind of money? I'm glad; I'm *really* glad!

What are the longest hours you've ever worked per day and per week?

I worked two 24-hour days in a row—48 hours in a row—in Alaska. That week I got 119½ hours; and I took home $1700.

That was take-home. The state of Alaska takes 15 percent in taxes; that's pretty high.

Usually I work about 86 hours a week and I only take home about $900: that's average. Plus you get free room and food. The only thing you pay for is cigarettes and toothpaste, booze and laundry. I make $13.10 an hour.

What was your income for 1976?

As of my last pay check, I'd made $38,000. In '75 I worked on the pipeline for three months and did odd-jobs like waitressing the whole year, and I made $17,000.

What do you think of Women's Lib?

I'm glad there's Women's Lib for the people that need it.

Who do you think needs it?

The people that don't feel confident in themselves to go and do whatever it is they want to do. I feel good about the British women and the women in the United States maybe ten, twenty years ago—everything that they did has made us able to do what we want to do now. I don't feel that I have to go to the Women's Lib and get them to help me; I do what I want to do.

From whom do you think you acquired your independent spirit?

My girlfriend, Sidney. She's two years older than me—I really looked up to her when I was growing up.

I was the oldest one in my family, so I didn't have an older brother or sister. I have a seven-year-old sister, a fifteen-year-old brother, and a sixteen-year-old sister. Sidney was the only person that set a lot of my ideals when I was really young. She had the biggest influence on me. Right now we're still really good friends.

Another major influence was my real father, and I'm still influenced by him, as far as men. He was an alcoholic. He didn't have much love. He was selfish, and he never paid much attention to me. When I was born, he wanted a boy. He was that type of person. He didn't want to even touch me after I was born, because I was a girl—that type of deal. All the time I was always tryin' to get his attention. Mom said that I wouldn't eat any vegetable except for peas when I was a kid, because he wouldn't.

This really makes me wonder now how I got into truck driving when he's a truck driver. I wasn't *trying* to be a truck driver, it just happened.

Another thing I learned from him, too, was what type of men *not* to get to know. He didn't have any feelings and still doesn't. He never tried to get in contact with any of us. [Collins was born September 21, 1956, on Guam. Her natural parents were divorced when she was seven. She has not seen her natural father since she was about eleven years old.]

What are your plans?

This is my plan. There's gonna be some work in Alaska in '77, but there's not gonna be as much. So I'm gonna have to be able to go to any town where there's work. If I can't get a camp job, I'm gonna need a place to live. I'm *not* gonna pay that outrageous rent and I'm not gonna let it keep me from goin'. So I'm gonna get a Winnebago, a mini Winnebago with the Dodge van on the front. I'll live in that for the next two or three years or however long it takes me to get enough money to buy some land and build a house. *Where*? I don't know. But I've *got* to have a year-round garden *somewhere*.

Do you have any secret ambitions?

Not many people know about it, but I want to sing. I want to take some singin' lessons in between workin'. I don't know if I'll do anything with it, but I really enjoy singin' and I like to hear myself sing.

Carpenter

Mary Ewing

The idea to become a carpenter started in college when I was a weaving major. I thought "Well, Gosh! I could weave all my own blankets and I could take a pottery class and make all my own dishes. Then I could make my own furniture. And then I could make my own house!

Like the vast majority of women in the United States, Mary Ewing had no background preparing her for the building trades. Her father died when she was six. Ewing and her younger sister grew up in a male-less home in Kansas City, Missouri, the city where she was born in December, 1948. From age thirteen she worked at "all the female jobs" except typing which she steadfastly refused to learn.

A physically small woman at 110 pounds and five-foot four, Ewing fits no stereotype. Her work life has not been easy. In 1973, Mary Ewing's sheer will and a determined male construction site manager opened a carpenter's apprenticeship program to her. The work was "hard as hell."

Somewhere along the line, sometime, I decided I wanted to be a carpenter. I didn't have any training. That was the problem, and I didn't have any friends who were carpenters. After I quit my go-go dancing job I went to HRD (Human Resources Development). They have a work-study program—three days of classes and shop work, and then two days you're actually out in the field. They pay just real cheap wages, something like $1.50 an hour while you're working. But they do pay you, and you get a lot of work experience. So I took the test, a small battery, English and math. It was about junior high school level, and I got 100 percent. So I thought, "Well, I'm set!"

I kept waiting for them to call me. They never did. Finally I called and they said it was filled with veterans. They told me that veterans were given preference. At the time I thought about taking them to court.

The woman in the HRD office just couldn't understand why I wanted to become a carpenter. I asked her, "How am I supposed to learn carpentry? This is my only chance." She said, "Well honey, go out and buy yourself some tools and jump in your truck and go find work." At the time I had no job, no money, and no truck.

They probably never had a woman in that carpentry program. And they probably don't now either!

I had a friend who was a general office manager at a hospital construction project site. Most office managers on construction sites are men. She ordered everything from nuts and bolts to curtains. She called me, said they needed some help doing part-time file work, and I didn't have to have any special clothes. I said, "Absolutely!" That was in 1973.

So I went out there. She had talked to the project manager and told him I wanted to be a carpenter. After I'd been there for a short time, he called me into his office. I guess he decided that I was really sincere about becoming a carpenter.

The problem was getting into the apprenticeship program. You have to get into the apprenticeship program, then the union lets you in. And then you get a job.

How did you get into the carpenters' apprenticeship program?

I had to take a test. It was math and tool recognition. So I bought some books and studied all the tools and the types of screws. I took the test and did well enough to get on the list to be accepted to the apprenticeship program *when* it opened. This was in February. The apprenticeship program is always closed in the winter; it doesn't open until May or June. But they *were* letting men in at the time I took the test—favorites, friends, nephews. It's all politics!

The hospital project manager started pushing his weight around, stressing the fact that he was running a federally funded project and the apprenticeship program couldn't afford to turn me down. He made phone calls, saying things like, "I don't care what your position is, this is what I *want!*" I was in the apprenticeship program in three days!

I was making around six dollars an hour. That was 60 percent of a journeyman's wage at that time. It was fantastic money!

What was your first on-the-job experience?

I didn't know which end of the hammer to hold when I started. I knew nothing about carpentry. And I went through hell!

I started in the panel yard, an area with a table saw where they build panels. You build the panels, then button them together with snap ties and pour the concrete in between the panels, and then strip the panels off and use them over and over.

That's where I learned to carry 2 x 4's and plywood, to drill straight, and that's where I started hammering. There's a way of letting the weight of the hammer work for itself, rather than forcing it, and not letting your arm get tired.

I was just exhausted. In the mornings I couldn't open my hand. It was so cramped up, I couldn't open it out of a fist. The hammering was the worst. Lifting and carrying is just a matter of balance.

The first six months, I would have to climb up panels leaning against the building. I thought it was pretty scarey. Now I realize there's nothing to it.

They wouldn't let me use the skilsaw [a powered, circular saw]. There's a ruling that says you can't use the skilsaw for the first six months. They never stuck to it until I came along. Then they stuck to the rules. It upset me. I just felt it wasn't showing much faith. But I was petrified to pick one up because I'd seen a lot of scars.

Now I love the skilsaw, even though I've cut my fingers. I could have lost one finger. It took quite a few stitches. I was ripping a 2 x 4—cutting it with the grain—and I ran this skilsaw over my fingers.

If the saw hits a notch or if you're holding the piece of lumber incorrectly, it can kick back on you, and the blade can run up your leg.

There are tricks to knowing how to handle all the tools properly. The journeymen might teach you tricks. Some are real helpful. A lot of them, though, are like cooks, they don't like to give their recipes away. They just watch you struggle.

How did male co-workers react to you?

I was working with two journeymen, probably two of the best carpenters. They were so patient. They never ridiculed. They were in their thirites. It was surprising; usually that age group is real uptight about women in the trades. I believe both of them were married.

It was the other men that caused me to cry. They'd laugh and they'd scream from the top of three stories, "Hit it Ewing, nail it!"

I was under incredible pressure. At the time, I was so bad, they just stopped and stared. And the more people that stared, the worse it got. Since that time I've learned to ignore it.

Because I'm a carpenter, most carpenters just think I'm strange. There's little effort made in getting to know me as a person. I did work with a young black surveyor once. He understood the kind of pressure I go through. He was the first person I've worked with who I felt I earned respect from as a person.

Have you been handicapped in any way because you are a woman?

I didn't have any knowledge of tools. A lot of men in the trade had fathers who were carpenters. They grew up with it, so they have quite an edge. I didn't even have a father—no older male to observe doing handiwork. My parents were divorced when I was very young, and my father died when I was about six.

There is an aggressiveness that I don't have . . . just a way of physically throwing yourself into your work. But I don't believe women are incapable of the work; women do have the physical strength to do it.

Women are taught not to push . . . the whole social scene. Women sit and wait to be asked on dates. They're not taught to be aggressive, and aggressiveness is really important in being a carpenter.

What are the physical demands of carpentry?

When I'm working, I try to gauge myself against the men. I've never given myself a hernia, and I'm surprised at that! The heaviest thing you pick up is plywood, high density plywood, and it's very, very dense. I know how to lift now, but sometimes I didn't use leverage to its greatest advantage.

I was really afraid of what was going to happen to my body when I got into this. I was afraid I would get ballerina legs—they did get larger, but my body didn't become grotesque. My arms, legs and pectoral muscles got larger.

I've had blisters, aching muscles. I find that I get muscle bound, so I do yoga.

I'm also a small woman. I'm 5 feet 4 inches and weigh 110 pounds. There are a lot of women who, I'm sure, are much stronger than I am. I've made up for it by having a good work attitude, and I think that's why they keep calling me back.

The carpenters who do work with me learn a certain respect for me because I really try. I'm a hard worker.

Do you specialize in any particular aspect of carpentry?

In my case I've done nothing but concrete work really, building panels, stripping panels, putting up tinkertoys [metal scaffolding].

I've found that carpentry is pretty much lost—the skill and the craftsmanship. Lots of carpenters, for instance, don't know how to build stairs; it's very specialized. Some people do nothing but build stairs all their lives.

What is your salary? Union fees?

When I started I made around six dollars an hour. Now I'm 90 percent of a journeyman, and my salary is $9.90 an hour. Journeymen start at $10.75 an hour and then it goes up.

I haven't taken my raises whenever I could. I have a personal thing about it, about being sure I'm worth the raise.

The union dues go up when the wages go up. The dues just went up to $19.50 a month.

It costs about 40 dollars to join the union. You're on probation for the first three months you're working, then you join the union.

What does the apprenticeship program entail?

The apprentice program lasts four years. Every six months the wages go up five percent, but you have to work 600 hours in each six-month period. You have to have 4,800 hours of work to become a journeyman.

When you're in the apprentice program, you spend three and a half years in school, going one night a week for five hours. The public school system pays for the apprenticeship schooling, and the courses are college accredited.

You get all your manual training on the job. There is absolutely no manual training at the school—you read your books. I've only taken two classes in which we didn't have a cheat sheet for the tests. A cheat sheet that goes around from generation to generation. The instructors are so hyped on passing you and getting you through that many of them are aware of the cheat sheet, and they don't care. [Ewing attends apprenticeship classes at San Francisco's John O'Connell Community College.]

The classes are stairbuilding, framing, concrete properties, concrete forms, using the level and transit . . . that's usually surveyor's work, but the carpenter has to know the instruments. Carpenters often have to use welding in construction; we call it "rebar," that's reinforcing steel.

What is your attitude toward unions?

The unions, I think, are much too big and much too powerful. They've got nothing to do with the working carpenter, as far as helping you secure a job or keep a job. I know of very few journeymen who go through a union hall to get a job, very few. The unions do fight for wages, though.

Have you done any organizing?

After my first year in carpentry, there was a wildcat strike. The union wanted to pull men off their jobs in a two-day sanctioned walk-off. Nixon's payboard had okayed this carpenters' contract, but when it came time to get the raise, the pay-board dragged its feet. The union wanted to call us off our jobs, but they couldn't guarantee that I'd have a job when I decided to go back to work. As an apprentice, the union doesn't get you jobs, you have to get your own.

We walked off the job. After the union said, "Okay, go back to work," the rank and file carpenters decided we weren't going back so that we could force the AGC (Association of General Contractors) to give us the raise that was coming to us.

I got cornered in a little hallway by plenty of large carpenters saying, "Okay Mary, walk off with us. We need you. We *need* a woman." And I kept saying, "No, no. You can't promise me anything. None of you have really done much for me. I'm not going."

One man said "Oh, to hell with her. Who needs her anyway?" That pissed me off, and I said, "Okay, okay. I'll show you who needs me." So I walked off and helped organize them. I set up a telephone communication line and a way of sending pickets out and a way of getting calls back in.

The unions didn't back us at all. They sent men to work through our picket lines. I learned a lot about politics. There were a lot of hateful feelings.

Some of us were off from six to eight weeks. I didn't have any savings, and my boss didn't want to hire me back. The union had gotten the general contractors to agree to hire us back, but they told me, "Well there's nothing we can do for you." I went to my local and they went out and talked, and after two days I got my job back. I hadn't worked for six weeks, and I didn't have any money coming in. I just got real, real upset!

As far as organizing during the strike, the men responded real well to my suggestions. They were relieved to have someone take over while they were out trying to harass other men off the job.

I went out a couple of times on what were called the "Doom Squads." I tried to talk men off their jobs. I found there was no respect for me because I was a woman, and I couldn't do a lot. I wasn't respected for my political beliefs.

Did you go to college?

I had two years of college. First I studied to be a fashion illustrator. Then I changed my major to weaving, because I lost interest in wearing high fashion clothes. I went to college off and on for four years.

An art major just seemed to be a luxury. I didn't feel it was a meal ticket to anything. I didn't draw or paint or weave much when I wasn't in school. I felt that if the only time I did it was when I was in school, then it was pretty worthless, because I wasn't going to be in school all my life.

Your formative years?

I was born in Kansas City, Missouri on December 5, 1948. My mother and father were divorced when I was three, and my sister and I went to California with our father. My father was a lawyer. He died when I was six, and my sister and I were returned to Kansas City where our mother took care of us. [Her mother is a teacher and has a master's degree. Ewing's sister is two years younger than she.]

How did the absence of males in your family affect you?

I think it helped me that I never learned to depend on males. I just wanted to be self-sufficient. When I'm ready to buy land and build a house, I won't have to have an old man to help me do it.

What was your employment background before you became a carpenter?

I've been working since I was thirteen years old. All the female jobs! [Laughs.] I was a page in a library. That was my first job, making 55 cents an hour. I worked as a salesgirl in an all women's store off and on. And when I was in college, I was a waitress at the Yuck Down, a beer joint in Lawrence, Kansas. Upstairs was the Yuck Up. [Laughs.]

The women were the worst customers. They'd come in with their old men, and I guess the short skirts put them up tight. Women don't tip very much either. You'd think they'd understand that cocktail waitresses are just trying to make a living! I guess there's a stigma attached to cocktail waitresses. A lot of people think they're not much better than whores. You get hassled enough . . . that's for sure!

I worked as a seamstress in Colorado for a short time. I was supposed to take care of the clothes in a head-shop run by a commune. But just too many people came to the commune, and a new shop just couldn't support 15 people. So once the first batch of clothes was sold, the money went to buy food instead of to new material.

Then I went to Canada to follow a man. That was when there were a lot of draft dodgers there. They were *real* tired of Americans and it was hard to get work.

I came back to the United States for various reasons in 1971. I just felt really at loose ends. I didn't know where I was going or what my talents were.

I lived with a man. I didn't have a job, and I just took care of the house. Oh, my God! I just became a bitch. It was horrible! I wasn't doing anything productive or taking care of my own life. I didn't work for almost a year until we split up.

I had refused to learn typing, so I'd never have to fall back on that. So I didn't have any skills.

The first job I got then was go-go dancing. It was clothed dancing so our place didn't do too well. It wasn't real hard work, but it *was* really boring. It didn't make me feel real good about myself!

After three months I quit my go-go dancing job and decided to learn carpentry.

Do you feel any responsibility to other women?

I've got to finish the apprenticeship program. I feel that I owe it to the women behind me. When I started, I heard "Oh, yeah, there was a woman in the apprentice program. She lasted three months." And "Yeah, there was a woman in the trade; she froze on the thirty-second floor, and they carried her down." Not real encouraging . . . so I feel I owe something to other women.

I just feel that women do have something to offer the trades.

They have a concern about what they're doing and a good work attitude.

Why did you want to become a carpenter?

The idea to become a carpenter started in college when I was a weaving major. I thought "Well, Gosh! I could weave all my own blankets and I could take a pottery class and make all my own dishes. Then I could make my own furniture. And *then* I could make my own house!" [Laughs.]

Donna Garrett

It's a very small, petty business sometimes.

A beautiful woman in her thirties, Donna Garrett is one of only 25 women active in stunt work in the Hollywood-based movie and television industry. [There are 250 stunt *men*.] She doubles for such well-known actresses as Raquel Welch, Angie Dickinson, Barbra Streisand, and Jacqueline Bisset. Her gymnastics training, physical strength, and confidence serve her well in hair-raising stunts she performs in movies such as "What's Up, Doc?" "One Hundred Rifles," "The Deep," "Fantastic Voyage," and the original "Airport."

Garrett adores her work and the intricate skills it demands, but the discrimination against women in her male-dominated field is appallingly widespread. Garrett is a frank, talkative woman who speaks out against the inequality she still experiences after twelve years in "the business." She highlights the blatant sexism that overshadows Hollywood, as she knows it, "behind the scenes."

I am a stunt woman in the movie industry. I double for actresses. The purpose of the stunt double is to do stunts, so that the actress does not get hurt in any way.

Even if it's an easy thing like maybe driving a car and near misses, or maybe going over a high gorge or whatever the circumstances, if the actress should get hurt in any way, they would shut down production and that would cost a lot of money. It's more reasonable for them to hire us.

I have been in stunt work for about twelve years. My husband is a stunt man. He was working in the business when I married him. I was a physical education major, going to school and also working and he suggested I get into the business. I said, "Well I don't know if I'd like it." And he said, "Well why don't you *try* it?" I said, "Okay!" So I got into the business. After about three months, I went on an interview to double for Raquel Welch, and I got the job on "Fantastic Voyage." I've been doing stunts ever since.

Most of us get into the business by doing extra work. We get in the Screen Extras Guild. Then as our reputation and experience progress we get into the Screen Actors Guild Union, which is the stunt union. Once you're in one guild, you automatically get into the other. All you have to do is get a job.

"Fantastic Voyage" was the first film in which I ever did stunt work. I did what they call "wire work." It consists of being in a harness, and there's a man who's up in the rafters and he sends you across the stage. And there's a man down on the floor of the stage, and he raises and lowers you. You're going about forty feet, depending on how high the ceiling is. Up and down and across. At the same time you're flipping and turning. You're in a harness attached to wires. This demands a *lot of coordination* between the men and yourself. [Laughs.] And if the wire should break, of course, you're in very bad shape! You'd be down on the ground!

How dangerous is stunt work?

I have to say that I think each stunt is very important and each stunt is dangerous within *itself*. The ones people usually get hurt on are the very simple ones. The very difficult ones always seem to come out very well, and nobody gets hurt. It's incredible! I think it's because you prepare for the difficult ones. You have everything organized and planned. The equipment's set up. You're very aware. Everything's proper.

With the easy stunts, you can think, "Well . . . this is nothing. *Anybody* could do this." And you *forget* to look at everything. That's when you get yourself in trouble. It's imperative to consider that all stunts are equally important.

What has been your most dangerous stunt?

The stunt that I feel was most dangerous? That's the one where—if there was a mistake—I would have been dead. This stunt was on the show "Shadow of a Hawk."

There was a gorge we had to go over on a suspension bridge. When they told me a "suspension bridge," I thought I would just have to hang over the side and climb back up. Actually, part of the bridge fell away in pieces under my feet.

The gorge was really there. It was 150 feet down and the bridge was swaying about fifteen feet and as we walked across, the planks fell out. And it was freezing cold. There was a helicopter above us that was creating the wind. If he had moved in any direction, he would have hit the trees and come down on us and we would all go down in the bottom of the canyon. So there were a lot of circumstances. There were three cameras going. It was a very technical thing. It had to be done right or not at all.

This stunt was a good stunt for a woman. There are a lot of times when women don't get to do the really good stunts.

Have you had any close calls?

One time I had a really close call. That was on a show called "Earthquake." They were tearing down some houses across the street from Universal. They were going to get the feeling that these houses were coming down because of the earthquake.

One house we went to was a very small wooden structure, about forty years old. A dozer man got behind the house. I was in the window frame. Two men are supposedly helping me out of the window. The house came down so *fast!* They had *no idea* it was going to do this. My back was to the frame of the house because I was coming out of the window. The men were facing the house. They could see what was happening. And I was very calm, nothing bothered *me!* [Laughs.] I could see the siding going because I was in the frame and in *my mind* I could see the speed of the frame on the siding coming down. And I thought, "Well I have just enough time to get out. Everything's fine. I'm not worried." But I forgot about the *roof!*

The roof was moving faster than the siding. The guys were yelling, "Hurry up! My *God!* The house is coming down! Let's get out of here!" We did, and as we proceeded to get away, there was another house in front of us. So that blocked our exit. The roof was coming down on us, and there was no place to go. It landed and finished, thank God, I would say less than a foot from our feet.

I've been in this business so long that, I swear to God, I thought it was *not real.* I thought it was fake. So I had to go up and try to lift a big beam of the roof, to believe that it was real. I couldn't lift it! I would say that incident was my closest call.

I hung over the ledge of a sixteen story building in "What's

Up, Doc?'' And that was at night; about three in the morning they finally got to us. All I had on was a towel, I got cold. It was winter. I *always* get cold.

Four times I went over the edge, climbed back up, fell over. And then the director came up—it was very *funny*—he said, ''I would like you to come out and jump out more and then grab hold of the ledge.'' I said, ''Yes, that would be fine. I'd love to do that. It will be no problem at all,'' I said. ''But I think I need another cable behind my back.'' My safety line was at an angle going into the window; the window was about three feet up from the ledge.

And I said, ''If I jump out, that cable will taut and slap me into the concrete ledge.'' He said, ''Well, how long will it take?'' I said, ''I don't know. You'll have to ask special effects.'' Special effects told him it probably would take about an hour. And he says, ''Oh! Well I don't think we have enough *time* for that.'' I said, ''Okay, then we'll just have to do it the way we're doing it, because I'm not going out there and *kill* myself!''

So we did. I fell over the ledge, and it was fine!

What does it take to be a good stunt person? Physical strength equal to that of men? Courage?

I think that a woman would never have the physical strength of a man. I think that a woman could, with leverage, probably produce as well as a man in the strength department. I'm extremely strong. But I realize I'm not as strong as a man. I never will be. Stunt women *are* much stronger than most women.

There's an area which I call *guts*. If you are a very good stunt person, you will go beyond the average ''courage.'' Let's say for instance going over the gorge 150 feet, how many times would you practice that? *Never!* So in that kind of situation, either you have that extra ''courage'' or guts, or you don't. And if you don't have it, you're not a good stunt person. I've always had it. If anybody'd dare me, I'd do it. I think it comes from self-confidence, especially in the physical department. I really enjoy being out there doing a stunt, when I'm physically involved to my best ability. When I do a stunt right, there's nothing that exults me more than that feeling. I really feel great! I don't go around bragging. I'm not that kind of person. What matters to me is knowing I've done a good job.

What I like best about stunt work is the unknown. It's very exciting, thoroughly enjoyable. I love that element of surprise, doing a good job . . . that *thrill* of accomplishment. It's a terrifically satisfying job. *I love it!*

Do you experience fear?

I think there's more of a fear of not getting the stunt done properly than there is a fear of getting hurt. Actual fear never enters your mind. If it did, you wouldn't be doing stunt work. You *do* want to do the stunt right the first time, if you can.

I think we're all *concerned* . . . that's the word for it. Even an actress when she's going in to do a scene, she has the same adrenalin, the same apprehension that we have. We want to do a good job and we want the stunt to look hairy *and* we want it to be *safe*. I have never had anything go wrong except in "Earthquake." That situation was not planned very well. Usually everything is worked out to the letter.

Who was your role model when you were a child?

I was born in the San Fernando Valley. My father used to work for a man who owned a lot of land: a property manager. My mother has always been a housewife.

I think that I never actually had anyone that I patterned myself after. The first four years I was being raised, my father was in the service, and he was gone. My mother and I spent a lot of time together. When my father came home, I never really got to know him very well. I never had an idol in the movies or in the music field. I know a lot of my friends did. I think the only person I really looked to was myself.

Because I was a girl, I was not *supposed* to go out and swing on the bars and not supposed to run track. That was the syndrome in our time. And I always excelled in those things. My mother always wanted me to be a pianist. But I always happened to have this incredible inborn ability. My mother had it before me but she didn't use it. She was always very limber, very gymnastically inclined, but of course in her time, they didn't do anything at all. [Laughs.]

My independence, I think, has come basically from my own inner ability. I've always had this I'll-do-it-myself and this *stubbornness*. I'll call it stubbornness! [Laughs.]

Does the erratic work schedule conflict with your home life?

I'm very fortunate. I'm married to a, shall we say, "liberated man." And he knows the business. Any time, say, if I get a phone call at ten o'clock at night saying they want me on the first plane at six o'clock the next morning, I say, "Yes, I'll be there." And I don't have to ask. And maybe if he comes home later I'll say "I have to leave in the morning." He'll say, "Okay, let's get organized. Let's get the kids organized." And I'm gone.

My husband's very self-sufficient. There isn't *anything* he can't do himself if he has to. My husband has really helped and encouraged me *tremendously*.

The children are very well adjusted. We talk to them—explain what's going to happen next. When we do spend time with them, it's 100 percent. They get to go to a lot of places and do a lot of things. They've been on the go since the day they were born, and they experience a lot of things most children don't. When they meet new people, immediately they adjust to the situation.

Usually either my husband or I are at home while the other is gone. That way the children (ages three and five) are aware that we are their main hold on life.

Where have you traveled?

I've traveled to Africa, Europe a couple of times, Bermuda, Alaska, Canada. When I get a traveling job that goes far away like that, I've just *loved* it. I've spent as long as three months at one time away from home.

What education have you had? Has it aided your career?

I got as far as three years of college, majoring in physical education. I didn't finish because I changed my mind and decided I just didn't want to be a teacher.

When I was in college, I used to compete in swimming, gymnastics, and diving. My background in physical education, particularly gymnastics, is definitely very, very helpful to me in stunt work.

How did you learn stunt work?

My husband is very good at all things. So as it came to different things like motorcycles, he taught me how to ride bikes. He's also an avid scuba diver, so he taught me scuba diving.

The high work, as far as high falls . . . that was *very* gymnastically inclined. That was very *simple* for me.

Horse work, we both went out and learned together from a very dear friend who has been in the business a long time. He's a terribly experienced person with many years "in the saddle" as they say.

You learn from different people. If you wish to know something, you can always ask a fellow stunt person. They'll be glad to help you.

Now you must be an all-round stunt person. In the past it was *very* specialized. The motorcycle people were one clique. The horse people were another. The films used to be mostly westerns, musicals. Now there is cops and robbers more. There's a lot more car work, water work—it's so *varied* now.

Adaptability is the main asset of a stunt person. They'll say, "Action! Now do it!" But you *do* have the opportunity, if you feel the situation is dangerous to you, to say, "This is *not* set up right. It's going to take another ten minutes. *But* it's going to save my life!"

You have to know where your body is, where it's going. You know it through experience. You just don't learn this overnight.

Describe the types of stunts you perform and the equipment you use.

We use different kinds of equipment. We have an air ratchet. It's a harness that uses compressed air, and snatches you away. For instance if you supposedly get hit by a rifle and they want the effect that it "blows" you across the room, they use an air ratchet.

There's the air ram. It's a box which has compressed air in it. You step on the door, and it catapults you in the air. It throws you. We use that in a car-hit. You hit it at the same time the car's coming by, and it makes you look like you're flying through the air. You go something like fifteen feet in the air and hit the ground. You just learn how to fall.

For wire work a harness is made to fit you. You use a harness for flying, when they want you to "fly" through the air. But you don't *always* use a harness. In high work, you could be on the rafters of the studio or on a tower.

For water work, you need to know how to scuba dive. I am a certified scuba diver. When they film underwater, it's usually thirty or forty feet under.

As far as water work with boats, I know how to drive a boat. I fall out of boats going about thirty miles an hour to thirty-five. I've water skied a couple of times in stunt work, too. My husband and I have a boat and we also water ski.

I did a stunt jumping out of a boat for Angie Dickinson on "Police Woman." We did a boat chase. That's one of the few times my husband and I really worked together on a stunt. He drove a boat for one of the actors and I drove the boat for her. We had a chase, near misses—it really was great *fun!*

High work is falling off roofs into an air bag. An air bag is a piece of equipment that comes in different sizes. It's blown up by a fan. It has little air vents which you open and close depending on how hard you want the surface or how heavy you are when you hit the air bag. The women in stunt work fall thirty to forty feet.

What about the men?

Men go higher. They go eighty feet. Women haven't developed it any higher because it's *never* called for in any scripts. Very seldom is there a script where a woman does a high fall that high—as high as men.

When you fall, it's a free-fall. We have no lines or attachments on us.

In the horse work, I doubled for Raquel Welch in "One Hundred Rifles." We were in Spain. Horse work . . . oh, that is *so* varied. There is so much to that. There are mounts and dismounts. There are chases. There are horse falls, saddle falls, rearing falls in which the horse rears and you fall off the back, jumping . . . Then they have the wagon department. You drive a team of horses—a one-up, a two-up. This is one or two horses. Women have only driven as many as two-up, I think. I am most proficient at doing mounts and dismounts and chases.

All of these things I've learned through lessons or actual experience. On occasion I have had to pay for classes. A lot of it just takes experience and time—a lot of time. Once you learn the basics, you must perfect them. Once I learned the horse work, I had to keep going and going and repeating on my own. A lot of things, too, you learn as you go along. You can't learn anything overnight. So I would take months, working every day on it, even if I might not have a specific job in mind.

The motorcycle work I learned from my husband. We would go out every weekend. I would go out and I would ride every day with him. And when the children came, we took them *too*. We put them in backpacks and on the front of the motorcycles when they got a little larger. It *never* slowed us down to have children! [Laughs.]

You do falls?

I do stair falls which are really very hard on the body. [Laughs.] In relationship to what we get paid for cars, I really think we should be paid *more* for stair falls. The idea is that *anybody* can do a stair fall. You start going and you roll down the stairs! In car work there's a lot of skill and a lot of ability and you have a lot at stake because you have a car. But it's *not* hard on your body! [Laughs.]

What stunts pay the most?

I really think car work pays the most, depending on the stunt. When I went over the gorge in "Shadow of a Hawk" that was a specialty. And when I went over the edge of a sixteen-story building, *that* was good money. Or when you're hanging from a helicopter, that's good money.

Compare the salary of stunt *men* and stunt *women*.

Stunt men make as much as 50,000 to 107,000 dollars a year. The women make between 15,000 and 20,000 dollars a year in stunt work. The work is so scattered, and there is a season for it, *especially for women*. Men can go through the seasons, but we can't. There's not enough work. Not enough jobs available.

Women should have equal opportunity to make equivalent salaries but we don't have equal opportunity to perform high paid stunts and coordinate shows.

The guys are doing a lot of the work we'd like to do, too. Under those circumstances, I would say we work six months out of the year, if you put all the days together, but they are spread out. The season is usually between June and February. From February to, let's say, May, it's pretty slow, because of television. Television isn't in production during those months.

Your work is more in television or movies?

There's more television work for women. I'd say 75 percent is television work and 25 percent is movies.

Because of the residual factor, television pays better than screen. We now get 100 percent residual return on what we do. Before, it was only something like 35 percent. When you do a job, you might not be paid as much now. But next year when they rerun the show, you'll be paid as much as you were the first time. In movies you get paid very good money for the *one* time you work and *that's it*. In television the show might rerun, rerun, rerun.

What is the rate of pay?

We go in on a base rate union scale of $172.50 a day. And after we do the stunt, we dicker for the price, depending on what we think it's worth and what they have in the budget. So it always is variable. You never can say just what any stunt is worth.

Explain why stunt women do not have job opportunities equal to those of stunt men.

In television now, as in all the performance industry, there are stunt coordinators. They are fellow stunt people who are now in a position of recommending people to work—basically hiring. They also have the power to fire and to set prices for different stunts. Now that there are stunt coordinators, it is sometimes very difficult for women to get jobs, because it's very political. In the past, before they had stunt coordinators, we'd get our *own* work through Production. A lot of times we set up our own stunts and we'd have to do everything ourselves. They've had stunt coordinators for the past five years.

With this stunt coordinator's position, it's more difficult sometimes for women to get jobs in television. In movies, there has always been a coordinator or person in charge. For movies, they usually take the men for stunt work. Because, if they go on location for two or three months, it's more economical for them to take a small man and double him for a woman than it is to take a woman and, let's say, use her for two weeks and send her home. So they use a man double.

In the Los Angeles area there are more stunt men than stunt women. And the scripts *do* call for N.D. work—that's nondescript work. Let's say there is a stunt scene where they have five cars. In the five cars, they will use *all men*. It's not specified in the script whether these people are men or women. We could get more work through this N.D. position, but we're *not* getting it. They just don't think of using women.

Especially in car work, a prime example. It's a very sad thing, but a lot of people have in their minds the old cliche "The Woman Driver." It's *very difficult* for them to change that idea. And when it comes time for us to do a driving job, they automatically go to production and say, "Oh! *She* can't handle it. *A woman can't do that!*" This is without even *asking* a woman first whether she can or cannot. So they use men. They sit them in a car and put a *wig* on them and you really can't tell. It's a problem!

I often am told that, "Well, you're a woman. And you should be *home*. And you shouldn't be getting as much money as a man because you're not supporting a family." Well, I don't agree with *that!* I mean if I'm doing a job and I'm doing it as well as a man, why shouldn't I be paid as well? And if I can handle a situation with a car like jumping it or turning it over, I feel that I *should* be given that *opportunity*. Because I feel definitely that in car turning over and car jumping, *I can do it!* Women just haven't been given the opportunity!

What stunt women would like is for Production to give us the opportunity to have the choice of first refusal [to double for actresses]. If there's a very difficult stunt to be done, we'd like them to call the stunt women and find out if any of them are capable of doing it. We're just asking for equal treatment, so that the jobs that call for a woman's double *go to a woman*.

When it comes to experience and ability, we've *got* it! If anything, we're making the men look great if they hire us. We get the job done in the first and second take, and we go home. The guys say, "Hey! That was really *good!*" So if we're that good, why aren't we being used on more jobs? It's a dilemma . . .

Is age discrimination a problem for stunt women?

That situation does develop in our industry. It *is* a matter of age. It's not fair, but that's *it* as far as women. Men can work until they're 67 years old in a stunt coordinator position or they still can do stunts if they want to. A woman who works until she's 40 is *lucky!* After that they say she's too old. I don't think that's too old.

There's a woman who's 45, maybe older. She does horse work. She's done it all her life. I worked on a show recently with her. One of the young girls tried to do some type of gag on a horse, and she couldn't get it done. This woman came up and did it the first time, because she's got the *experience*. You can't trade that in for youth, I'm sorry!

The men don't admit it because it's a *game*, but they *want* the young girl. The men have the power to hire, so they're going to hire the young girls because they're more interesting to *look* at . . . and *enjoy*. [Laughs.] I was born in 1942.

What are stunt women doing to eliminate this discrimination?

The Stunt Women's Association was formed six or seven years ago. At the time the stunt coordinator was not in the position he is now. Now he's in a much more powerful position which jeopardizes our work. With that in mind, the Stunt Women's Association is trying very hard to make Production aware of the fact that we want the choice of first refusal and that we also would like the opportunity to become stunt coordinators, *especially* for the predominantly women shows now on the market.

We're asking for the predominantly women shows like "Wonder Woman," "Police Woman," "The Bionic Woman." All these are governed by men right now. There's no reason a *woman* couldn't handle those stunt coordinator jobs.

My hope for the Stunt Women's Association is that we can get to the producers and make them realize what's happening. I don't think they're aware of the situation. They *do* have the power to make it work. They have to *change* the situation.

It's very difficult to change people's minds, especially when it comes to a male and female role. They assume the stunt coordinator position is a male's role. They just *think* that a woman would not be able to handle it, and they use the excuse that a woman is too emotional.

Why don't stunt women instigate legal action?

We could always use the Equal Opportunities Act, Title Seven. But this business is so *darned political!* I say this because of a situation that just happened recently at Universal. We went to Universal for three months, talking to them about the idea of having a woman stunt coordinator. Universal is very good about listening to the idea of changes. Members of the Stunt Women's Association went in for a meeting. The man we were talking to said, "Well, we have a *very good* situation going for you. We have a co-stunt coordinator position available on a movie."

Two hours later they chose a woman co-stunt coordinator, but unfortunately she did not have the experience that our women have. The fact that she was not with the Stunt Women's Association was not the problem, because there are women who are not with our group who are excellent stunt women, who have put their time and their dues in and have really worked hard.

We wrote a letter, stating that we felt it was very unfair that they hired an inexperienced woman and that the job was given away as if it were nothing, as if you had to have *no experience, no talent, no nothing!* We wrote this letter to the heads of Universal, to the producer of the show, and to all those involved in the situation. It was taken as a very bad move, supposedly, on our part. They condemned us totally. And now the men are totally against us.

Any time we make any waves or try to promote an idea, a lot of personality problems and political conflicts result. It is *so difficult!* You just don't know where to turn . . . what to do next. You could use the Title Seven . . . yes. But the person or the group who uses that will be *castrated totally,* I'll *guarantee* you. They'll bring in *other* women to take our place. So that puts *us* out of work.

It helps us if the actresses recommend or ask for us. Sometimes there's a sad situation. If an actress recommends someone, the person in charge might want someone *else* because of *politics.* So they will tell the actress "Well, I'm sorry, she's *busy.*"

It's a very small, petty business sometimes. I never would have believed it. I've always felt equal in my household and I never was aware of the facts of this industry until I had jobs taken away from me. And I knew I could do them. The men generally don't understand. They say, "That's all right. Just turn the other cheek and go the other way. And if you *don't,* you're *not* going to be working!" I used to turn the other cheek all the time. But now I'm tired of turning. It doesn't do any good.

Inez Ruth Hills

*I looked him in the eye and I said,
"That depends on the kind of woman
you hire!" He looked up at me and he
laughed. He said, "I guess you're
right," and he hired me.*

Forklifts, twin band resaws, rippers, trim saws: you name the equipment in a cedar fencing mill, and Sandy Hills mastered it long ago. A "foreman or supervisor" for the past eight years, Hills started near the bottom of the mill ladder doing piece work and climbed up rung by rung, hand over hand.

The first woman employed by Quinault Pacific Corporation in Shelton, Washington, Hills says, "I learned all the jobs from the man I think the world of, my employer." As both a trailblazer and standard-setter, Sandy Hills opened the mill's doors to other women who, today, comprise "over fifty percent" of Quinault Pacific's employees.

The youngest of ten children, Inez Ruth Hills was born in Waldport, Oregon (population 2,000 she estimates) in 1930. Because of rheumatic fever, she quit school after the eighth grade, and left her parents' farm at age fifteen when an older brother "took to striking" her and knocking her teeth out. She then lived with family friends who gave her the name of Sandra. "They didn't have any children," she says, "and if they had had a daughter, they would have named her Sandra. I've carried that name since . . ."

Hills became an avid horsewoman; breaking horses and riding competition "for fifteen years." After her first job as a waitress at age sixteen, she went on to fish filleting, trailer-home finishing, hotel desk clerking and Christmas tree shipping.

Christmas Tree Town, U.S.A., as Shelton, Washington is called, today provides a livelihood for Hills' entire family. Her two grown sons have followed their father's footsteps to Simpson Timber Company. The elder "runs the big stacker" in the dry sort yard where her husband "bucks logs"; the younger son works in the mill. Meanwhile Sandy Hills, age 46, arises at 5:30 a.m., dons her jeans, sweatshirt, heavy shoes and takes her supervisorial place in the Quinault Pacific mill, the niche which she carved with two primary tools: equal opportunity and a clear sense of her own personal work ethic.

My job is really a hard one to describe because I have to do so many different things. But basically I am a yard and grade supervisor of Quinault Pacific Corporation, a cedar fencing mill in Shelton, Washington.

It's a mill where you bring in logs, put them through a saw mill, cut them to certain dimensions, run them through other machines and end up with a product of fencing pickets, fencing rails, and fencing posts of all dimensions.

I supervise usually from 20 to 30 employees, men and women. It varies, depending on how busy we are. We might be running a seven-day week schedule with two supervisors. Sometimes we are both in there seven days.

On an *average* we have 40 employees, and normally there are about 24 women employed in the mill. The figure varies because of the amount of work and the availability of women that really want to get out and try this kind of work.

You supervise more women or men?

I would say that in the remanufacture department where I'm most active, there are more women than men.

I direct them on grading. This is the various grades of fencing which you have in any type of lumber. You have grades that you sell it by. The employees have to learn each grade and package sizes, according to whether we're going to rip it or trim it or sell it as it is.

We want correct grade. And we want them to work consistently so that we know, day by day, what we're going to put out and what we have to sell. They will automatically pick up speed as they do this. But we want consistency in the grade of lumber so that our customers *know* that when they order a carload of a certain thing, that's *exactly* what they're going to get.

You must be quite competent in your job?

Well, my boss thinks so or he wouldn't have kept me ten years! [Laughs.]

Are you the first woman to work for the mill?

Yes, I *was* the first woman to go to work in that mill. That was on September 9, 1966.

I was hired to learn to grade and, what we called at that time, "string-tie" bundles of fencing picket. That was on piece work.

How much were you paid?

At that time it was pretty low. It was pretty hard to make a wage out of. I was paid four dollars for a thousand pieces if they were just graded and stacked, and I was not paid for the low grade, only for the number one. For the string-tying it was eight dollars a thousand pieces.

I got to where I could make 20 dollars a day. That was working *pretty fast!* [Laughs.] Because I just got paid for the number one materials.

This was heavy work?

Yes, at times. Sometimes you got real light lumber. But when it comes to string-tying, I was putting ten pieces of 1 x 6, six feet long, into a bundle, then picking it up and stacking it. Those bundles probably weighed anywhere from 25 to 40 pounds, depending on whether they were wet or dry. But I didn't find it too difficult because of the way I was raised. I've always been real strong.

Wasn't that wage terribly low?

I thought that I wasn't really being treated fairly on the piece work, where I had to handle so much low grade and was only paid for the number one. I went to Al Johnson, my boss, one evening about two months after I started working there, and I told him that I felt this way. He said, "If you *don't* think I'm a fair man, you *can't* work for me!" I said, "Well, do *you* think you're being fair?" And he said, "Well, maybe I don't know what's going on!"

I said, "Well, would you like to walk with me to the dry shed?" He said, "Certainly." So he came out, and I showed him the day's run of low grade that I had stacked, free, gratis, and the amount of high grade that had come out of it that I got paid for. At that point, the break-down between high grade and low grade was about 50-50.

He put his hand on my shoulder and he said, "Sandy, you're absolutely *right!* You'll be put on an hourly wage starting tomorrow morning." [Laughs.] He had no idea of what was going on because the foreman was handling this, and the male foreman at that time objected to women.

There was discrimination from the foreman?

In the beginning. I was the first woman there, and there *was* a definite feeling that women didn't belong in that mill. But it *soon* changed. [When Hills began working at the mill, there were "about ten" employees.]

Have you ever been a sex object at work?

No way! [Laughs.]

Have male co-workers *ever* displayed sexist attitudes?

Right in the beginning there was a mild amount from the men—they didn't want women there.

When you went across the yard to go to your job position there were whistles, catcalls, that sort of thing. When they found out I wasn't even going to *look up,* they quit it. [Laughs.]

It wasn't *too long* until they found out that all I wanted was to do a job and earn a paycheck and that I wasn't up there to look at them or play with! *Then* it was great!

There was one man, Randall Carpenter, who was just great! He was at the mill when I went to work there. He was a head rig sawyer in the big mill. Where the other men *just* didn't want me there, not me particularly, but just didn't want a woman there—he was just *wonderful.*

I always took my breaks right where I worked in the big shed that I graded in at that time. I would never go in the men's lunch room, and I never had my lunch there. I left them *strictly alone,* to do their jam sessions or whatever they do in there. He would come out and bring a big thermos bottle of coffee for me and sit down and talk and give me encouragement and companionship. I just thought the world of him. He was kind of a father type image, my own father having been gone for years. He was just a real great guy.

What was your reason for working there?

I didn't start out to be foreman at all. All I did was go to work to help my husband pay for a home and raise our two sons.

What was the application process?

[Laughs.] Oh, it was kind of funny really; I walked in with this other lady. [Laughs.] He [Al Johnson] said, "Yes, I have considered hiring women but we don't have any bathroom facilities for women. Really, I'm not too sure it would work because you would have the problem of men *and* women working together, as far as male and female go." I'd never met the man before. I looked him in the eye and I said, "That depends on the *kind* of woman you hire!"

He looked up at me and laughed. He said, "I guess you're right," and he hired me.

I learned all the jobs from the man I really think the world of, my employer, Al Johnson.

His wife, Gloria Johnson—I really feel *great* about this lady—went along with her husband hiring a woman in the mill, to try them there and see if they would work. She always treated me with real *great respect* and understanding.

She could have been very jealous, but she wasn't. He's a nice looking man and he has a nice way about him. He holds a real high regard for women.

You were grading lumber until your promotion?

Yes, I still grade lumber, really. I went from there on to the extensive grading system, a round table is what we call it. It looks like a big wagon wheel and lumber comes out of the machine and drops on it. The graders work around that.

Then a woman friend of mine, Ella, was hired. She was the first woman hired after I was. Al Johnson told her I was to be her boss. I didn't know anything about *that!* I told her, "He's full of *baloney!* He's just pulling your leg!" [Laughs.] I didn't know it, but it was the truth. [For about five years Hills did "seven inventories a month" and "used to do all of the recording of production for eight different departments," in addition to supervisory duties.]

How *did* your promotion come about?

After I'd been there about two years, Al Johnson called me in and said, "You're going to have a new boss in the yard." Of course Ella and I kind of slipped our cool because we didn't want a new boss. We were yelling, good naturedly, back and forth. Then he said, "Well, I hope you like him, because it's *you!*"

I said, "Oh, come on Al! I don't know anything about it!" He says, "You're *going to try it!*" That's how I got started about eight years ago.

How many bosses do you have?

Just one.

You're second in the chain of command?

I think there's probably about four of us that share that position. Ella is one of them. I taught her and I'm just *real proud* that she's got up there. Two of the four are women. [Hills' salary is $1,300 a month.]

What equipment do you run?

I learned to drive forklifts to move the logs and to load boxcars.

I used to have to take two forklifts down into the log yard. A log truck would unhook its trailer and we'd get a lift on each side of the trailer and pick it up, and the truck would back under and we'd let it back down. Things like that.

Was that dangerous?

At that point it was a little bit because of ground conditions. This was eight or nine *years* ago, and we've improved greatly since then. This was a *real mudhole*. There were ruts and it was difficult to control the lifts sometimes to make certain that we didn't drop the big trailers.

It's been a constant thing of grading and driving forklifts, running trim saws, and resaws.

What is a resaw?

We have a twin band resaw, which means it has two blades on it and you feed dimension sized wood like a 2 x 4, 2 x 6, 2 x 8, through the saws, and they bring them down to a nominal one inch. And these go over a grading belt and are graded.

How great are the occupational hazards?

Well, there aren't really any great deal of them if you use common sense. I tipped [laughs] a forklift over once with a big load of lumber on it, but this was due to ground conditions and a truck driver that didn't want to move his truck. I tried to bring the load off, and me, forklift and all went over, but I wasn't hurt.

Does the weather create a problem in your work?

Yes, it does. For many years we were right out in the open with no roof over anything. But now we have *most* of the people under cover. The lift drivers and the supervisors still trudge around in the rain and snow.

"Under cover"?

It's not exactly a building. It has a huge roof over it but it's not covered on the sides. So it *is* cold.

What is the lowest temperature you work in?

Oh, it's gotten *real* cold! We've gotten as cold as 5 below. But that's rare. We do occasionally in the winter get some deep ice and snow. We had to shut down just once because of too deep a snow.

How do outsiders react to you?

The people from the outside, for instance, the truck drivers that come in to be loaded, do react. I have three women forklift drivers and they can load these trucks quite well, but my basic loader is a man, he's a real cracker jack. But people are amazed when they see a woman on a forklift. They back up about *forty feet!* They just can't believe their eyes. This is the first mill where they've seen women doing this type of work.

This is a medium-sized cedar mill. There aren't too many in the country. I know of another cedar mill that also puts out fencing, but I don't think any women work there.

Are women quite rare in mill work?

They have been I guess. To these truck drivers it is unusual. They come in with loads all the way from Canada, take them to Denver, places like this, and they're just astounded. We've had a few that said they did not want a woman to load their trucks. So they go to whatever boss is above. We have never had one of our bosses go along with it. "If you don't want to be loaded," they'll say, "pull out of the yard!" After you put about half a load on the truck, the driver changes his mind; he gets real friendly.

What other jobs do women perform at Quinault?

They run trim saws a great deal. In fact the mainstay of the mill is those women trimming that lumber. They have to know the grade and be able to trim it out.

How do male employees react to you as their supervisor?

When you first hire a new male employee I think you have a—I hate to use the word—but I think it's a jealousy type thing.

They seem to think it should be a man's position. They get a little bitter with you for a little while. And if you're not easy going about it, you never would have a man working for you. But there are ways to work around that. I'd say within two months, if they stay, they change their minds completely. I think they do come to respect me. I *have* to feel that way.

Have you found any difference between male and female employees, as far as hard work?

You're going to get me in *trouble* there! [Laughs.] The difference I *have* found is that if a woman wants to work, she is a *better worker* than a man.

Why is that?

There've been so many years of discrimination in the past decades when women couldn't get a job that paid anything, maybe 75 cents an hour like when I started to work as a waitress, or $1.25 when I was a desk clerk. You couldn't make anything.

I think it's still an appreciated fact with the women that they can come to the mill and make the same wage that a man makes. I think it causes them to work harder.

Are most women strong enough for the work?

We find this to be a big problem. They'll come in and say, "I really want to try it. I know I can do it, because I've raised three kids. I do housework. I work in the yard. I've helped my husband build a home."

We try to explain to them that it's a little bit different when you're working eight straight hours. They really get the sore muscles, and some of them won't even come back the next day. They're just too sore, and they quit just like that.

But if they come back and work for three or four days, then those muscles start to tighten up and they become harder and firmer. It's real good for their health. Once their muscles get firm, they'll feel better. It's just a matter of sticking with it. Heavy-set people trim right down and they get proud of themselves. It's really kind of nice to watch.

What work do women do best in the mill?

Grading. Because they're faster with their hands. There isn't one person—man or woman in any type of work in the whole mill operation, from the big guy down to clean up kid—that won't agree that women are faster with their hands! And this is what it takes to grade fencing. They're coming at you a mile a minute—that's just a figure of speech, but they're coming very fast.

I have seen about two men who were just about as fast with their hands as women. But in general women are completely faster with their hands. I think this is because of women's basic way of life all these years. We do housework and we take care of the kids at the same time. It's the ability to do more than one thing at a time. Men will do one job at a time and that's it.

What are your personal goals?

It's hard to phrase, but I really want to be part of my company's success. I want to see better working conditions and wages for our employees. A comfortable profit for the company will, in turn, benefit us because we're on a profit sharing plan. This helps our community, too, if we can provide jobs.

I feel real good about helping to create a place of employment that women can come to and be treated equally, have equal pay. If they're willing to work hard, they'll make a good wage. To me it's good work, it's outdoors, and I think it's good for your health. It'll help their husbands, or if they're divorced, it will help them raise their children. I feel real good about that.

How has your occupation changed you?

In some ways I have changed. I feel more satisfied with life. I like the place and I feel like I'm part of it. It seems to give me a reason to strive for better things and to see that I could actually help other people, whether it's women *or* men in that mill, to strive for better working conditions for them. It just kind of gave me a goal. And it *has* made me more capable and understanding about people and their problems and how to run a profitable business.

The only thing really I *had* to change was social life. You cannot socialize with your crew. If you go out and have a few drinks with them and one or two of them starts to get a few too many, then if anything's been bothering them on the job, that's why it comes out. And all of a sudden you have horrible feelings. And if *that* doesn't happen and you just have a good time, why the next day on the job they kind of take advantage. So you learn to socialize outside of the circle of people that work for you. This has to be a rule.

What is your reaction to firing other employees?

Horrible! Horrible! I just had to fire two men this morning. There was complete disregard for our company. There was nothing I could do about it.

Does it drain you emotionally to have to fire other employees?

Very much. Sometimes I can't even eat supper at night. It could be my check as well as theirs. I guess you could say that this is a disadvantage of my responsibility. I've *never* enjoyed firing. I don't think I ever will.

You do hire employees?

Yes. Each supervisor is allowed to do their own hiring and firing.

I've hired almost all of the women here, except after Ella got on, she hired a few. They aren't all here now; some of them you have to let go. I've probably hired twenty, thirty men, and probably fired that many men *and* women. If they work they *stay,* if they don't, they *can't!* [The starting wage is $3.00 an hour. Hills has the authority to give raises as well as hire and fire.]

You mentioned that you never entered the men's lunchroom. Is this still true?

Yes. We have a real nice lunchroom for women. It's my doing. I think it keeps down on a lot of jabber, for the *wrong* kind.

We had a problem one time with a male and female employee who were both married to other people and looked good to each other. *Boy!* The race was *on!* There were a lot of problems, a lot of hurt feelings on both of their families' sides, and I put down a hard, steadfast rule that there would be no more of it. The women would eat *there* and the men would eat *there* and they would *not* be together on lunch breaks. [Husband and wife teams can have lunch together in their cars, but, Hills says, "I still don't allow the men to come into the women's lunchroom, and the women do not go in the men's lunchroom."]

What is your most important trait as a supervisor of other people?

The hardest thing for me to learn was the personalities. I found that if you didn't stop and study the personalities—male or female—you're going to be *lost*. Right at first, I just wasn't willing to take that much time. I was in a hurry. I had been handed a job and I wanted to do it. But I learned that you have to be sensitive to the people, or you're going to be lost, because each person has to be approached differently to get the best working capacity out of them.

You've got to be willing to listen to their troubles and show them that they are appreciated. If they're doing a good job, let them know it! Talk to them. Give them a raise. Maybe you're so tired that you want to go home—it doesn't matter. You have to listen to that person's problems. The men bring their problems to me and are as frank about them as the women. [Ages of mill employees range from "sixteen to about 57."]

What personal conflicts have you experienced from your work in what is usually regarded as a male capacity?

It bothered me quite a bit for awhile because you have to dress quite masculine. I try to wear a white blouse, something like this. But you begin to have people say, "Hey, Mister!" when they come into the yard. When you turn around they immediately apologize, but they're not expecting to see a woman in this position.

How do you maintain your sense of femininity?

You just plainly have to. When you leave your back door and go to work, you become a supervisor. And when you come back into your back door, you become the woman again.

Are you a traditional woman at home?

Yes. At home I do the housework and that sort of thing. My husband helps, however. He's real good about it. He was just doing the dishes a little bit ago. [Laughs.] We've been married 28 years. My husband has quit the falling and bucking [cutting] and is in a dry sort yard now. They bring the logs into this big yard, put them out on the ground, and he bucks them. He doesn't have to climb the mountains to do it now.

Have you regarded yourself as a trailblazer?

Well, I never did for a long time, until it was brought to my attention by Mr. Johnson's wife. She said, "Do you realize what you've done?" I said, "No." I thought I was in trouble! [Laughs.] And she said, "Have you looked at how many women are here?" And I really hadn't up until that point.

I have set high standards for the women. They either *do* the job and conduct themselves in a correct manner, or they don't stay.

Do you take vacations?

This year I'm planning to take my first vacation in ten years. The first year I went to work there, I put in for a leave. I was the only grader and the foreman came out and said, "Sandy, we've got two boxcars that have to go and I don't have a grader. If you leave on vacation we're shot down."

I said, "Okay, I'll stay." It's been sort of like that every year since.

Was your childhood rather economically deprived because of the depression?

Yes. My folks raised ten of us. I was the last one.

My folks were *financially* poor all their lives to their death. But we didn't really feel poor because we had plenty to eat. We lived on a farm. My Dad hunted, fished. We had plenty to eat, never were hungry. [Hills was born December 12, 1930 in Waldport, Oregon, "a small town on the Oregon coast," where she lived until her family's home burned when she was twelve.]

What people affected you the most?

My father. My father raised us kids all to be independent, to learn to do for ourselves. He taught us what hard work was, and to always do a job the best we could no matter how big or how little it was. He was a very firm, strict man, but a good one.

Did you finish high school?

No, I went through the eighth grade, started high school, got rheumatic fever and had to quit.

What occasioned your leaving home?

Well, one of my brothers and I couldn't get along too sharp when he came home from the service. He took to striking me quite often, knocked my teeth out, so I decided I'd leave home.

When was that?

About 1945. I talked to my father. He went along with it, and I went to live with some friends. I stayed with them two years and I rode horses for them and rode competition for many years [a total of fifteen] after that. I broke and trained my own horses and some of theirs.

They were real good friends. I worked on their farm for them and was raised like their own child. They were great people.

What about women's lib? How do you feel about that?

I believe strongly in equal rights. I think this is good. If a woman does a man's work, she *should* be paid for it. If a man is doing the same work, he should be paid equally. But women's liberation, where they break into men's clubs and they have to go there because they've never been allowed to go there . . . this is more or less *degrading* the male and female aspects of life. I just don't believe in it.

Rather than raise a bunch of heck and cause a lot of static with everybody and bring the whole world down, I think they can just prove themselves. I think that home and marriage is the best background you can get. I really would like to believe it.

What do you feel the most effective way of obtaining equality in employment is?

Proving you can do the job and doing it graciously and not being a horrible-type person about it. If you go in, keep your mouth shut, do your work, and I believe they'll learn to respect you.

Kay Holloway

*I think motivation is the important
factor.*

Only four women in the United States are chiefs of police, according to Kay Holloway, the "number one law enforcement officer" in
Coalinga, California, population 7,000. An agrarian community
bordering the San Joaquin Valley, Coalinga has "a small town, rural
atmosphere. Cotton, tomatoes, and melons are the three crops,
and there is a lot of cattle ranching." But Coalinga is a community
with a difference, a difference so great that Kay Holloway, competing with seventeen other applicants—all of them male and two
of them already police chiefs—was offered the position. Since
August, 1975, Kay Holloway has headed Coalinga's police force of
eleven sworn—all male—officers.
    Born in 1934, Holloway is mother of four and newly married to a
California Highway Patrolman. She cut her professional teeth in the
Los Angeles County Sheriff's Department. Holloway calls herself a
"Christian woman," and displays the candor and honesty that such
a description implies. In April of 1976, she was appointed by California Governor Jerry Brown to serve on the state's ten member POST
commission which "sets guidelines and standards" for police training across the state of California. Chief Holloway is also "the only
female on *that!*"

You come into an all-male environment and expect to find
some resistance, some resentment of the fact that you're a female, and none of this materialized! I couldn't ask for anything
better. That's one of the major surprises of the job.
    From the beginning I've had an excellent staff. Our police
department, for the city size, is extremely professional and very
well educated.

109

I am paid more than my predecessor, who was a male, which is rather unique when a woman is put into a position formerly held by a man. I came on board for $1,300-something a month in 1975. It's now up to $1,640.

I took a thousand dollar a month cut in pay to come to Coalinga. In Los Angeles I was making $2,400 a month. The job in Coalinga was originally advertised at $1,030, but when they saw, in Coalinga, what I was making in Los Angeles, they offered me the $1,300-something. I accepted on those terms.

I filed for the test along with sixteen males. First they did a rating from your resume. Out of the seventeen applicants, they invited nine people to a civil service oral.

Two of the people I competed against were chiefs of police, so it was quite an *accomplishment* for me personally. [Laughs.] And I don't feel this is a case of reverse discrimination. I don't feel like the token woman.

What is your role as chief?

I am basically the number one law enforcement officer in the city. I'm responsible for all law enforcement functions. I administer a department of eleven sworn officers, five reserve officers and five civilians.

There is actually no typical day in law enforcement, but I am responsible for hiring and training of police officers. Of course, we are a service agency, and our only reason for being is to provide service to our community. I am responsible for the budget and making sure we do things, not only within the framework of the law but within the framework of our financial support which, of course, comes from the city. I am a sworn officer, but my functions as chief are basically administrative or executive in nature. I don't work the streets.

I'm responsible to the city manager of Coalinga who in turn is responsible to our city council. Because we do have a full-time city manager, I, in essence, have one boss. We have an excellent city manager.

What are the crimes in Coalinga?

The same kinds of crimes occur here as everywhere else, it's just a matter of degree. Where a large area will have many more, our numbers are much smaller, but, per capita, probably our totals come out very similarly. Since I've been here, in the past year, we've had armed robberies, assaults, rapes.

We lost one of our patrol cars to a dynamite bombing, and our dog catcher's wagon was dynamited. We were very fortunate that no one was hurt in either one. It was just a miracle that someone wasn't hurt in the police car. The officer had just parked it and gone into the police station. We could have lost the station, but we just lost the windows out of the station. It was a fuse device, planted up under the car.

With the aid of federal authorities, we put two people in jail for that particular crime. We called in the ATF [Alcohol, Tobacco and Firearms]. It's the federal agency comparable to the FBI, but their specialty is bombings and any crime using firearms or involving alcohol.

The bombing was the worst incident dollar-wise and as far as the horror and fear it puts into a city. We had two bombings within a two-week period. One person was involved in both incidents. He had a different partner each time.

We did have one rape case. I worked with the victim because I'm the only female sworn officer in our department. Most departments, if they have a female officer, will let her do the rape investigation because it's much easier on the victim. Our victim was an elderly lady, and she was having a hard time talking to male officers. We were able to apprehend the man, but we lost it in court on a technicality.

We have a very high burglary rate. That's probably our number one major crime. Usually that's a grand theft, either from a locked automobile or from a dwelling—breaking and entering types of things. We have a lot of drunk drivers because we service Interstate 5.

I maintain a regional jail, which most small police departments don't. We book prisoners from four different agencies, who go to different courts for their appearances.

You head investigations?

I have the ultimate responsibility for all investigations. If it's a major case I would be on the spot overseeing activities, for instance a bombing or a homicide. But we haven't had any homicides since I've been chief.

The first thing that is done in any major case like the bombing of the patrol car is to seal off the scene, so that you protect the evidence. The next thing you do in any small town—and this is done in many large agencies, too—we call in the people from the federal authorities who are specialists, and we assist them. They took over the investigation. In that particular case, we worked about 26 straight hours. At the end of that 26 hours, we had two suspects.

How do you keep going?

We survive on a lot of coffee which is plasma to law enforcement. But when you're up for long hours working on something that's very demanding, adrenaline and the fact that you're uniquely interested in what you're doing are what keep you going.

You are on call constantly?

I'm subject to call 24 hours a day, seven days a week. I do have a captain who takes my calls if I'm out of town, but even then they know where to reach me.

They call me out on any kind of major crime, in other words a homicide or a very bad accident with multiple injuries usually, or anything involving one of my officers. For the normal routine drunk driving and petty thefts, they don't call me out. I read the reports the next day.

How does small town police work compare with the metropolitan?

In all honesty, the thing that I was totally unaware of, coming from a large metropolitan agency in middle management, is political climates. Now I'm in a small town, I feel the environment. I see the interactions of the political structure and all the workings of government. Of course, you're far removed from these things in the large metropolitan area.

What are the dangers of police work?

We have had threats. One Halloween night my house was under guard. We received threats that my house would be the next one to blow, so I took my children out of the house and friends kept them. Of course I worked all night anyway. There was an armed guard on the back of my house and on the front. Nothing ever happened, but that was immediately after our patrol car had been bombed. You don't take these things lightly.

You live with potential danger all the time. You're not sure just what will happen, particularly in a jail situation.

You carry a weapon and keep weapons in your home?

I do carry a weapon on duty. There are all kinds of weapons around my house from a .22 caliber to a shotgun. It doesn't worry me for my children. My children know not to touch guns.

When these kids first expressed interest, I took a gun, unloaded it, let them handle the gun, explained that it's something that kills, that it's never to be touched. None of my children have ever attempted to touch any weapons.

How did your police career begin?

I was a secretary to begin with. We had a big cut-off in the aircraft industry around 1963, and I was looking for a job. One of the jobs I applied for was police matron. Of course I conjured up a great big heavy-set matron that we see in the movies. I wasn't *that,* so I felt that I wasn't qualified. But I took the test, and I came out number one on the exam. That's a written and an oral. [As a matron, her salary was 434 dollars per month.]

I went to work and continued college. I started as an education major—I was going to teach. After a year as a matron, I decided I really wanted a law enforcement career. I changed my major to police science and took a test for Los Angeles County to become a deputy sheriff. I was hired and went to the Los Angeles County Sheriff's Academy in June of 1964. [Her starting salary as a cadet was $575 a month.]

How rigorous was cadet training for women?

There were nine females in my particular cadet class and more than a hundred men. We took all the training that the male cadets took, with one exception: we did not have to scale the six-foot wall. Lady cadets, today, do that. We did have a modified P.T. [Physical Training] program, with ladies' push-ups instead of males'. It was not tremendously modified; basically we had the same kind of training. We had firearm training, classroom, lifesaving, swimming.

It was like bootcamp. It took six weeks, but there was a minimum of 400 hours within that six weeks! [Laughs.] We worked from 6 o'clock in the morning until 6 o'clock at night, six days on with one day off to clean your uniform and get ready to go back to the academy. [Laughs.]

What was your first assignment?

After the training, I was assigned to the Jail Division as a deputy sheriff. This is basic for almost all L.A. County deputies; almost all of them go to the jail. I was sent to Sybil Brand, the women's jail.

[During her early years with the Los Angeles County Sheriff's Department, Kay Holloway became a senior deputy in the women's jail, training and supervising other deputies. After three years, she took a voluntary demotion—giving up "corporal stripes, in essence," so she could transfer to the Detective Bureau.]

Why did you want to work in the Detective Bureau?

That's where law enforcement is—in the investigation of crimes. It's in actually putting all the pieces together and actually making the arrest. The Warrant Detail was a beginning into the Detective Bureau. From there you transferred into other units within that Bureau.

I was a detective assigned to the Warrant Detail. I was one of the first two females on that assignment. It had previously been all men. It was desk duty, but that was the step into the Detective Bureau. We were the first women to take that career route into the Detective Bureau.

I wasn't there very long, and I came out number one on the Sergeant's List, and I went right back to the jail. [Laughs.] I had taken the written exam prior to going to the D.B. You don't expect to make it on the first exam. You usually take it for experience the first time, and then you get serious the next time around.

I was sent back to Sybil Brand as a sergeant, supervising the deputies on a particular shift. I took primary responsibility for training new officers, making sure there are schedules, that everybody shows up, uniform inspections. You deal more directly with inmate problems. You have more responsibility and of course you're paid more. [As a sergeant, her salary "started at about $1,600" per month.]

After I had been on as a sergeant for two and a half years, I took the lieutenant's exam and came out high enough on the list to be promoted. That put me in charge of the p.m. shift [3 p.m. to 11 p.m.] at Sybil Brand.

I went on maternity leave, and when I came back I went on graveyard. [Early morning shift from 11 p.m. to 7 a.m.]

I was the Watch Commander for the early morning shift, which means that you're in charge of the entire jail for the eight hours that you're on duty. The number of inmates, the vast majority of the time, was between 700 and 800.

What experience did you have in supervising male officers?

When I was lieutenant at Sybil Brand Women's Prison, 57 people of various classifications reported to me. About 35 of those were sworn officers, including two male sergeants and five male deputies. So I was not new to supervising males when I came to Coalinga.

How do you explain your rapid promotion through police ranks?

I *wanted* the jobs. I *did* want to be promoted. I don't know that I'm very smart, but I did study very hard. It's my career. I think motivation is the important factor.

I've always had a great deal of energy, so I was able to work, go to school, keep up with the children and maintain pretty well.

You were married at the time?

My husband, of that time, was very supportive. There was no problem with that. I had helped put him through college when he got out of the service. One of the agreements we made was that when he finished school, I would go. He did a lot of baby sitting and everything so I could go to school. It worked out fine.

You worked and attended school?

During all this time I was going to school constantly. It took me ten years to get my bachelor's in law enforcement. But, of course, during those years I had four kids.

Somewhere along the line, too, I picked up a teaching credential. [Laughs.] Then I started working two jobs, just prior to the birth of my last baby. I was teaching in the junior high school part-time and working graveyard. [Laughs.] I was teaching law enforcement half-time to junior high school students. I like teaching!

I went on to teach in the Sheriff's Academy. I taught "Sociology for Police Officers," with special emphasis on the family and alcoholism—things we have to deal with as police officers. I have a minor in sociology.

Now I'm twelve units shy of a master's degree. [Laughs.]

What problems did you have with your roles of policewoman, teacher, mother, wife?

You have to live a different kind of life when you're trying to sleep days, have young children, and work nights. I got a little tired of that, although I enjoyed my job in Los Angeles. More than four years of my career were spent on graveyard shift.

The only real serious problem that I had in dealing with the many different roles—trying to be mother, wife, a cop—was that I had one little girl who became ill while I was in the Sheriff's Academy. We lost her two years later. That was a tremendous, traumatic time and a very *difficult* time. Lots and lots of pressures. That's probably a major reason for the failure of that marriage. Tremendous pressures build up while you're watching your child die and knowing that you can't do anything about it.

What motivated you to leave Los Angeles County Sheriff's Department?

Of course a dream of mine has always been to go upward. I've always been an upward mobile. The chances of a female making captain in Los Angeles were *very* slim. Since I left they *did* promote a female captain, in 1975. There was a female captain who retired many years ago, and they replaced her with males. So my career path there looked like it had come pretty close to the end.

How did you learn of the post in Coalinga?

Some male chiefs of police, friends of mine, sent me job announcements. That's how chiefs are recruited. They send announcements of openings to other police departments. Actually the chief's position in Coalinga was advertised. A friend sent me the clipping and said, *"Here's your job!"*

Why did you apply for the position of chief, a traditionally male occupation?

I came to Coalinga to see if I could compete with a male peer group at this particular level.

Professionally I felt competent, and I *wanted* the job. I had really fallen in *love* with the town. And being the only female, I wanted to do well. So there was a tremendous amount of built-in pressure.

There were nine of us after the screening. The first letter I got inviting me to the oral was addressed to "Mr. Kay Good." [Laughs.] [Good was her name prior to her recent marriage.]

The response from the male competition when I arrived was the really fascinating thing! All the final applicants were there at the same time. They invited everyone for the same hour and then they decided how we would be interviewed! We sat in the courtroom. So all these men show up and they're looking at me like, "I wonder what *she's* doing here!"

Describe your oral interview and response of women on the board.

We were interviewed by the local civil service commission which is five members, plus professional law enforcement officers. The commander of the local office of the Highway Patrol, a chief of police, and a captain of another police department sat on my board.

You had eight people to respond to. This is a very large oral board. Normally you'd have three members.

There was only one woman on the board, a civil service commission member. Surprisingly enough, I was *not* all that glad she was there! [Laughs.] She was of Mexican-American background and interested in my ability to speak foreign tongue—that sort of thing—which I don't do well. She was the most apprehensive.

The oral test is to see how logical one is and how you verbally respond to questions. How you really handle yourself.

Your formative years and early influences?

In 1934 I was born in the little town of Baltimore, Ohio—a wide spot in the road. My family moved to the Puget Sound area where I actually grew up.

I guess you'd say Mother was very working class. She was left alone with five children when I was seven.

Mother scrubbed other peoples' floors. She did day work. She worked very hard and very long. My mother was first generation Swedish-American, the youngest [adopted] of twelve children. She had a tremendous love of education, but she was not able to pursue her education. Once a girl in the old rural family got through the eighth grade, she had to go to the city to continue school. Mother's parents weren't willing to turn her loose from the farm, so she was never able to fulfill her desire for education—plus having five children kind of put an end to the possibility of education.

We had a very happy family life and very church-centered. I was brought up in the Baptist Church. My mother was the mother of the whole world. Our house was a center of all the country activity. I had a very loving relationship with my mother.

Her hopes and dreams of education had a strong effect on me

personally. But I'm the only one of her children that went through college. I was second to the oldest.

What path did you take after high school?

I was given a scholarship to go to college when I got out of high school, but I wasn't able to come up with the train fare to get to the eastern part of the state to *use* it! [Laughs.]

I pumped gas in a service station. That was my first job. I was eighteen. I made 65 cents an hour. [She first married about that time.]

From the gas station I went to a men's tailoring factory, making men's work jackets. Then I worked in a factory making men's work gloves, running heavy duty sewing machines. That was all that was available. They *were* sweat shops.

When a job became available, I went to work at Pacific Telephone in Tacoma as a long-distance operator. Then I resigned to have a baby.

The next job I got was for a cemetery, working in the office. I started as a PBX operator, learned the clerk-typist work and went to school to take shorthand so that I could become a steno. After a while, I went to work for Trans World Airlines as a secretary. I left there to go to work as personal secretary for a newspaper publisher. I had several other secretarial jobs in the aircraft industry. From there I went on into police work.

How did your lack of a father figure affect you?

From childhood, I really felt insecure from not having a father in the home. Now I have a positive self-image which came later in life. My mother did marry a very fine man who adopted us all, but he only lived for a few years after they married. She was widowed again when I was fourteen.

Does your position as chief create conflicts with your husband?

My husband is a cop, too. He's *not* on the Coalinga force. I would never do *that!* [Laughs.] He's a Highway Patrolman. We don't have the same hours, but having been in law enforcement for a long time, we've learned to adjust.

My husband is a unique individual! He's a traffic officer assigned to the local office. It *has* to be tremendously difficult for any man whose wife—in any career field—more or less outranks him, even though I'm in a different agency. I'm at the executive level while he's at the entry level. He's a very, very unique person and is able to handle the transition.

Are your roles traditional at home?

Of course my husband is boss at home, and I *know* it.

Our family is a very typical traditional American family. He's the father, and I'm the mother. He's in charge of all the financial kinds of things. We do make decisions together, and probably one of the greatest things about our marriage is that we have excellent communication. He arranges his days off to travel with me as much as possible, so we have companionship when I'm on these trips. [Laughs.]

The house is *my* primary responsibility. My husband does help me. We can together. He makes pickles and jelly, and I do pretty well with the canning. He's from Kentucky.

Do you recommend law enforcement careers for women?

I believe that law enforcement is an excellent career for some women. I firmly believe that the best female law enforcement officers are those who want to do those things they can do well: all phases of investigative work, juvenile, supervision, and administration. There is a role for women in recruitment, community relations, training, transportation, custody. In fact, most phases of law enforcement are ideal for women, but, in my opinion, the patrol function is best left to male officers.

Is your job fulfilling?

I like my job because it is always interesting and challenging. One day is very different from the next, and you never know what to expect. There is little chance that boredom will set in. Above all, you have the satisfaction of knowing that you are doing a very necessary job and providing a valuable service to the people in your community by making it a better place to live. Our product is service, and we have many opportunities to affect the lives of others.

It is very fulfilling to know that you are needed and that you can respond to these needs. We often are able to assist in times of crisis, and the vast majority of person-to-person contacts are positive.

Other rewards?

The opportunities for travel are *fantastic!* My city is very progressive. They want me to become active in law enforcement groups. One of the first places I went as chief of police was to Denver, Colorado, to the International Association of Chiefs of Police. I was the only female chief of police there.

What are the intangible rewards of your work?

I am a Christian woman, so one of the things that has been rewarding to me is working closely with our local ministerial association. We have a prayer breakfast once a month where all the people working with youth in our community get together for breakfast and prayer. All of our ministers work together.

Another unique thing about our police department is that we administer the Salvation Army fund locally. The police department is the only place in town that's open 24 hours. When people need help they come to us.

One of the most rewarding factors of this job on a very personal level is having Saturdays, Sundays, and holidays at home with my children—the more regular hours.

Emily Hanrahan Howell

> *When I was in high school there was*
> *nothing available. When they asked*
> *you, "What are you going to do?" I*
> *said, "Be a waitress I guess..."*

Emily Howell has made history in modern aviation as the first female captain and first woman pilot of a U.S. scheduled air carrier. Howell is also the *only* female member of the Airline Pilots Association, the union with membership of some 40,000 pilots!

Born in 1939 of financially poor Catholic parents, she sought her first job in a drugstore at age fourteen and has been employed ever since. Howell's formal education ended with high school. Today she says, *"Anything* is possible if people just work at it. And this is the best country in the world for opportunity." In January, 1973, Denver-based Frontier Airlines hired Howell as second officer on a Boeing 737.

At the time of this interview, Howell stated that there were only about six women pilots employed by the 50 commercial airlines in the United States. That was three and a half years after Emily Howell first set foot in Frontier's all-male crew room, her heart in her throat.

Surprisingly, Howell says that although some 25 articles have been written about her, she has never been contacted by publications connected with the women's movement.

Emily—Captain—Howell lives in Denver with her young son.

I'm a captain on a de Haviland Otter. It carries nineteen people. I go up through Nebraska, and most of my stops are in small towns in Nebraska.

Frontier Airlines has 22 Boeing 737s which hold 97 people each. We have approximately 30 Convair 580s, each of which holds 50 people, and three Otters. We serve over a hundred cities in seventeen states *and* Canada—Winnipeg. More cities than United Airlines. [Laughs.]

I've been with Frontier three and a half years. Before that I worked with Clinton Aviation Company here in Denver. I started to learn how to fly in 1958.

What was your motivation?

Ironically, I wanted to be a stewardess when I got out of high school. I didn't know whether I'd like flying or not. [Laughs.] So I bought a ticket on Frontier Airlines to go from Denver to Gunnison and back. I was mainly looking to see if I'd get airsick and watching the stewardess' duties. On the way back the airplane was empty, and it was early morning, a *beautiful* morning. I asked the stewardess if I could go forward and see what was going on. She got permission and I went up and rode the rest of the trip back. You couldn't do that *today!*

I just fell in *love* with it, and the co-pilot said, "Well, gee! If you like it so much, why don't you take flying lessons?" [Laughs.] He told me where to go. So the next week I started flying lessons, and I've been flying ever since.

The first license you get is your private license, and that took me about a year. I was working at the May Company and I was making 38 dollars a week. A flying lesson was *$12.75* a week, so I didn't have a *lot* of extra money! [Laughs.] I just *lived* for my flying lessons. I was living at home; I was fresh out of high school.

I got the airport bug. I looked all over the airport for a job, and my instructor said, "I think they have an opening here." So I went to work at Clinton as a receptionist and worked there for almost sixteen years before I was hired by Frontier. [Laughs.] I've been in aviation a long time. Clinton is the Cessna dealer in Denver, and I was taking lessons from Clinton.

What jobs did you have at Clinton?

I started out as a receptionist. Then I was a flight school secretary, which really taught me the flight school business. After a year and nine months I got my flight instructor rating, and then I went from flight school secretary to flight instructor. [Her salary as a secretary was $300 a month.]

You were the only female instructor with Clinton?

Yes, I was. I think I was the only *woman* instructor in Denver at the time, too. I started instructing when I was 21. As I recall, there were five men and myself. In 1967 we had about twenty flight instructors.

In 1968 I became a FAA flight examiner, a pilot examiner. With that designation I was able to give flight tests. And I was assistant flight school manager. [Of approximately 500 people Howell taught to fly, only 25 were women.]

How many women were flight examiners in the United States at that time?

I rounded up statistics to find out who the women flight examiners were in the United States, and there were 40 at the time. *Fifteen* were in California. I was the only woman out of 40 flight examiners in Colorado.

When did you join Frontier?

I was running the flight school, and I had kind of given up hope, because I had applied for Frontier, United, and Continental. I would upgrade every year. I had talked to the chief pilot for Frontier in 1967, and they weren't hiring at the time. He said the best thing I could do was to get more time and my ATR rating. ATR is Airline Transport Rating, kind of the last rating you get. I got that rating in 1968.

How did you obtain the ATR rating?

By studying. *Most* of it was on my own. There's a written and a flight test involved. I had to pay for it on my own again, get instruction and take another flight test.

What chain of events led to your being hired by Frontier?

I didn't hear anything for a long time and the airlines weren't hiring. Then in September of 1972, I heard through the grapevine that three of my ex-flight instructors were hired by Frontier. They had worked *under* me at Clinton. One of them had about the same amount of time I had and also was my *age*, and I said, "Well, *heck!*"

One flight instructor told me that he had an interview with Frontier, so I knew they were going to have another class. I spent 'til midnight writing a cover letter with my application. I sent a letter to the man who had interviewed me before and one to Andy Hoshok who was the interviewer. The main thing I wanted to get across was that I had been applying since *1967*. I went to the Frontier office bright and early the next morning and the little gal said, "What are *you* applying for?" I said, "A pilot," and she said, "Oh, is that right? How many hours do you have?" And I told her, "Seven thousand." She said, "Oh! My *goodness!*" [Laughs.] She went back to the head office guy, told him, and he said, "Well, have her leave her application."

That afternoon I called a couple of friends of mine who worked for Frontier, and I asked one fellow, Jack Howland, "Jack, do you think I can do it if I get hired?" And he said, "Well, *certainly* you can!" He boned me on my ATR, and he pretty well knew my flying ability. Then I called another friend, and both of these fellows started helping me, telling me what to study in case I had to take a simulated ride, which I *did*.

Then I called Jack Gardner who worked in the Frontier offices. I asked him to let me know if he heard anything. He kept me *very* well posted.

That same afternoon this other fellow called me and said, "Hey, Andy Hoshok stopped me in the hall. He asked me all about you." He needled me a little bit. He said he told Andy, "Well! She does *alright* for a *girl!*"

A week later Jack Gardner called me back and said, "They've *really* been talking about you, but I don't think it's going to go beyond Andy Hoshok's office, because they don't know what to do with you. If I were you, I would get *over* here and some way I would see Mr. O'Neill, vice president of flight operations. I'll meet you and I'll get you in there *some way.*" So I went to the office. We met in the coffee shop, and Jack said, "Okay, give me *exactly* three minutes, then come into his office."

So I walked in and he said, "Well, *Emily Howell,* what are *you* doing here?" Big stage! [Laughs.] And I said, "Well, I'm here to try to see Mr. O'Neill." And he said, "Well, let me see what I can do." So he poked his head into Mr. O'Neill's office and said, "Mr. O'Neill, there's someone here I'd like you to meet." The timing was just *perfect!* So I went in and talked to Mr. O'Neill for about ten minutes, and he knew exactly who I was.

One of the things I told Mr. O'Neill was that I knew this was going to be quite different and that he might even have to talk with Mr. Fellman about it. Mr. Fellman is the president of Frontier. The next day I got a call from Frontier Personnel Office. I had another interview with Mr. Hoshok and Mr. O'Neill and they were firing questions back and forth. Then they said

Mr. Fellman would like to meet me and set up another appointment.

At that next meeting, Mr. O'Neill said, "Well, before we make a decision, we would like to give you a simulator ride." It's a Convair simulator on the ground, that simulates the airplane. They wanted to see if I could handle the force, if I had enough physical strength for it. He said, "Let's try to do it right now, if it's open." Luckily, it wasn't available, so they set up a schedule for six that evening.

In the meantime I called my friends Jack Howell and Bob Wilson, and I spent 45 minutes with each of them on the phone. They were commercial pilots with Frontier and *very* familiar with Frontier procedures. I really studied right up until six o'clock.

I was waiting in the Frontier lobby. I think sometimes things happen that give you courage. This little gal came out and said, "Oh, you're Emily, aren't you? We heard you have a simulator ride tonight." It's funny in a company how word really shoots around, and she said, "We're all rooting for you! We *really* want you to get on!" It was like a real shot in the arm. [Laughs.] Then Mr. O'Neill came up, and we went back to the simulator room.

Another lucky thing happened. Jack Rawlins was the instructor for the period. And I said, "Well, Mr. O'Neill, are you going to fly in the left seat?" Poor Mr. O'Neill hadn't been in the left seat—the captain's seat—of an airplane in years. The instructor pipes right in because he was running the operation, and said, "Gee, I think that'd be a *good idea*, Ed!" [Laughs.] So it was kind of a neat situation.

If the pilot in the left seat had been pretty sharp, pretty on top of everything, it might have been a little hard for me. But with Ed sitting there and the instructor standing behind both of us, it was a better situation. The period went exceptionally well. I was *really* amazed. We flew about two hours simulated flying, doing all the maneuvers.

At the end we were shooting an approach to runway 3-5 at Stapleton in Denver. I was just dead tired, and it wasn't the best approach. I was getting more tired all the time. There's a lot of pressure on you—I was trying to get a job! But I got through the approach all right. Then Mr. O'Neill said, "Gee, would you like to do some more?" And I said, "It's up to you, Mr.

O'Neill. Whatever *you'd* like to do." But I thought, "Oh, God, I *hope* he doesn't want to do any *more!*" [Laughs.] And he said, "Oh, I think that will be enough." And I was . . . you know, *whew!* [Laughs.]

You were then hired?

Then we sat out at this long table outside the simulator. Mr. Rawlins was talking and went into how hard an airline pilot's job is, the hours that you have to work, the fatigue, family life, on and on. He was painting a bad picture and really trying to discourage me. I turned to Mr. O'Neill and said, "Well, Mr. O'Neill, I *know* I can do it. Give me the *chance.*" I said it again, "I *know* I can do it!" He said, "You have the job, if you *want* it. But I want you to sleep on it tonight and give me a call in the morning." The next morning I did call him first thing and said, "I *do* want the job." He said I'd be getting a letter from personnel.

This must have created quite a stir?

Some way the news got hold of all this. Frontier called me about ten o'clock in the morning that same day. The newspapers were calling but Frontier's office didn't even *know* about it! [Laughs.] The P.R. director was almost in hysterics. He said, "I just found out you've been hired!" He said he really needed to have a meeting with me and that the press wanted to meet me. I went to Frontier that afternoon, and they handled it very well. That was one nice thing about Frontier. They never pressured me into doing press things or anything like that. Everything was natural, taken care of as it came along.

What was your salary?

I think it was about 650 or 700 dollars a month as second officer in a Boeing 737. That lasted nearly a year. Then I went to first officer's position on the Twin Otter. The end of 1973, I was first officer. That was in the right seat. Second officer is sort of an engineer. [Left seat is the captain's.] I flew the Otter, and then I went to the first officer's seat or co-pilot in a Convair 580. I did that for quite awhile, back and forth between those two airplanes. Then with our scheduling, new contract, and so forth, quite a few people moved up. That's when I was lucky to get a bid in the Otter as a captain. That was June first of 1976.

It's really unusual in an airline to get a captain's seat on *any-thing* that fast. At United Airlines it would take *eight* or *ten* *years*.

We're in a good position right now. Frontier is a small air-line, and when a small airline expands, people move faster. [Frontier employs 540 pilots, all of them male except number 369 on the seniority list—Emily Howell.]

What are the duties of the captain?

The captain is in command of the ship and has the responsibili-ty of making all the decisions for the safety of the flight. We work as a team—the captain and the co-pilot—and we share the flying. I'll fly the first leg, and the co-pilot will fly the second leg. But the captain makes any pertinent decisions that have to be made, sort of like the boss. [Howell's salary as a captain is $24,000 a year.]

You're the first woman pilot with Frontier. What other firsts?

I was the first woman pilot to be hired by a scheduled U.S. air carrier. There are probably close to fifty carriers. There are 40,000 pilots in those airlines. I was the first woman pilot to be hired and the first woman captain. [At the time of her inter-view, Howell was also the only female among the 40,000 mem-bers of ALPA—Airline Pilots Association—"the only union in the world run by employees," according to Howell.]

How many women pilots fly scheduled air carriers now?

There are about six. Two with Western, a couple with Braniff. And North Central and American have gals, and that's about it. None of them are captains.

A woman *did* pilot commercial planes around the thirties?

Yes. Her name was Helen Richey, and she was a co-pilot on an airline. At that time there were no scheduled airlines; they came into effect in about the 1950s. But she *was* a bona fide pilot with a cargo route in the east I believe.

Helen Richey was the first woman pilot on an airline as far as I know. There *have* been gals that have run their own charter outfits. And there've been all the women that worked in the WAFS, the Women's Air Force Ferry Command with the U.S. Air Force. They ferried B-17s and all *kinds* of planes. So they were actually captains of big airplanes. That was during World War II. [These World War II pilots were actually the Women's

Auxiliary Ferrying Squadron, part of Air Transport Command. Helen Richey, during the thirties, was co-pilot of an air mail transport plane for Central Airlines.]

What is it like to be the first woman pilot?

When I started, there was so much going on that it was kind of hard at first. The first year everyone was wondering if I was going to stick around. I felt pressured somewhat. But within about a year, the attitude of the other pilots began changing and they started accepting me as one of the fellows.

Have other pilots evidenced negative attitudes toward you?

Yes. When I went out for my second trip with Frontier, I introduced myself to one pilot. I put out my hand to shake his, and he said, "I don't shake hands." I knew I was in for it! [Laughs.] He didn't say three words during the whole trip to St. Louis and back, except, "Don't touch anything on the airplane!" But since then he's really come a long way.

I did fly a whole month with a captain that intensely disliked me. He still *does!* [Laughs.] He's the only hold-out. When he comes into the crew room, I usually leave because of the remarks. They kid about it. I think in a way he's sorry he started this, because he doesn't know how to get out of it now. Once you establish yourself as an S.O.B. . . . [Laughs.]

What psychological problems have you had?

I think the *biggest problem* for me to get over was that young women used to grow up being programmed to be a nurse or housewife or secretary. Doing anything else was a little *extraordinary.* So I had to get psychologically over this myself. I put a lot of pressure on myself and got through it alright, but I had to go through a period of readjustment with *myself.*

I think the hardest thing for me was going into the crew room where you get ready for your flights and so forth. It's *all* male. The first few times, I *hated* to go in there.

Things are much better now. The pilots really are nice; they accept me. Once I'd gone through some training and then flown with quite a few of them, the word started to get around that, "Boy! She really *can* fly! She does alright!" That *really* helped.

[Frontier "trained" her before she was assigned to a plane as second officer; this was largely "an indoctrination to the company." Her "first real school was the Otter school," a two-week ground school in Denver and a one-week "flight portion" at Great Falls. "The next school was in Convairs, including ground school, simulator, *and* flying time. Co-pilots have recurrent training once a year, and captains, twice a year." A captain's initial training is usually two weeks. Frontier trains all its own pilots.]

Have you ever believed that you are the token woman?

No. But when I got hired, I did feel pressure because I wanted to do a good job, mainly *for* women.

I wanted to do a good job so I probably put more pressure on myself than the average individual would. If there had been other women in the same capacity, there wouldn't have been as much pressure.

When I went to Frontier, I was glad that I had almost sixteen years in aviation. That background really helped me with a lot of things. Not just flying, but dealing with people and with other pilots. The flying aspect wasn't the only thing I had to contend with.

When you were hired by Frontier, you had 7,000 hours of flight time. How did that compare with other incoming pilots?

Probably I had the *most* time. I'd say they have from 2,500 to 5,000. You have to have at least 1,500 hours for an ATR rating. Now I have about 8,500 hours. That's quite a few hours.

What has been the most difficult aspect of flying?

I think probably the mechanical part of it. You have to know all the component parts, the main systems of the airplane. The Convair 580 has several systems. You have to pretty well know the whole electrical system, the whole hydraulic system, and the structure—like on the gear. There could be ten different mechanisms that you have to know in the gear.

The electrical system has AC/DC, the inverter system that inverts DC to AC. That was really hard for *me*. We have written tests on this.

They have *fine* instructors. And I have to say that a couple of these instructors really helped me through it at Frontier. They explained it so I could understand *but* I really had to work at it.

You *really* enjoy being a commercial pilot?

Oh yes, I do. I love my job. I *love* flying! I think it's the ever-changing, the challenge of it. Flying is never the same.

Every day you go out and fly an airplane, everything's different. Different conditions. The air. The colors. The wind. It's never the same. So I think that's the biggest reason that I like flying.

Of course, it's also the challenge of getting the airplane off the ground, the challenge of being able to fly bigger airplanes all the time. And learning new things keeps you really alive mentally.

How does it compare with your former jobs?

It is the best job I've ever had for security, for working conditions. And who else can get in a million dollar office and go from Denver to St. Louis and back? It's not like sitting in an office and seeing the same scenery all the time.

There *are* times when you work harder, when you have bad weather and you're shooting approaches. There's a lot of *hard training* you have to get through all the time, where you have to work on an emergency procedure for example. This is all part of the whole thing, part of the challenge, part of making the job safer.

What are the occupational hazards?

Really, I consider there are none, unless it's the unusual that happens. I've been flying a long time and there are very few times that you're really scared.

Have you had any frightening experiences?

Oh, there have been times when I've had an airplane pass close or something like that. I always worry about the possibility of mid-air collision; I guess that's the biggest worry any pilot has. Sometimes you feel like it's kind of an uncontrolled thing in a way. But the FAA constantly works towards safety, and our new radar environments really help.

Weather—all pilots are concerned with thunderstorm activity, I think, more than any weather phenomena, because of the violence that a thunderstorm can bring. They've been known to tear an airplane apart—the wind and sheer gust factors inside a thunderstorm. But that's improved too, because nowadays they have weather radar so ATC [Air Traffic Control] can help you when you're flying. You have airborne weather radar in the airplanes too, so you can almost find your own path through weather. In the old days they didn't have this; they had to go by guess work. A lot of times they were in real deep trouble. Flying has really come a *long way*.

How much do you fly?

I fly 75 hours a month. It takes about sixteen to seventeen days a month to do that. For instance, I go out this afternoon and I'm back tomorrow afternoon. I'm on duty approximately 24 hours. In that time you get nine hours flying time in. At present, I probably cover about 900 miles a shift.

This sounds like a rugged schedule.

It hasn't been difficult to adjust to. I really like it because I'm home part of the day. And they're really the *best* parts of the day for my little boy. Of course, all schedules don't work out as well as the one I'm on right now. The only thing I have to do when I'm gone overnight is have my mother babysit. [Howell's son is eleven years old. She is divorced.]

Does your job affect your private life?

No, I don't think it creates any problems. I'm engaged to a real nice fellow. He's a big fan of mine! He doesn't like me to be gone at night *real* well, but it works out fine. When I have two-day trips with the airline, he doesn't like those. I'll be gone on the average of eight nights a month.

What are the negatives?

Oh, I think it's the long hours. You do get a little tired of being away from home so much, but I think every job is not perfect. It's the best job I've ever had, as far as time and doing what I want to be doing. I would say that the pluses definitely outweigh the negatives. [The travel benefits Howell has include no-cost flights on Frontier and passes on other airlines for flights at service charge rates of twelve to twenty dollars.]

What is the life expectancy of your job?

It depends on the equipment you're in. Hopefully, as the airline expands and if there's enough retirement from the top, the next step I could probably go to would be the first officer seat on a 737—a co-pilot. From that position I would go back to captain on a Convair 580, and then from there I would go to captain in a 737. That would be the top position with our airline right now, unless we get bigger equipment. Most people work up to retirement at 60 years old.

Your physical condition must be tip-top?

Yes, and we're required to take a medical every six months as a captain. If you're a first officer, it's once a year. It's a pretty stringent medical.

Which of your senses is most important?

Vision and hearing are most important I imagine. [Laughs.] And then the *heart*—very important!

What physical strength and stamina do you need?

I'm a real tall gal. I'm five foot nine and weigh 140 pounds. And I've got a lot of stamina. So I haven't had any problem with physical strength with the airplane. The new airplanes are all hydraulically boosted and there's no physical problem there, of course. The Convair 580 is a pretty heavy airplane to fly, and we have quite a few of them. It takes a lot of *muscle*, but you learn how to use trim and differential power and so forth. Somebody told me before I started flying the 580s, "*Gee!* That airplane's like flying a *cement truck* with four flat tires!" After I went through training I told him, "Hey, you were *right!*" [Laughs.]

We spend long days. Frontier hits a lot of cities, and we'll average, oh, ten landings in a day. And that's hard. If there's weather connected, you'll make ten instrument approaches. So it does make for a long day.

How do you minimize the physical exhaustion?

Using technique and varying your technique. Once you've learned how to fly the airplane, you start using different techniques to make it easier. Your seat position even makes a difference, how close you are to the rudders . . . These are all called techniques. And pretty soon you get into your own techniques, your own grooves. This makes the flying easier.

You constantly exert energy at the controls?

It's just a matter of constantly flying the airplane. On take-off, there's a pretty good pull. After that there's no *big* problem. When the air is real rough, the airplane becomes very rigid— this is the Convair 580 I'm talking about. It's very tiring because you are flying it constantly and it's moving. It feels like it's a solid block sitting in the air. Rough air is very tiring.

How did your childhood influence your individualism?

When I was growing up, I was very much a tomboy and a leader of a gang of boys and gals—mostly gals—on the block. We'd play baseball and softball. I was the organizer of games and stuff like that.

I think probably the biggest *step* in my life for independence was when I got my first job as a freshman in high school. I was fourteen, and we were all talking about getting jobs. I said, "I really want to get a job!" And we were at this drugstore and somebody said, "Why don't you see if you can get a job here?" And I said, "I think I will!" And I walked back to the druggist, the owner. I asked him for a job and he said, "Well, when can you start?" [Laughs.] I think that started my independence more than anything, because I've worked since then, since I was fourteen, with one job or another.

What did you want to be?

I didn't really *know*. When I got to working at the May Company, I really enjoyed retail sales and I enjoyed displaying. That was part-time. I worked to the point where they offered me an assistant buyership at a new store. The only reason I couldn't accept it was I didn't have a car or a way to get to the store. That was probably *another* lucky break because that might have led me down the retail path.

Right after that is when I got into flying. I have a cousin who was a stewardess at one time. I always admired her. So that's probably how I first started thinking about being a stewardess.

What about your parents?

My mother has been a housewife. She's never worked, just in the home. We were *very poor*. My younger brother Dennis and I have talked a lot about it. I think the reason we've worked so hard and are ambitious is because we didn't have anything when we were kids. There were six kids in the family. My folks worked *so hard*. We saw that poverty so much, and it was always hand-me-down clothes. I think we just wanted to strive to do something better and get somewhere.

My parents were such good people and tried to give us what they could. They did give us a good upbringing. My dad was a driver for the Railway Express Company for years and he retired there. [Howell and her twin sister are second to the youngest. Her twin is a nurse and captain in the Air Force. Two of her brothers obtained college educations: Dennis, who has a dry wall construction business, and another who is a forest ranger. Two other brothers are employed as an auto mechanic and postman.]

Has your formal education been beneficial to your career?

I think it helped. I went to parochial schools. You wear uniforms all the time, so I've never really gotten away from that. It was a real good school and I got along real good with the teachers. It taught me a sense of discipline.

My little boy is going to parochial school. That's one thing I do like about them—they have a little more discipline.

Do you have regrets regarding your education?

It's never been a drawback. I wish I had gone to college. But I got so involved with aviation that that's all I studied for years. And now I *do* miss not having college, at least a couple of years. I think I'm lacking a little bit there because I didn't really get into the deeper subjects. [Her twin is working toward a bachelor's degree in nursing.]

How do you see yourself?

I think that I'm attractive. I get along well with people, and I really endeavor to do that. I like people. And I really kind of want people to like me. I think I'm well-organized and I get things done. If I have a job to do, I'll get it done—in clubs or anything like that.

Are you aggressive?

I'm not real aggressive. I'm more of a quiet aggressive, if you know what I mean. I wouldn't have sued the airlines to get on the job, but I *did* pursue it. I've got the stay-to-it-ness—perseverance. And I get a little bitchy at times. [Laughs.]

How do you command respect?

Just having patience and trying to do my own job—a good job—and being friendly. I always try to be a woman. I didn't ever try to be a man in a man's world or play the role. I think this is probably the biggest thing.

Men have generally been very encouraging to you. Is that true?

Yes. When I was working at Clinton and just starting out, my boss was my first flight instructor. He really opened a lot of doors for me. He'd give me a lot of opportunity, knowing I would work hard at it. I think that's the secret.

At Frontier, the people I talked to were convinced that I would do a good job for them and that I would try hard. I think that by talking to them I took most of their fears away. I let them know the experience I had and that it was a *career*.

Have you ever been a member of women's consciousness-raising groups?

No I haven't. I belong to a couple of women's organizations and I have for a long time. Like Zonta International. It's a businesswomen's association. *Zonta* is an Indian word meaning "friend" or "friends." The members are all professional people— doctors, lawyers, and every chapter has a professional housewife.

When I was hired by Frontier, I kind of expected *Ms.* or somebody to get hold of me, but they never did. It was curious. I haven't had to deal with that. But I do believe in women's lib to a certain extent. I don't believe in the bra-burning and all that stuff, but I do believe that the whole women's movement has really helped, along with equal rights and everything else.

I had a great job, and I was in aviation for so long that I didn't have to fight the bureaucrats or the really unequal times that people have had—the gals who *do* work so hard and never get anywhere. I never had to fight that, but I can sympathize. I understand how women are held back terribly.

Dairy Officer

Judy Jensen

I work with the inmates in castrating, dehorning, milking. Some haven't seen a cow before, and it's a new experience when I need them to help me deliver a calf or treat a cow down with milk fever.

She works with prison inmates—convicted robbers, rapists, sodomists, murderers—teaching them the ropes of dairying. She is the first female vocational officer at Utah State Prison Dairy Farm.

Judy Jensen was hired in December 1975, despite the misgivings of prison officials. Jensen's credentials were excellent; she had, with her sister, run a ranch in Utah, and she held a degree in dairy science. Her qualifications were no problem, but Jensen was a *woman* and "a dairy officer had been killed a few years ago" while on duty. How would the prisoners respond to a female officer?

Today Judy Jensen works shoulder to shoulder with male prisoners. She has never doubted her occupational choice. In an "Employment Performance Appraisal" by her supervisor in April 1976, Jensen was rated "outstanding." Prison officials are apparently delighted with their decision.

An all-male environment is old-hat to Jensen, the first woman to graduate from Utah State University with a bachelor's degree in dairy science. Jensen was born in 1943 and reared on her parents' farm in Utah.

After her interview, Jensen was promoted to "Dairy Farm Vocational Instructor Supervisor" at a salary of over $1,000 a month. At the time of her promotion, she had worked at Utah State Prison for less than a year.

I really didn't think they'd hire me. I went all out to apply. I called the prison and asked for an informal interview, because I felt that when they got the application, they would think it strange for a woman to apply. I wanted them to meet me personally, so they would *know* who was applying.

George Brown gave me a personal interview. I'm sure that he was mostly responsible for me being hired. I went to the prison and he gave me a tour of the dairy. He told me a dairy officer had been killed a few years ago. It really shocked me. And he told me that the hazards were so great that I'd have a hard time convincing others to hire me. He introduced me to one officer in the dairy. The guy didn't even say hello; he just started laughing. Since then, we have a good relationship. He tells everybody that he hauls hay with me and he's *puffing* and I'm still going.

I think being able to do equal work and the fact that I feel qualified has helped me overcome this kind of bias.

What is your capacity at Utah State Prison?

I supervise and instruct eleven inmates. We milk about 114 to 125 cows in the milking herd. We have approximately 50 to 63 cows that are dry, a lot of beef animals that go to the slaughterhouse next door, and a lot of heifers that we keep to replace them. Our total animals is over 400.

At this time I'm assistant supervisor at Utah State Prison Dairy Farm. The supervisor is not happy with the work and he's threatening to quit. Hopefully I'll be put in that position. [At the time of this interview, Jensen's salary was 871 dollars a month.]

The supervisor is in charge, but I very seldom work with another officer. When I'm out there I'm the *only* officer.

What was the competition for your job?

I really don't know how many people applied for the job. But I know that one guy that applied called while I was sitting in the interview and said that he just couldn't come because he was *afraid*. And he was a pretty big guy.

I think that was a factor in hiring, too. They were kind of desperate when I came along, and I had the qualifications.

Most people would not want your job because of the danger?

Yes. A dairy officer was killed out there four years ago. He had caught two inmates using drugs or engaged in homosexual acts, no one's really sure. I don't have the details, but I think maybe they hit him over the head and put him in the silage pit. He may have suffocated if they didn't kill him by hitting him.

What are the occupational hazards?

There's the people that I'm working with. I work with murderers. I've got two now that are in for sodomy. One raped his five-year-old child, then he raped her again when she was seven. I thought maybe they'd screen sex deviants. I'm getting them all, but there hasn't been any problem.

How are inmates chosen to work in the dairy?

They all have to have a job. They all have to work. If they show an interest in the dairy and the prison doesn't think they're a security risk, they usually send them out. Some of these guys have been in before.

Are you afraid on the job?

No, not at all. I have no fear, but I'm aware of the dangers; I would be foolish if I wasn't. I guess it's because of how I was brought up all my life to look out for myself. I always feel in control. I work with the men, and I don't ask them to do anything that I wouldn't do. I treat them all as my equal. I don't feel that I'm superior to them and I convey my attitude to them.

Sometimes I'm there as late as midnight or one in the morning if I have a cow that is calving. I might call one or two inmates out to help me. There is *absolutely* no problem. [Usually she works until 8 p.m. with no other officers on duty. "Sometimes a milk processing guy" works with her; he leaves at four p.m.]

I don't carry a firearm; I carry a two-way radio. All the dairy officers are supposed to carry the radios. They cost $1,100. The last time a dairy officer had one, he laid it down, and it was stolen and may have been used in a break.

I feel a little better working with *some* of the men, but I try not to show this. I had a bloated calf last winter. I tubed it with a hose, and I couldn't relieve the pressure. So as a last resort to save its life, you make a puncture into the rumen. I handed the instrument to the inmate working with me; I said, "*Here.* Make the puncture hole right here." He picked the instrument up like a knife and he said, "I just *can't* do it, Judy." I said, "*Boy!* I really have to worry about my safety with *you*, don't I?" [Laughs.] So I did it.

Another time I was moving lumber with two inmates and they uncovered a nest of mice. They said, "What do you want us to do with these?" I said, "I don't care *what* you do with them! I *hate* mice." So they picked them up and moved them over to where they were sure the mother would find them.

The inmates respect you?

I've been told that the inmates respect me not because I'm an officer but because I'm a woman. I've hauled hay since I was ten years old. I've had Shetlands and calves, and I grew up on a farm. Some of these guys are city boys. They will be driving a truck loaded with hay, and I'll jump on the back and start throwing hay off to the cows. They'll think it's another inmate, and then they'll see me and they'll be *shocked*.

Do you believe that the prison dairy farm is beneficial to inmates?

Oh, *yes*. I had an inmate tell me just a few weeks ago that the prison's done more for him than any other institution. He's been in trouble since he was eight years old. He even told me he learned how to count. He'd come out and work with me as much as twelve hours in a day, and he's only required to work six hours.

I definitely believe that the dairy is helpful to the men who work there. Some of them ask me if they can work extra hours. They say, "I want to donate my time. I go *nuts* sitting on the inside." I say, "*Sure!*" [Most of the inmates are required to work seven days a week.]

Are the animals dangerous?

Yes, I'm working with 1,500 pound cows. When they get milk fever, I'm the one that hits their jugular vein and puts in the calcium gluconate. Milk fever is a depletion of blood calcium. In these high-producing cows, it's a strain on them producing that much milk. When they produce a calf, that's another depletion of calcium, and they go down with milk fever. I've had a few cases of that. I treat all the ailments, and if I can't, I get a vet.

It *is* dangerous working that closely with cows when they're sick. I've been told by the inmates, "If anything happens to you, if you get hurt by a cow, we might have a hard time explaining that it *was* a cow. We're *worried* about your safety." I say, "Well, you better take good *care* of me! You better help me all you can."

If I get into a dangerous situation—like if I get into a corner with a cow—they're worried about it. And they *are* very helpful.

What qualifies you?

I grew up on a farm with three brothers and one sister. My parents were really neat, because if my sister or I wanted to drive a tractor or something, they didn't say, "Well, *you're a girl! You* shouldn't be out driving a tractor!" In fact, my sister *beat* one of my brothers in a tractor-driving contest. I think she was twelve years old. The contest was backing trailers, and she beat them. [Jensen is the youngest of the five. Her sister—seven years older than she—is Jensen's closest sibling in age.]

My *brothers* were good about it too, because we worked side by side with them and it was never the feeling of, "My sister can outdo me on this or on that." There was *never* the feeling of competing with each other on the basis of sex.

My parents always wanted us to do what we wanted to do. It's *fun* driving a tractor when you're a kid. It's fun for the boys, and it was *fun* for us too. And it gave us extra money. I could come home when I was in high school and go out and do jobs for neighbors and make extra money.

When Faye and I had our own haying business, hauling hay, we had a couple of guys working with us, throwing hay off. It would be hot, and they'd get right off the truck and say, "I feel like I'm going to pass out. I've got to go sit in the *shade.*" And Faye and I would finish unloading the truck. Maybe this just comes from doing it more than other people.

When I was twelve, I used to straighten bales for my father to haul. He bought me a Shetland pony when I was eight. I raised Shetlands. I had as many as ten or eleven at one time. These were to sell, except that I could *never* sell them; I'd grow attached. It was *supposed* to be a little business venture, but I never sold them. [Laughs.]

When I was in high school, I would go around to dairies and buy calves and raise them. But this was all something that we wanted to do. We weren't ever forced to work. We *wanted* to do it!

I understand that you ran a ranch?

In 1965 my sister and I leased the Hi-Ute Ranch, just the two of us. I was 22 then. We boarded about 250 cows and we had about 50 of our own. Sometimes we'd take calves as payment. We also boarded between 45 and 60 horses.

We worked on the Hi-Ute for four years. We leased it for two, and we put the hay up for two. We left because Faye wanted to go to college, and I wanted to go also. I wanted an education so I could do what I wanted and have a more secure future.

How did others behave toward you when you worked the Hi-Ute?

When we were running the ranch, and I'd go up to the station to get gas in one of the trucks or something, I'd have cowboy boots on and Levis. And I'd get *stared at* like I was some oddball. I wanted to walk up to them and say, "Well, I'm *sorry* I can't always wear a *dress!* But I've been down branding cows!"

It's better now. It *has* changed. But what I don't understand is just because you're a certain sex, what's that got to do with what you want to do and what you *can* do. I don't understand it.

What other work have you done?

I've had other part-time jobs in the wintertime when things would slow down, but I was always grateful that I could quit them in the spring and go back to what I wanted to do.

I was catering banquets when I was sixteen, at the University of Utah. My father worked there as a baker on the side. My mother worked with my father.

You are an accomplished horsewoman?

I've been around horses since day one. I've always had a horse.

Have you had any accidents?

I was thrown off a horse when I was fifteen. I have a pin in one hip now. It knocked my hip out of the socket, but they didn't know it was out for a year. [As a result of this injury, Jensen was in a wheelchair for six months and on crutches for another six.]

I received a brain concussion when I was chasing a cow up at the Hi-Ute. There was a little bit of snow on the ground. I got too close to the cow. She slipped and went down, and my horse did a somersault over her. I was down on the ground and I thought, "This is great—I'm *okay!*" Then my horse was getting up and kicked me in the head. I was dazed, and my sister rushed me to the doctor. He told me to stay in bed for a few days, which I didn't do.

I've been thrown from horses lots of times, but I've only been hurt twice. I have a horse now that I'm *sure about*. I've had him for twelve years. He's never bucked with me; I don't think he knows how. And I don't ride strange horses now. I'm getting too old. My bones won't heal as easily.

You seem to take potential danger for granted.

I'm not afraid of things as potential dangers, but if I weren't aware that they exist, I would be very foolish. My mother, especially, is freaked out that I work down at the prison. She really tried to discourage me from taking that job. She said, "Oh, *Judy!* There's *other* jobs around!"

But when I was at the Hi-Ute I lived alone for half of the time I was there. That was in the wintertime. Faye would go to Salt Lake and sell insurance, and it was just too far to drive back and forth. The winters are *horrible* up there.

Kaelbeck and Lance, two of our greatest murderers here, were on the loose at that time. A body was found about two miles from where I was living. They had dumped it on the side of the road. After that happened, I got a gun and slept with it by the bed.

You say you left the Hi-Ute to go to college. What is your education?

I wanted to be a veterinarian. I went to the University of Utah for two years. They don't have a veterinarian program, so I had to transfer to Utah State. But the chemistry and the physics . . . I don't have that kind of a mind. The competition is great, and unless you're an A student you're out of the running. And back a few years ago it was harder for women to get in vet school. I understand it's becoming easier for women now to be accepted.

In any agriculture-related class or animal science class, I'd get A's. I changed my major to animal science, and I thought, "Now *what* am I going to do with animal science?" I talked to a counselor, and he said the department understood there were a lot of jobs in dairy science. Dairy didn't sound as glamorous to me as being a rancher did, but I wanted a future and I wanted to stay with animals. My father had a dairy when I was young. Most of my experience, however, has been with beef cattle. I really needed more experience with dairy cattle, and I feel that I got most of it by going to college. I was very happy with the education. I started in September of 1969 and went to school for five years.

Utah State was receptive to you?

I had lots of encouragement from Utah State University. They were very receptive. I was the first woman there to get a B.S. in dairy science.

At my meeting with the department head in dairy science, I

asked, "What about the other women who have graduated? What are they doing?" He said, "I don't know. We haven't *got* any. You'll be the first!"

The reaction was complete *non-negative*. I did have one instructor up there when I first started. He was a vet. He said, "Oh, why don't you just give it *all* up and get *married!*" But he was an exception. Other than that, the professors at Utah State were very encouraging.

Women in dairy science are obviously quite unusual?

Not very many women have studied dairy science. I think that if they *really* wanted to pursue this field, the doors would be open. Some women might be afraid of what labels would be put on them while doing non-traditional things such as artificially inseminating cows. But I was always accepted in my classes by the male students as well as instructors.

What do you like about working with animals?

I saw a calf two nights ago that was so *bloated* it was like a balloon. All my inmates had gone in, and I was out there alone. I put a hose in its stomach twice. The next morning it was just fine. I just get satisfaction from the work. I just love animals.

Your education has been almost sufficient for you to act as a veterinarian?

The physiology and anatomy of an animal have really helped me. I've got the education, and I have the experience. I had the experience before I went to college. But *now* I wish that I was in the classroom again, because I'd like to ask a *million questions!* Every once in a while, I'll go up to Utah State and talk to my professors.

I hated high school; I loved college. I barely got through high school. I just didn't go to school. I didn't lie to my parents; I'd say, "Oh, I don't want to go. I'd rather be out baling hay or something."

How do you explain your reaction to high school?

One of the biggest reasons was because I had to wear a *dress* to high school. And I didn't have that many clothes in high school.

What was your parents' economic status?

They've always been about middle. We never lacked for anything, but my mother doesn't sew and couldn't help me by making dresses. And then I didn't like keeping up with wearing something new *every day*, keeping up with so and so. On days when I could wear levis to school, *those* were the greatest days.

Then, too, you *have* to go to high school and I didn't *have* to go to college. I didn't get any encouragement to go to college. When I told my parents I wanted to go, they said, "Judy, you'll *never* make it. And we hate to see you waste your money." I guess this was because I hated high school. But they *could* have given me more encouragement, and they didn't give me any monetary assistance. I got government loans.

Is your family strongly religious?

My mother is religious. My father isn't. Faye [her sister] once served in the two-year Mission for the Church of Latter Day Saints, but she's no longer active in the church. And I'm not religious.

Do you experience loneliness at the prison?

No, I don't feel any loneliness, but I'm kind of isolated at the dairy. I really don't know very many prison employees, and they don't know me. I think maybe some of them might be afraid of me. The secretaries probably regard me as being tough, like women that portray matrons in prison movies. I'm doing something they wouldn't want to do, nor *would* they do it. They don't know me personally.

My days go very fast. There's always more to do than I have time to do.

What training did you receive at the prison?

I got firearms training and a little bit of judo. We discussed case histories on problem inmates. [She learned to fire machine guns, among others.]

I was advised to go in and read the folders of the inmates I work with, but I haven't. I don't want to because it might change my *feelings* toward them. I really don't care if they're out for murder or what they're out for, I'm going to treat them *all* equally and as potential risks.

I've never had any real problems with inmates. I tell them, kidding, "There's no escaping on *my* shift. If you're going to go, go on a guy's shift! *Don't* go on mine!" [Laughs.]

What physical strength is required of you at the dairy?

It's not really required. I'm supposed to be a supervisor. The first day at the dairy, I jumped on the truck and helped the inmates haul straw. My supervisor came out and said, "You're not *supposed* to be doing that. You're supposed to be supervising." I told him that I can supervise while I'm working. I can't be sitting and asking someone to do something that I won't help them do. It belittles the men, I feel. So any job they're doing, I'm out working with them. I just *can't* think highly of myself if I'm sitting somewhere telling them what to do.

Is the strength you use comparable to a man's?

Oh, no, I'm not as strong as most men. People see me out hauling hay and they think that I must lift weights or something. I'm not *that* strong. But I've hauled hay, and I know leverage. Like lifting a ten-gallon milk can—I'd never do that all alone. I protect myself that way. [She is five-foot-seven and weighs 145 pounds.]

How does this job fit in with your financial and personal objectives?

One hundred percent. At some point in time I plan to have my own farm. I'll take backers if I can find them.

How has the work at the prison affected you?

I feel better about myself. When I worked at the Hi-Ute and would go into town and those people were staring at me because of the way I was dressed—it made me *feel bad*. I didn't understand why it had to be that way. I was doing what I loved to do; I was good at it. Now I'm accepted more, *and* I have the education. The world has changed. Although women are not completely accepted yet, they are freer to *be*, which only tells me that I never should have felt bad in the first place!

There are lots of rumors about me among inmates on the inside and even officers. The inmates that have worked with me—that's great! *They* would go to bat for me, because they know me, but most people there don't know me. They've had bets that I wouldn't last six months. I know, because the inmates have told me.

The inmates told me one day, "Well, we won a carton of cigarettes on you!" Another inmate said, "Did you go to *court* to get this job like we heard?" I said, "I *sure didn't!* I just applied and got hired." Another rumor was that I was a woman cop on the outside. I lift weights—that's another rumor. Those people just don't know me.

Nancy Johnsen

> *I do have dreams of some day becoming a corporate giant. I have this fantasy of a female-owned corporation . . . with 900 outlets across the country.*

In 1973 Nancy Johnsen took a long hard look at her secure job as an ad agency production supervisor, decided she didn't like it, and quit. For what? She wasn't certain. She was 28 years old, held a degree from Columbia College of Communication, and had been "in" advertising since her college days. By most career standards she was successful, but there was a major obstacle: Johnsen, who had once bought all the "myths," no longer believed in the worthiness of her work. Cat litter, a product of the firm's major account, was the unlikely catalyst that made Johnsen see herself, in a moment of humorous truth, as "a professional cat shit pusher."

While collecting unemployment one Christmas season, Johnsen made gifts from wood scraps and realized how much she enjoyed working with wood. She began to build bookshelves, tables, and landed jobs—basically teaching herself every step of the way. Handyperson Enterprises was born, with Johnsen doing part-time office work in order to insure the rent and be her own boss *most* of the time. Integrity was important.

At the time of this interview, Handyperson Enterprises—envisioned by its mentor as a nationwide female-run corporation—is at the fledgling stage. But if Johnsen's pluck and enthusiasm are any indicator, her venture will be a mighty and quick success.

Born in 1945 in Chicago, Johnsen was reared in Crystal Lake, Illinois, population 8,000. She describes her parents as "very open-minded people, very heavy into the community." Her father is production manager of a sewing machine company and her mother has had "off and on jobs." Johnsen has two sisters; the elder, by two years, is a housewife and mother of three sons. Her other sister, ten years younger, is working toward a master's degree in child development and is "interested in establishing a day care center."

An active member of the National Organization for Women, Johnsen articulates the problems of women who would learn a trade and work with their hands. She sees the educational system, unions, and union contractors as flagrant obstacles.

I went to school thinking that I really wanted to be a radio dramatic writer. Between 1963 and 1967, everybody *laughed* at anybody who wanted to be a radio writer, because the thing was disc jockey, hard rock, and there was no need for radio dramatic writers.

Because I was paying my way through college, it occurred to me that if everybody's laughing at being a radio writer, I could major in advertising, work in an advertising office and use the facilities of the agency to get through school. This is exactly what I did.

I went to Columbia College in Chicago for four years. I have a bachelor's degree in mass communication and a degree in advertising. I graduated in 1967. That year I moved to San Francisco and got a job as assistant in the production department of an advertising agency in the financial district. The company is now called Botsford-Ketchum.

I was with Botsford for seven and a half years. I was production supervisor for five of those years. In September of 1973 I quit my job.

Why did you quit?

Well, I started putting things in perspective. Before I quit, I was working primarily on the Clorox account, one of the biggest accounts. I was working on a product which was a cat litter.

You spent your time promoting cat litter?

Yes. And one day I sat down and I figured out that for me to maintain my job, I would become a professional cat shit pusher, because if the cat didn't *do it,* I didn't have a job! [Laughs.] Once I thought about it in those terms, suddenly everything looked a little different! [Laughs.]

I decided what I was doing was not really important. I didn't feel good about it, so I couldn't take doing it.

What led to this change of attitude?

I can't really pinpoint it for myself. But I have talked to a number of people who have changed their careers somewhere between age 28 and 30. I was around 28.

The only thing I *can* pinpoint is that when I started in the advertising business, I was right out of high school. I just fell into it really. I was good at it, and I never had to think about what I was doing. The avenue was just there; I never really had to choose, and I bought all the myths—that it was indeed a fun place and that you could make a fortune in the business. I had a third cousin-in-law by marriage, removed a number of times—that kind of relationship—who lived in Hollywood. He was our wealthy relative, and he was in advertising. So I bought the idea that I could probably make a sizable living in the business. Suddenly I had some time to think. My decision was, "Well, I am very good at what I do in advertising. I am only 28 years old. I have some money in the bank. I'm in a position to take some time off, look around and see what I *can* do. If I fall flat on my face, I can feel comfortable knowing that I can always go back into the advertising business."

What did you do when you quit the advertising agency?

Nothing for a while. I collected unemployment for as long as I could, something like a year. First I had taken a part-time job that ran out. I was production assistant for a photoengraver. That's when I realized that working part-time is a highly civilized way to live!

You can live on the income and your free time is so much more valuable. I really appreciated that. I was writing a novel.

What's become of the novel?

It is still sitting there. It has been rejected twice for very valid reasons. It's your basic love story, started on the assumption that if the man who wrote *Love Story* could make a fortune, I could too. The novel is about 12,000 words; the title is *No Right to Mourn*.

How did you make the transition to the handy business?

Christmas was coming along, and I had to do something for gifts because I was not working. That was Christmas of 1974. They had been constructing a building across the street from where I live, and I had been collecting scraps of wood for my fireplace. I went down there and I looked at all these pieces of wood and I said, "Okay. What can I make?" I have three nephews who were on my Christmas list, so I started making little buildings out of these wood scraps for a kind of mini-town.

I had never done anything like that before. I had been to camp and carved a million letter openers, but that was about as far as I'd gotten with it. I found that I really enjoyed working with wood.

I also had a friend, a guy, who did a lot of basic repair. I decided I wanted to make a stand for a telephone, so since I had the time and he had the tools, I designed what I wanted and he showed me what I needed to know. I was extremely *proud* of that telephone stand, and I just went on to other items. Since then I've made a parson's table, a nightstand, bookcases.

Were you selling these items at first?

No. But after I made some of these things, my roommate came home one day and said that a woman that she worked with needed some bookcases built; would I do it?

I took on that job, and I realized that there is a whole market out there of people who really don't want to spend their time doing it. So that's when I started looking for people of that vein who needed jobs done.

How did you go about locating them?

I had become a member of the National Organization for Women. I was still collecting the dregs of my unemployment, and N.O.W. was having a convention in Philadelphia in 1975. I really thought I wanted to go, and I knew that unemployment wouldn't take me there; that's for *sure!* So I thought if I could find some people who needed some jobs done, I could go to Philadelphia.

So I placed an ad in the *N.O.W. Newsletter* just offering my services for that particular purpose, and the response was pretty good, considering. I had strange, different kinds of jobs. I made some bookcases. I put some peepholes in doors. I caulked some windows, did some painting—miscellaneous things.

What other advertising have you done?

I produced some little flyers and took them round to real estate offices, thinking that people who buy houses or buildings might want someone to come in and paint it, fix it up, that type of thing.

I got a couple of calls, enough to pay for my flyers and time distributing them. The rest of the work I've gotten primarily by word of mouth.

You're teaching yourself?

You rely an awful lot on people at building supply companies and hardware stores and on the terrific amount of detailed instruction in books in libraries.

It's not that hard to know what to do to start out with. Read it once, talk to somebody and after a couple hours working on it, you get pretty skilled.

Are you utilizing any particular skill more than others?

I'm doing more painting now than anything else, but it fluctuates. This just happens to be the painting season.

There was one time when I was building a staircase and building a bookshelf and building a table all at the same time. I've also built a concrete stone retaining wall and patched a chimney among other things. [Laughs.] I do basic home repair. I can fix washers; I've put in a garbage disposal. I have a surplus of power tools—drills, sanders, power saws. Except for bookcases and painting, I don't think there's a job that I've done twice or exactly alike.

You must have an innate ability?

I happen to be quite mechanically minded. I can see how things fit together and that's a definite attribute.

You have a business license. What was the procedure for acquiring it?

I have just filed as a business. It just means that I'm getting a license to do business in the City and County of San Francisco and in the State of California, registering under a fictitious name, that type of thing.

I'm also filing for a Resale License so that if I want to pick up a used piece of furniture at a flea market, strip it down and sell it, I can.

One thing that I want to do is get a storefront type of area, with a big workroom where I can set up tools and a workshop where people can come in and use the facilities or take lessons.

Who are your customers?

The interesting thing is that my market, as near as I can tell, is primarily women. Either they don't know how to do the work or they don't want to. Besides that, they give me the keys to their apartment and home. They're trusting me; I get the feeling that they trust me a little more because I'm a woman. I try to give the keys back just as quickly as I can! [Laughs.]

What do you charge for the work?

At the moment I charge $5.50 an hour. If it's something that I haven't done before and I have to spend a lot of time teaching myself about it, I don't charge for that, because I don't think it's fair. I would estimate it by the project. I would say, "Okay, it may take me 20 hours to do this, but it's only worth fifteen bucks." I can't charge more than it's worth.

Are you making a living from Handyperson Enterprises?

Because I'm just getting started, I'm registered with a temporary office service, and I have a friend who owns a company where I do some typing two days a week. It just barely pays the rent, but at the *moment* at least I can guarantee having my rent paid. If my friend doesn't need me, I call the temporary agency.

Why did you really decide to go into this business?

There are some people who are meant to work for other people, and there are some people who are not meant to work for others! I finally learned that, for myself, I have to work for *me* because nobody else should put up with me! [Laughs.] And too, I'm not an office worker, not really. Especially not pushing people for somebody else.

I decided that I really wanted to go into this business. The government cut me off—*justifiably!* [Laughs.] I was on my own, and I had to fend for myself in terms of economics.

Being your own boss is important to you?

Being my own boss is something *terrific!* Every brush stroke that I put on means something; it's really a reflection of the image of my company and future. If I don't do a good job, I am the one responsible.

I'm so proud of myself it's unbelievable. Everytime I do something I just sit back and think, "*I* did that and *I* get the benefit!"

I like myself a whole lot more! I'm sitting here thinking that I can do *anything,* and I'm *not* selling myself.

What are your ambitions for Handyperson Enterprises?

I do have dreams of someday becoming a corporate giant. Once I set up my storefront here, in ten years I want to have 900 outlets across the country. I don't know if this is ambition or dreams, but it's there.

I have this fantasy of a female-owned corporation and what it would be doing. I *can* see myself with 900 outlets across the country. I would spend at *least* one day a week actually going out and working, painting a wall or staining a bookcase—whatever.

One other thing that I would do is change the concept of women working with their hands. I want to change that concept in our educational system. Young women need to get basic repair type of instruction in school, just as they get home economics.

It's just so important! There are so many things that women find themselves not being able to do, things that they *ought* to be able to do. I think everybody should be given the opportunity of working with their minds and working with their hands. I don't mean that people who work with their hands don't work with their minds, but they should have that choice between labor work and office work. The opportunities ought to be shown to everyone!

You foresee having all female employees?

My thoughts go two ways. I think I would prefer to have female employees, primarily because of the trust factor. The other thing about it is, if the present situation exists ten years from now, women are still going to have problems getting jobs through unions and union-hiring contractors. I think there's *got* to be an outlet for women who want to work in this kind of field, without having to deal with that type of situation.

You have no need or necessity to be a member of a union?

I would *not* be a member of a union if my life depended on it! I do see a definite need for unions, but I am appalled by the power that union leaders have obtained and the disastrous effects they can cause on society just by trying to wield that power. Even if they're *not* successful, it's disastrous!

What are your observations about union discrimination against women?

I was talking to a woman who was a full-fledged journeyman—as they still call them—in the carpenter's union. She said that the problem is not necessarily with the union itself, but with the contractors. You can be a union member, but if the contractors don't want you—tough! You can pay the union dues, but if you don't get the work, what good is it? And the contractors *aren't* hiring women.

The unions only have so many apprenticeship openings each year. And you have to take a basic entrance test. Until women are given the industrial arts skills in the educational system, they aren't even going to be able to pass those basic tests. And what woman, who doesn't even know what a plane is, can pass that test?

Do you anticipate union problems?

I definitely think that if this company gets as big as I hope, unions are going to be my biggest problem. In San Francisco I think that you're not going to be hassled until you hire three people. When you get to three employees, they're going to stop by and say hello! [Laughs.]

If I get into having a staff and a couple of outlets, I *can* expect to be visited by the union. I can also expect the people working for me to think about joining the union.

Would you offer any benefits particularly geared to women's needs?

One thing I would like to set up is an insurance policy that would cover the special needs of women. I'd like to have a decent child care center available to them, too. Unions don't care one *bit* about this!

Do you regard yourself as physically strong?

Yes, and getting *stronger!* [Laughs.]

Has any of your work—like building the retaining wall, for instance—been a strain physically?

That was kind of interesting, because that was the first time when I really *had* to test my strength. I had to carry 80-pound sacks of dry cement from the front of the house to the back, and I said, "I think I have met my limit!" Eighty-one pounds would have *killed* me, I'm positive!

So strength is a consideration?

Yeah, but it doesn't bother me that much because I take very seriously the California labor laws that limit weight to 25 pounds without a mechanical device. I should have had something to transport that cement.

Have you found that you must be more aggressive to function well in this work?

Assertive, yes. Aggressive, no. I did have a tendency to be aggressive rather than assertive, and I had to curb that.

How do you distinguish between assertive and aggressive?

Well, aggressive is, "You better *not* do that because that's a *dumb* thing to do!" Assertive would be, "Could I suggest this way, because otherwise I just have to let you know I don't feel right about you doing it that way." Expressing your feelings in a positive way rather than just coming on strong.

Do you ever have difficulty in being assertive?

Sometimes I do have trouble asserting myself when I find my time being taken for granted like, "*Uh,* while you're here painting, would you mind dusting the floor?" I have to assert myself and say, "No. That's not what I'm here for."

In other words they think of you as a cleaning person just because you are a woman?

I think so, yes. Or maybe it's just a question of whether I can be conned into doing it. If the price is right, I'll do anything! [Laughs, jokingly.]

This happens with women, since they are primarily your clients?

Yeah, and it's primarily a *habit* reaction. I don't blame them for asking, because I know where they're coming from. They've got something that needs to be done; I'm there and maybe I could do it.

How do your male friends react to your work?

They think it's neat. But I only deal with a *select* type of man! [Laughs.] They think it's neat because they're in my narrow-minded circle of friends.

Which means broad-minded?

Yes. [Laughs.] I haven't run into the bigotry type of thing among my friends. All of them make the offer of, "Let me know when you need some help." I have run into some women who can't understand why I'd want to do something like this.

Do you know these women rather well?

No. These are women who I *don't* know rather well!

How does your family react?

My family's cool about it. When I first quit my job at the advertising agency, since my father has worked for the same company since he was sixteen, I thought he really would be upset that I'd given up my job without having another one. But they have not bugged me about it.

A couple of years ago I injured my knee playing softball, and I was home at Christmas to help my father paint the house. The only thing he said was, "I'm worried about your insurance." I said, "Don't worry about it." He said, "Okay."

How are you covered in case of accident?

I have my own personal liability insurance.

Have you had any accidents?

Not on the job, no.

Do you regard your work as hazardous?

Oh, sometimes. I'd say the hazard that I have is dropping something on my feet, so I wear my steel-toed hiking shoes. There's also the possibility of falling off a ladder.

How do you use your creativity in this work?

My creative interest comes through when I get to design something like a piece of furniture or I have a neat project. I made a phone stand with a hidden compartment, and I had to ask myself, "Now how do I do this?"

Do you ever question your capabilities due to the fact that you are female or your background?

I can't really separate the two. My background is based on being a female child. What I was taught I could or could not do as a youngster carried over, and I have to make the dividing line: can I *now* as an adult human being working with my hands, do something, or can I not do something because of what I think I am as a woman?

Electrical Mechanic

Sophenia Maxwell

*Death, man, you can come any time,
because I feel that I'm really whole. I
feel like I can fit into anything, that I
can* do *anything, that I can go* anywhere
and be *anything.*

Since November, 1974, Sophie Maxwell has worked as an apprentice electrical mechanic for the Southern Pacific Railroad. All available information suggests that Maxwell is the only female electrician—apprentice or journey—employed by Southern Pacific. (Southern Pacific *does* claim to have *two* female locomotive engineers in the entire United States.)

Of all the women I interviewed for CONVERSATIONS, Maxwell was probably the most charming. I first visited her in her warm, stylish San Francisco home, and met her again during her twenty-minute lunch "hour" at the Southern Pacific Yard. In both environments she was equally personable.

While visiting Maxwell on the job, I talked with her co-worker, Leonard D. Ticehurst, an electrician with Southern Pacific for 28 years. One must remember that Ticehurst is a middle-aged Caucasian male unaccustomed to working with women to appreciate his "fond uncle" remarks about Maxwell. "She's my girl," he says. "Most people are afraid to get dirty, but *she's not.* She works *hard!*" For Sophenia Maxwell, a "positive attitude is the key" that opens doors.

I'm an electrical mechanic apprentice. That entails maintenance and repair of electrical equipment on Southern Pacific transportation trains or gallery cars. It's a commuter fleet running up and down the (San Francisco) Peninsula. I maintain and repair that.

What motivated you to become an electrician?

At one point in my life I decided that I needed to have a skill. I have a five-year-old son. And I needed to be able not only to survive, but to live. Therefore I wanted something that couldn't be taken away from me, something that I could *always* have, in case I wanted to go into anything else. There are a *lot* of fields I'm interested in. I thought I should have a skill. Most of the *men* I know can do a number of things—electrical work, plumbing—and they may be lawyers. So I said, "Well, *look Sophie!* If you want to do something like that, if you want to go into another field, you better have something that no one can take away from you—that you can *use* and build on."

Electricity is something that goes far and beyond. Now it's into medicine and anywhere else you go. Everything's electronic. So I figured that would at least give me a loop-hole.

I decided I would divorce my husband. [Laughs.] That's when I started looking into things. I looked into plumbing and a lot of other things. I kind of like math. But I wanted something that was basic, that I could always get a job in.

I was about 24. Now I'm 27. It wasn't too long ago. [Maxwell was born in 1950.]

I *really* did some thinking! I had a manual. There was a project going on in San Francisco, and they had sent out brochures on apprenticeship programs. Plumbing is good but is rather limiting. And this wasn't. Plus it wasn't as heavy and as bulky, and I could do it on the side. If a friend has something that needs fixing I can fix it a lot simpler. My tools are relatively small and I can deal with them a lot easier. They're less cumbersome.

How did you prepare yourself to become an electrical mechanic?

The first thing I did was look at the requirements, and that included math, and a B average in high school algebra. That was for the union, Local 609 Electricians Union. That's called the outside union. Mine is an *inside* union, the railroad union. It was so long since I'd had algebra, and I wanted to be up on everything. Being a woman you *have* to be better. So I took algebra and physics and another basic electricity course, and I started on electronics. I went to John Adams, an adult school, and John O'Connell [both in San Francisco]. It took me about a year to prepare. Meanwhile I was working part-time as an art teacher. [Maxwell worked for the telephone company for nine months as a clerk, then married and had a child. To keep her "interest going" while she was married and to earn some money, she took an apprentice course at the San Francisco de

Young Museum art school and taught art at a neighborhood center. In addition to her other interests, Maxwell plays the piano and sells real estate.]

After you took the preparatory classes, what happened?

First I got in touch with Advocates for Women. They're an agency that helps women who are interested in non-traditional jobs. They helped me along with job leads. First the Local 609 Electrical Union was open for apprenticeships. That was in April. Their test was coming up, and I had to drill for that. Then Mare Island Naval Shipyard and PG & E (Pacific Gas and Electric) were looking for apprentices. I was really in there plugging away. I was going to school in the morning, and I was in a cram group through an agency for minorities. At night I'd go to Advocates for Women. It *wasn't easy*, and that's what makes me feel so good that I got it! It makes me feel like I can do *anything* in the world!

What was the test?

It was basically an aptitude test. They're trying to determine your aptitude, mechanical aptitude, your interests and so on. We took the test one morning for four hours. It so happened that the union test and the Mare Island tests were the same day. I was really tested out. Then I got a call that Southern Pacific was looking for an electrician.

By that time, I had been interviewed by this person, that person. I said, "I am *sick* of this!" I walk in—I'm a woman, and I'm not trying to be anything else! I want to support my child. I walk in there looking my best. Men look their best when they go to interviews. So I wear a skirt, and they'd ask me some of the weirdest questions, like what my father and my mother thought about it, and why didn't I go into modeling?! Really, there were a lot of little sly things, and when you're being interviewed they have ways of trying to get you off the track. I'd stay with it, but I'd never gotten any jobs. So I was disenchanted.

The woman at Advocates said "Look, Sophie, just go down and *try* it!" I didn't go. She called me back and said, "Sophie! Get your ass down there *right now!* I'm going to call and make the appointment." I walked in. They looked at me and asked a few questions, and they *really* looked at me again. They asked things like, "What are you going to be doing in the next ten years?" And I said, "Hopefully I'll be a journeyman electrician!" So I got the job! I was floored. I said, "*No test?* No *nothing?''* I sure wanted to be able to take the test [laughs]. I guess they got the answers they wanted. I've been working there since November 1974.

Describe the training program.

I'm still in training. It's a four-year program. You work with a journeyman electrician and you learn tools, basic electricity, how to handle tools, what tools to use, and which ways they can be used. Learning what combinations, what wires, what things you can substitute for other things. Learning how to *think* mechanically. Learning to trouble-shoot.

As an electrical mechanic, I'm dealing with an engine, so at this point I'm learning about smoke—if it's gray or white or black, what the trouble is and where to go. Also AC air conditioning, heating, lighting, and engines.

About every six weeks we change who we work with, and it's another mechanic, an electrical mechanic. My title is Apprentice Electrical Mechanic.

This is the same as an electrician?

There are different types of electricians. There's an inside wire man who does your house wiring, and an electrical mechanic who works on the electrical systems of the train or car. Every six months there's a change, and I go to another point; now I'm where they work on the engines themselves. I'm working on cars, which is what the engine pulls. Next I'm going to work on the engine. They're almost *all* electronic so that's going to be another fascinating thing—totally different—dealing with diodes and transistors. More sophisticated, *and* it gets into computers. The whole huge thing has so much power. [Laughs.] That fascinates me! To think that I'm going to be able to deal with that!

What have you found to be the most difficult aspect of this learning process?

I think the most difficult thing is for me to realize I'm just learning and not to get discouraged at not knowing. That is something I have to deal with every day. Telling myself that just because I turn the screw wrong this time, I'll still get it. [Laughs.]

You have to think mechanically. To me this means that when you take something apart, you're aware of exactly how it went, so you *know* how to put it back.

And *organization*—every screw, bolt, you *know* where it is. Some of them are *very* tiny, some of them are very *big*. I think that's one of the most important things, knowing how to put back what you take off. If you miss one little washer, just a flat piece of metal, *that* can throw the whole thing off because some things are *very* precise. You have a gauge; it has to be *just right!*

What do you find most interesting about the work?

I think it's when I'm finished with a job and it works. It comes in and it's not working; you fix it, wipe it off, clean up the engine, and it *works!* I feel like a *doctor* sometimes. We go out with our different meters—gauges for testing the oil pressure, gas pressure, the voltage.

Because of my work, I've realized that there are so many other things I can do and that nothing is really closed. It really is wonderful.

Probably the most challenging thing is trouble-shooting. Maybe there's a short somewhere. Each car has to hold maybe 250 volts. Sometimes a car will not hold that. The air conditioning, the heating, the lighting circuit, and all add up to that amount, that load. When you turn all that on, maybe the engine will quit. Trouble-shooting is figuring out what the cause is and why.

Describe what you do on a daily basis.

The trains come in in the morning and passengers unload. These trains sit; they'll probably be going out later in the day. I inspect them. I make sure the air conditioner is working properly, the heating and lights are working properly. I check the engine speed. I make sure the doors are all working properly, that there's no smoke coming out, and that everything is pretty much okay. If I find anything wrong I write it down. Later on, about 9:30, after everything has been checked and the last commuter fleet is in, everyone reports down to baggage, and if you had any problems you tell them what it is. Then work is assigned. I may be assigned to air conditioning, maybe it's cycling. So I go in and check that, and if I find something wrong I fix it. Say, if it's cycling, that sounds like it needs Freon so I'll add the Freon. Maybe it's the compressor, or the generator, or maybe it needs a whole new engine change. [Each day Maxwell works on about twenty trains, each with four to seven cars.]

When you make the survey of the train, would a journeyman be with you?

Right now I'm a set-up electrician. That means that after a certain period, they decided I could work on my own. I get a journeyman's salary, but I'm still putting my time in as an apprentice. I'm still an apprentice, according to the union and to Southern Pacific.

As an apprentice you have to have a number of days or hours in. I'm "set-up." That means maybe an electrican retired, and that job needed to be filled. They didn't have enough electricians to fill it, so they said, "Okay, we will set you up. You'll be getting *our* rate of pay and working as an electrician, but still every day you work will be accounted to your time as an apprentice." The apprenticeship program at Southern Pacific is four years.

What about the union?

I feel good about the union, and I attend the meetings. An apprentice doesn't have any voting rights or anything like that. But an apprentice is really a good thing to be, because when lay-off time comes, you usually won't be laid off. You're on a different roster altogether than the journeymen. In Southern Pacific, there has to be maybe one apprentice to every seven journeymen, so we're really pretty well protected. Instead of laying me off, I'd be moved to another point. *And* being a *woman* does not hurt me. [Maxwell is the only woman in her union, as far as she knows. Her initial union fee was $50.00, and her apprentice dues are $8.50 a month.]

"Being a woman" *is* helpful?

Extremely helpful. Well, because they have to have their quota. [Laughs.] They're always asking if I know any women who are interested. I don't know, maybe it's just talk.

How do your former salaries compare with the present?

They don't compare with the present job. The highest salary was about 100 dollars a week. My salary now is about $300 something, and that's a *week*. My take-home is over $200. Every two weeks I gross $650. Hourly it's seven dollars and something. The railroad is pretty cheap. Outside electricians make between 12 and 16 dollars an hour, maybe even more.

Is physicial strength necessary?

I find that it's not all in physical strength. It's in leverage and knowing how to use what you have. I have to pick up heavy tanks, between 90 and 100 pounds. It's Freon which is what you put in your air conditioner. You have to put the tanks on a truck in order to get them on a train. Sometimes the train will be at the depot and the Freon is at the storage place, and I have to lift it up and put it on the truck. I've learned which end of the crowbar to use and the way you place things, angles, and how to push things over, the pressure you exert. [Maxwell is 5'8" and weighs 143 pounds.]

I was talking to a fellow—I was having trouble doing things—and he said, "You know something, you ought to go to a health spa." He said, "I work out every day. Most men do." Usually a man has something in his house that he exercises on. So I started going to a health spa, the Golden Venus. And I took dance lessons. I swim. I was more physical. I took *sailing* lessons, even. I just did as many things as I could. In sailing I learned rope-tying which you need sometimes. It was really helpful. I was able to use the knots to tie something around or keep something on the truck. It really did a lot of good things for me.

Going to the health spa was really great because I was able to improve my physical strength and tone up my muscles. I was going about three or four times a week . . . swimming, exercising the upper torso, the leg muscles. Sometimes if you're pushing something, you push from the legs. Maybe you'll have a foot on one part of the car giving yourself that extra push-off. You almost need to be a *dancer!* Sometimes you are in a cramped space and you need extra force.

Is your work dangerous?

Yes, it is. The *trains!* You're going over tracks. The trains are going back and forth, constantly being moved and put on tracks getting ready to load. And they are extremely quiet! *Extremely!* In fact, just last year a man lost his leg. This happens all the time! They're always having safety meetings, every week. Periodically someone might come up to you and ask, "What's the safety rule of the week?" It's very hazardous. If you're thinking of going back to the shed to get a part, say, and you're thinking about where it is, you may not hear that train being moved and creeping in on you. That's what happened to that man! I have to be extremely alert all the time. Maybe I'm thinking about something else, and I look up and there's a train. Sometimes they don't have whistles you can hear, or you may *not* hear. It's dangerous.

Sometimes you have to get up in the trains, up in the upper

part of the compartments where the compressor tanks and some of the heating elements and that kind of thing are.

Then, you have to lower fans, about 25-50 pounds each on a rope; there's a man down at the bottom. I've been on the bottom at times. If *anything* happens to that rope, that motor comes down on you! When you're taking the bolts off, you may be holding it with one hand. Things like that can happen all the time. The Freon tanks can possibly explode.

And of course you can get shocked dealing with 220 volts. The higher the voltage, the less danger you have. You can be knocked out, but if someone is there *immediately* they can get your heart going again. Then you can go like *that!* (Slaps her hand.) Your lower voltage is more dangerous because your heart will tremor, instead of just stopping. If it's just tremoring there's nothing you can do.

Have you had any psychological problems with your work?

When I started, I felt *black*. I felt a racial thing, certainly. My fears were about being black and working with the kind of men I was going to be working with. They haven't always been earning a decent salary, and those are the ones that feel the greatest threat. Being black *and* being a woman, I thought I would feel that. But they did a very good job of covering it up, because I didn't experience any of that. See, we have been taught . . . we've been put against each other. And then when we see each other and I talk to them, and they talk to me, we find out, "Hey! You're not so bad! You're not lazy! And you don't do this and do that." And it was okay. It was all right!

That's extremely important, and I think that's why integration is so important, so we learn about each other. And being a woman, I could bring certain points to them, and they related to me. We can communicate with each other.

Do the men at work accept you?

I've had a fantastic reception! *Beautiful!* I always work with men. Sometimes I work with three or four, if there's trouble. If they've finished their work and they see you still working on something, they'll come and help you. Really beautiful! Really fine! That's the way they are. It's because I wanted it! *Nobody* could have done anything to me because I knew what I wanted to do. So they have to respect me for that. I'm sure they all have something to say, but because of my attitude they can't be anything but positive toward me. A positive attitude is the key.

You are *totally* accepted?

You can't change a person altogether, and they've grown up with certain outlooks and things that are ingrained in them about women. I am a woman, so they still open doors for me and I *definitely* let them. If they see me carrying something heavy, they'll take it. If I see them carrying something heavy, I'll come and help them with it. They have little names that they call me, like "Little One." [Laughs.] As big as I am. I feel embarrassed.

I think you run into those types—one who says, "Well, if you're a women's libber, *you* do it!" So they'll give you *everything* to do. There's the one that won't let you do anything. And then the one that will understand and help you if you need it.

I think the men really *want* me to be a good mechanic. They give me little tips and hints about doing things.

Right now I'm working with a fellow on an outside job wiring someone's house. That's really been a chance! I'm learning how to bend conduit and things like that.

Do you have friends at work?

Oh, yes. There's the fellow I'm working with. A man asked me to do some wiring in his house. And I said, "Oh, okay. I'll get my buddy and we'll come over." So I went and I asked my buddy, Art, who works with me every day, if he'd go with me. He said, "Sure, I'll meet you there at six o'clock." And so *boom,* we're working on that job together. [Laughs.] And that's nice!

Have you experienced *any* discrimination?

No, I can't say that I have. It's *great*, isn't it? That *needs* to be known! I was out at an apprenticeship conference. Some women's group asked me to be there. And there were all these men looking for apprentices and so on. I started talking to them and relating, and we were *laughing* together! We *laughed* and we *talked*. There was over a *thousand* of them.

When I got ready to leave, they *all* came up to me and said, "Look, we really enjoyed you!" You know, there's bad flowers in every bunch. And you'll find that some of the men are the *laziest* people! But usually the women who get those jobs are better. Usually they chose to be there. And they have a reason to be there! I think they'll probably start looking for *more women!* [Laughs.]

Do you enjoy the work?

Truthfully, I can say this is one of the happiest times of my life and one of the fullest times of my life. I always say, "Death, *man,* you can come anytime because I feel that I'm really whole. I feel like I can fit into anything, that I can *do* anything, that I can go *anywhere* and *be* anything." And therefore there's nothing I have to prove. I've already done it. And I feel so good about it, because I *chose* what I wanted to be. I chose it. And I *got* it! And *that's* what makes me feel so good!

How have your personality and approach to people changed due to your job?

I am much more open now. *Much* more open. I have something in common with these men, that I wouldn't ordinarily. I can talk to them, and I know about their lives and what they go through. I know how important it is for women to get out and try to liberate our men. I really understand that. A lot of them may have wanted to go into different fields. Most of them, I find, are not in this by choice, like I am, but it's something they knew they could get a job doing. They may have wanted to be something else. It's tough!

What do you mean by liberating the men?

I mean if we take some of the responsibility for our families, not only financially. I don't think our world would be in the shape it's in if we had taken more responsibility as human beings, and as women, and as thinking people. We have to interject that. We *must,* in order to save it.

What about roles? Do you see a division between "male" roles and "female" roles?

No, I don't. I think all work roles are important. To me, some of the most important people in this country are your janitors, your streetsweepers, *and* anyone in the home. *That's* one of the most important jobs there is! It's important for that woman to have her head together and to be in as many things as she can to be aware, so that her children will not be ignorant. That's an extremely important thing!

Would you describe yourself as a "women's libber"?

A women's libber? I'll tell you . . . being a black woman, we've always been women's libbers. What they're advocating now we've always had. We've been *forced* to advocate that. As you know the work force mainly has been black women and white males. We've always worked. But now, as a black woman, I'm able to make more. Instead of wiping his wife's kitchen, I'm working with him! I think black women have always been women's lib. God *knows* we have always been *per se* liberated but we needed a different kind of liberation. We definitely need it. I think women's lib can help us achieve it.

The black woman has been confined to menial and demeaning work in the past?

I would never call my grandmother's work demeaning. Nobody can make small my *grandmother*. Never! Never! Because of her and her spirit. My grandmother could work in somebody's kitchen and call them "Lily" and never in her life say "Miss" to anybody! Never in her life! The thing is that *my mother* was a housekeeper. And we had a dishwasher before the people she worked for! My mother is an extremely shrewd smart woman. [Laughs.] She is! *She is!* And *that's* the kind of people I grew up with!

Who in your background, men or women, set a standard for you?

My mother and my grandmother. My mother was a house-keeper and my grandmother was a laundry worker. They are *too much!* And my mother, [Enola Maxwell] ran for the San Francisco Board of Supervisors in 1975. She got 22,000 votes. [Laughs.] And that's my mother. My mother is too much.

My grandmother always told me—she worked 22 years in this laundry and she was late maybe once—she said, "I don't work for anybody but *myself!* I don't have *any* bosses! *Nobody!* I call *no man* my boss. I'm my *own* boss." And she said, "When you go to work, when you're on top, you're doing that for *you*. I'm only working for myself."

I'm the youngest in my family and I have one brother and one sister. My brother's going to UC Berkeley right now. And my sister is a cosmetologist. She's always had her own business. My father too. My father's great!

My family, that's all I ever really knew. It's just my mother and my grandmother. We were living in the projects. My grandmother was earning 22 dollars a week and my mother about the same. And those two bought a house. And they did their own electrical work, and they did their own plumbing, and they laid their *own* tile, and they cut holes right in this house! And they bought this house, still working for those same people.

Then, one day when we were living here, my mother decided she would have to get a new job, and she decided to work for post office. She worked there for a while, then she came home one day and said she was going to become a minister. "I'm going to have my *own* church," she said. "In that way people are going to be able to smoke in my church and drink coffee. That way they won't have to leave early." A couple of years later my mother became the first woman Presbyterian lay-minister in this city. She said she wanted to be a minister, and she *was* in a couple of years.

I remember asking her, I said, "Mom, can you see me as an electrician?" She said, "Sophie, I can see you as *anything* you want to be." I said, "Okay!"

Was your father at home when you were growing up?

Well, sometimes. They got married twice. I guess for a couple of years there was a male figure. They're *very* close. My mother and my father are very good friends. He's a building contractor.

When you were growing up what career did you want?

I thought I would be a psychiatrist. Then I went to a boarding school in Utah. It was college prep—study hall, bells ringing all the time. And I said, "I don't think this is for *me!*" [Laughs.]

Are you a member of any women's organizations?

I'm affiliated with Women for Peace. It's an organization of women who have been fighting for peace a *long* time, even before Vietnam. They were in the civil rights movement. A lot of fascinating women. And Black Women for Action. They're really into politics and social things like that.

You encourage women to enter trades?

Women *need* to make more money. And there is definitely more money in the skills. To a certain extent we're getting more into a skill-oriented society. Social workers are kind of going. Teachers are overdone. So I think women have to go to other things, to learn about what's happening around them. Women have to be more independent.

I think you can be *more* feminine and *more* self-confident if you aren't afraid to lift something or get greasy or dirty.

What are you striving for personally?

Well, I am striving to make money. I want to send my son to a nice school. I want to have a house.

Most men have been able to raise families, buy a house, have a car, on their salaries. Well, I should be able to do the same thing. I enjoy being a woman, and I enjoy being an *independent* woman. I don't feel like I need anybody else to make me a whole person. I think I can get everything that I need, and that's why I'm working so I can try to achieve that. If I can't do it *this* way, then I'll figure out something else.

Judith Grant McKelvey

*The best part of the women's move-
ment, which I think is very important,
is that women have begun to value
themselves and to examine their own
goals . . .*

Born in 1935 of Catholic parents, Judith Grant McKelvey grew up in Milwaukee in the forties and fifties when women equated their worth with their desirability to men. McKelvey somehow escaped that myth. She credits her parents, particularly her dentist father, with her decision to opt for a profession and independence.

The only woman in her graduating class of 400, McKelvey took her law degree from University of Wisconsin School of Law in 1959 and went to work for the Federal Communications Bureau, thus avoiding another traditional route, that of teaching. Law firms were closed to women attorneys, but the federal government was not.

Eventually McKelvey decided to teach for a year at Golden Gate University School of Law in San Francisco. Finding teaching to be an "affirmative" experience after all, she taught at the "unique" institution for six years, involving herself in various committees. In 1974 she was named dean, a title that carries with it "total" responsibility for the academic life today of 750 law students; 38 percent of those students—fifteen percent above the national average—is female. There are 168 accredited law schools in the United States; according to McKelvey, deans of only three of those academic institutions are female.

In this interview McKelvey reveals her views on the Women's Movement and women's need to become "critical thinkers." Her observations, honed on the experience of her own life, are timely and astute.

I'm a lawyer, and I am presently dean of Golden Gate University School of Law. I became dean in the summer of 1974. Before that I had been with the Federal Communications Commission for a period of three years as an attorney/advisor between 1959 and 1962. Then I lived in France for three years, spending most of my time traveling; that's how I became interested in teaching.

I came to California, and, while waiting for bar results, it occurred to me that it would be interesting to do some part-time teaching in a law school. So I applied to teach at Golden Gate University Law School for part-time purposes, and I was offered a full-time teaching job, which seemed to be a good thing to do for a year. That was in 1968. I found that I liked teaching so well that that was what I *really* wanted to do, after all that time. I was someone who had gone to law school to avoid the prospect of ever having to teach, but I guess it makes a big difference if you do something out of choice rather than from force.

Many women, at the time I was going to undergraduate school, viewed teaching as one of their major choices, if they wanted to avoid doing secretarial work with an undergraduate degree.

How did your appointment as dean come about?

I had taught for six years at Golden Gate University Law School. Then the prior dean made it known that he was going to be leaving. Interestingly enough he suggested that I might want to apply for the position. It's an *unusual* institution!

I submitted my name and went through the interviewing process and, somewhat to my surprise, I was appointed about six months later.

What was your reaction to assuming the position as dean?

To some degree I did it with trepidation, partly because I was very interested in teaching; teaching had been an extremely affirmative experience and I had really loved it. However, I did feel that there were some things that the law school ought to be doing. So I came to the work with the feeling that I may or may not be the right person to do it, but because I did perceive some things that the institution should do, I'd give it a whirl. It was with some concern in terms of what I was getting myself into.

I would not have described myself as an administrator . . . but I had a very deep interest in the institution as, by the way, most of us do at Golden Gate. I thought the time was ripe for a great number of things to be done. The Law School was just on the verge of becoming a *major* law school.

What are the actual responsibilities of the dean?

Before I became dean, I couldn't figure out what they did all day, and now I *know!* [Laughs.] One of the interesting things about it is that I had to change my concepts of what success is and what makes a good day or a bad day. As a teacher, if you have a successful class, you get good feedback from students; you know whether things are going well. In administration, your results take much, much longer to come about.

The responsibility is a *total* one; you are in the position of being a constant problem-solver, the long-term planner, the budget planner. You have to run a successful recruiting and admissions program—that is, you must fill the school with good students. Then you must be certain that the students are getting a good legal education with *all* that that implies, that they're getting good financial-aid advice and good counseling, and, finally, that they are being helped with job placement. You are also supposed to be a catalyst for the faculty so that they do creative work and get the kind of support they need, and you also have to see that you have the money to hire and keep good faculty. Then there's the development side: you begin new projects and programs, and you develop an alumni program and get involved in fund-raising. And, of course, you attempt to relate the school to the community.

So the dean is a manager in every sense of the word. You are responsible for plowing the soil in which a good law school and, thus, lawyers can grow. You can't do that alone, but you are trying to create a climate where education can take place and where people have the goods and services they need to perform and, in the long run, you hope that all the things you do have some impact on improving the quality of legal education and the way in which lawyers relate to society.

I learned that running a law school is really no different than running anything; this was a great surprise to me. In running a law school, you are running a *business* of a certain kind, but your business is to produce good lawyers, to have a good library to serve those people, and to integrate your law school and your graduates into, and to serve, the community. [The budget she deals with is "in excess of a million and a half dollars. We're obviously responsible," she says, "for producing the income as well as staying within the expenses." McKelvey's salary is $38,000 a year.]

How many women law school deans are there in the United States?

I think there are presently three deans of the 167 accredited law schools. These are the American Bar Association accredited law schools. The University of Miami at Coral Gables is headed by a prominent law teacher from the University of Chicago, Soia Mentschikoff. Dorothy Nelson has been the dean at USC [University of Southern California] for a number of years. Then there is myself. There was one other person, a woman by the name of Judith Younger, who was at Syracuse, but she's no longer the dean.

You are the first woman dean of Golden Gate. What qualified you for that position?

We had no factions within the school, which was an important kind of thing. Because of my interest-areas, while teaching I had involved myself in various kinds of committee work. I had worked very hard at it, so I had been intimately involved with administrative activities.

Because of those activities, I suppose there was some perception that I would *work* at it. On occasions, because of working in the administrative structure on committees, I had expressed ideas about what I thought we ought to be doing. I suppose that led to some assurance that I had the health of the institution in mind.

There was a sense among us on the faculty that the law school was growing and that there were some very good things on the horizon for the law school. So the thinking may have been that I was a person from inside the law school, knew it and thought well of it, and had its best interests as my own interests. I suppose I appeared to be dedicated to the school.

What were your qualifications before joining Golden Gate as a teacher?

I suppose that anyone who becomes dean of a law school first has to have some interest in a law school. Obviously you have to have a law degree. I had done my undergraduate work at University of Wisconsin and obtained my law degree there in 1959.

I've concluded that the way people probably become deans is through teaching in a law school and gaining an on-site kind of experience. That probably qualifies one in the best way for becoming a dean. In my case the teaching experience and an interest in *this* institution were absolutely essential.

Golden Gate also has a female director of admissions?

Yes, and in addition the associate dean of the law school is a woman. Her name is Mary Minkus, a graduate of Stanford Law School. I think this says something about this particular institution. [Mary Minkus became associate dean "a year and a half or two years" before McKelvey was named dean. Patricia Ostini is director of admissions.]

Golden Gate Law School seems to have a good female representation in administration?

It's interesting because it would have been very easy for the institution to have said, "My God! There's a woman in the administration already, and if we have another woman as dean, that means the total law school administration is female!" I think that was one of the most fascinating parts of being selected dean. The fact that there was already a woman in the administration was one thing that I thought would cut against me most. If it was a problem, I never heard about it! [Laughs.]

There is no suggestion of tokenism?

Absolutely not!

They might have been a little worried about it. I'm sure they considered that the projected image of the law school would be totally female. And I guess they had to say, "Well, it's okay! We will just have to take whatever risks that may raise."

How many women were on your interview board?

There was one female in the group, a student, out of seven committee members. [The Dean's Selection Committee was composed of members of the Board of Trustees, the President of the University and two law school students.]

As dean, have you experienced any difficulties because you are female or any resistance to female administrators?

I haven't really experienced a problem in that regard. Again, I think that's due to the very same forces that allow one to flourish in this atmosphere. I have never had any problems with students, with administrators or faculty. I have never perceived being female as creating a problem here. This undoubtedly says a great deal for the rest of the people in the institution. [Laughs.]

It's a *unique* institution. I suppose that my decision to stay after first coming here to teach probably had something to do with the very affirmative, open atmosphere of the place.

My experience in the context of this institution has been that it is *virtually* of *no* importance at all whether one is female or not female. It just hasn't been a factor. It's amazing to me.

What is the percentage of women law students at Golden Gate?

We have 38 percent overall, with approximately 44 percent in the first year class. [The law school, she says, has 750 students. Two-thirds are day-time students, and the balance is in the part-time division.]

The breakdown of female and male instructors?

Of the twenty full-time faculty members, two are presently women. I was one, of course, who came out of the faculty, so that made one less.

Of the fifteen or so part-time faculty, probably 25 percent is women.

What percentage of law students in the United States is female?

I think it's about 23 percent now. It's really climbing. There is, I would guess, a total of about 110,000 law students in the country.

In the mid-sixties, women constituted probably about five percent. There's been an enormous growth.

What avenues were open to women attorneys when you obtained your law degree?

When I got out of law school, one didn't think in terms of getting a job with a law firm. You just didn't *think* in those terms!

You thought in terms of precisely what I did; you went to work for the government, which is probably why there are as many women attorneys and engineers as there are with government. You'll find them relatively high in the Civil Service because that's where those women professionals went to work after school. Law firms were almost impossible to break into. Usually there would be some sort of tie through a relative or a husband. It was *very, very difficult!* And it is *still* true that women are not properly represented—in my judgment—in firms. It is much better now, but there is still a long way to go!

In retrospect, thinking about women attorneys being so unacceptable to law firms, I find it extraordinary that there wasn't even much anger about it. It was just understood. It was just a fact!

How do you account for that attitude toward women lawyers?

I think most of us accepted the world as a man's world, and law was regarded as a man's profession. There weren't very many women who went into law, so women weren't particularly noticeable anyway. A lot of sex discrimination is at the subconscious level. There was no doubt in most firms about how their clients would relate to women, as well as an attitude that women did not have the stamina and the aptitude to be good lawyers—the sort of stereotyped view of how women handled themselves, that they weren't aggressive enough and that they were emotional beings. Typically, women who did get into firms probably practiced in areas where they didn't deal with clients to any great degree and where they didn't get into much litigation. They did not enter areas of practice that would bring them into conflict in courtroom situations because of the question of how juries and clients would respond to them.

A lot of firm prejudice *was* at the subconscious level, and women themselves didn't think of going into the legal profession.

You were an unusual woman and probably regarded as a little odd if you went into law. You were regarded by many as reducing the chances of ever getting married, because it was *thought* that no one would want to marry someone better educated or threatening intellectually. So law schools and law firms just grew up without thinking of women as potential lawyers.

What work were you doing with the FCC?

I worked in what they call the Office of Opinions and Review. It was interesting work. I was doing a lot of writing, reviewing various kinds of briefs and preparation of commission opinions. It was like the kind of work that young lawyers do for judges. I was there for three years.

Was that a constructive experience?

I think it was. Although I discovered that I am interested in a more active people-oriented role—one that's not desk-tied, in a sense. In administration you're constantly involved with other people. At the FCC there was a lot of research and a lot of writing which was interesting but not what I would want as a total career.

Were there any other women attorneys in your FCC office?

There was one other woman. But there were many others in the agency. The government generally was very good about hiring women.

How many women were law students at Wisconsin when you were there?

In my class when I started, there were four or five women out of about 400 students. I was the only woman to graduate. [McKelvey graduated in the top 15 percent of her class. She states that she had no difficulty in gaining admittance to law school.]

You are an advocate of women lawyers?

Yes, I am. One of the reasons why I am a great advocate of women becoming lawyers is that they become critical thinkers, and I think that's good for everyone, including women. It also prepares them for any number of work opportunities. Lawyers can do and do many things in our society.

Why did you go to law school?

I was a philosophy major as an undergraduate and, as I said, one of the things I thought I wanted to do least in the whole world was be a teacher. I think that most people in philosophy ultimately train to be university professors. I wanted to do something besides go into teaching. Also, I wanted job independence. I have to give credit for my decision to go to law school to one person in a major way—my father.

How did your father influence you?

He had four daughters and one son, and his attitude towards the children generally was to treat them like individuals. He had no sexual stereotypes in terms of the way he treated his children.

I remember going to him for advice about being a philosophy major, asking "What am I going to do with this?" I remember him saying to me, and I guess I was a sophomore in undergraduate school at the time, "Don't you want to do something that will make you independent?" A great question! He said, "If you *don't* like it, you don't have to stick it out." It seemed like a good idea to me. [McKelvey was the second oldest child in her family. Her oldest sister is a professor of dance. Her brother recently completed law school. One sister graduated from undergraduate school with a major in art history, married, had a family and has just started working again. Her youngest sister did not finish college but is considering going back. "She married and had a family, and is probably about to become what you would call a re-entry woman.'']

How would you describe your parents' economic status?

Good solid middle class. My father is a dentist. My mother went to college. My father is a professional and valued education, so it was expected that we would go on to college; it was really never much of a question.

Did you attend public schools?

I guess I had what is known as a ''good Catholic girls' education.'' I went to a parochial school—it was not a girls' school—through eighth grade. Then I went to a public high school. I started at private high school, but I didn't like it, and my father got me out of *that!* [Laughs.] He's a good fellow, and I must say, too, that my mother encouraged me. There was never any real pressure to get married and have a family. My mother encouraged me very much to do something like be a lawyer. She thought that was a *fine* idea. That was very rare at that time. I think I was very lucky.

Did you find parochial and public schools to be a negative or positive influence in defining female roles?

I think there is some concern about sexual roles of young women and young men. In terms of the substantive grade school parochial education, the education was good. Academic excellence was rewarded, and certainly as much was expected of the girls as the boys.

Was being ''smart'' in high school a social handicap?

Sure. Certainly in the fifties, that was something that young women tried to hide. I very well remember that it was far more important to be popular than it was to be smart.

For young women in the fifties, I think the dilemma was all of those approach-avoidance things of being thought smart and wanting to be popular. I think that the biggest impact on young women was the subconscious pressure *not* to think of themselves in terms of real goals. Probably the most destructive aspect of that was that your worth was largely tied up with what you regarded as your desirability to men. Young women did not think of themselves in goal-orientated situations. They didn't ask themselves, ''What do *I* want to be when I grow up?'' And that's what I think is the subconscious destructiveness of sex discrimination.

Have you encountered any other discrimination toward female attorneys?

I lived in Virginia for one year shortly after I was married and before I went to France; I remember that it was an *extraordinary experience*, just extraordinary!

I didn't become a member of the bar, because I was just going to be in Virginia for one year and it isn't necessary to be a member of the bar unless you're actually going to be in the courtroom. I was living in a small town, and I went to one of the major local industries to look for a job, and I could *not* get by—honestly—the Women's Employment Entrance! [Laughs.]

Women's Employment Entrance?

Women's Employment Entrance, that's right! They literally had *two* doors. There was a women's employment area and a men's employment area. A woman stopped me in my tracks and told me that if I couldn't type, I might as well just forget the whole thing.

Have you observed that women themselves often discriminate against or resent women professionals?

There is far less of that now than there used to be. All of us went through it in some way.

To be one of the small number of women in law school, for instance, was a *very* interesting experience. There was a special status accorded to you because you were one of a small group, and it was ego-satisfying in a sense.

You made it on your own in a man's world, you were accepted by your instructors and your fellow students, and *they* decided you didn't have two heads. It was seductive in the sense that you began to think of *yourself* as special. One of the things that you began to believe about yourself was that you weren't *like* other women.

Older women—those over 35—have not been very supportive of other women in the past. I think that this is something we've all had to come to grips with, because the tendency has been not to identify oneself with what one *thinks* of as the stereotypical woman. This has been very *destructive!*

I think this is changing and *has* changed enormously in a very short period of time. Most women, regardless of age, have become very supportive of one another. I think that women first had to learn that it's okay to lose your special status and that you didn't really lose very much once you stopped believing your own press notices—that is, that you're different from other women. And that's a *tough* thing to learn, especially when it had given you status.

How would you describe yourself?

As a compulsive worker! [Laughs.] I have a real work ethic. I also think I get along relatively well with people and can get people to work together.

What makes your work rewarding to you?

I suppose there are two levels of reward. I see people—faculty and students—in a situation where there is an enormous amount of good intellectual interchange, the best kind. I find that the best way people can relate to each other is probably around ideas that interest them. That's one reason teaching appealed to me so much, but I still have the company of these people as an administrator. I have found that intellectual stimulation has continued. Secondly, I find administration can be creative. You are always planning and building.

You believe this is a real contribution to society?

Oh, yes. I also think that what has happened in legal education in the last ten or fifteen years has had a positive impact. I think lawyers have an extremely important role to perform in society.

I happen to think well of lawyers, and I think that for the most part they are intelligent people. They also are trained to think well. As society's problem solvers, it seems to me that they can and ought to make great contributions to the development of society. The law school is an institution which should be a center of learning and also *serve* the present and future community.

How do you deal with the pressures of the work?

I make sure I get a lot of exercise.

Have you had difficulties in interpersonal relations because of your profession?

Not a *hint* of a difficulty! It's of continuing interest to me since I am married to a man who is twenty years older than I am. He is a very liberated man. By the way, he's retired.

This creates no problems?

Absolutely none.

A subject that interests me on a variety of levels is that my husband was a bachelor when I married him, and he had never been married. I think that he was never interested in a relationship where he had to be the one on whom somebody else was dependent. He's an independent human being and he likes to associate with other independent human beings. So my career, rather than being a threat to the relationship, appealed to him. He's really a marvelous human being.

He was in the Army, but his education was in English literature and [laughs delightedly] he writes poetry. He writes well, *and* he also takes gorgeous pictures of wildflowers! [Laughs.] [This is McKelvey's only marriage.]

Have you any children?

No. I decided when I was twenty years old that I did not want to have a family.

Why was that? That was an unusual decision in the fifties, especially for a woman of Catholic background.

I decided that I wouldn't be a very good mother. I also wanted the kind of independence that I knew a family would not permit.

I thought myself a *very* selfish person for a very long time. I used to find myself kind of apologizing or taking a hostile attitude if anybody asked me why I didn't have a family. Now I know it's just a choice people make.

What is your attitude toward the women's movement?

I think it's *critically* important. The women's movement is really all about the equality of opportunity in all its ramifications. This means that you're a person trying to do your best, that you have an opportunity to develop your talents. Society as a whole benefits if this is true of all its members. The best part of the women's movement, which I think is *very* important, is that women have begun to value themselves and to examine their own goals, which is a legitimate thing to do. In the past, many women didn't have goals or were unable to realize them if they did. Also, value was too wrapped up in whether they appealed to somebody else in a marriage sense.

Have you felt pressured by a sense of responsibility to other women?

I certainly think of that as an aspect of my behavior, but I have to admit that I don't think of myself as *having* to do something that *I* don't want to do.

I do think it's important to do what I can to see that the position of women is improved at any level. It's important to me to devote time to activities that accomplish this, and I spend a lot of time working toward these ends. But in terms of making a major personal decision in life-direction, it has not been the deciding factor. I think I can do the most for women by doing what I think I do best. I think this is true of each of us.

Chaplain

Diana Moore

> *A great case for discrimination could be*
> *brought against the Southern Baptists.*
> *There's no doubt in my mind.*

Former Miss Kentucky and model, Diana Moore is the first woman chaplain of the United States Army National Guard. She grew up in the Appalachian Mountains of coal-mining, poverty-stricken eastern Kentucky, strongly influenced by her Southern Baptist Church. In college she led her sorority sisters in weekly prayer and meditation, graduating summa cum laude, listed in *Who's Who In American Colleges and Universities,* 1971. In 1974 she was one of the first women to receive an in-depth Masters of Divinity from Southern Baptist Seminary in Louisville.

When Moore began knocking on Southern Baptist doors for a pastorate, there was no place for the attractive minister in her own church. In 1976, when Moore was 26 years old, the National Guard opened its ranks to her. Today Lt. Moore ministers to the religious needs of more than 2,400 men. She is one of only five women chaplains in the entire Army structure.

At first I considered active duty, full-time. Then, after talking to various people, I decided that right now my heart is in a local parish rather than in active military duty. The major reason for this decision is that I'm involved in this really exciting church in Louisville where I'm living. It's a small community church and people are actually living out a radical kind of commitment, which is where I am with ministering.

As it is today, the church—and I use that as a kind of blanket term—has not made a great deal of difference. If I'm going to buy into the whole Christianity thing, it's got to be total for me.

What are your duties with the National Guard?

My responsibilities are to provide chaplaincy coverage to the 103rd Service and Supply Unit in Richmond, Kentucky. I'm the one and only chaplain responsible for those five units—approximately 2,500 guardspersons, about fifty of whom are women. I hold usually two regular services on a Sunday and provide counseling. [She is paid 50 dollars for each reserve day she works. Her rank is first lieutenant.]

I do the same sorts of pastoral things that a regular minister would do—preaching, counseling, communion, the whole thing. I'm excited about pastoring. That's where my heart is!

How did you enter the Guard?

This chaplaincy is voluntary. I was checking into opportunities in Kentucky, new ways of ministry, really. And there were no women chaplains in the National Guard.

I had an advocate, a person who had been in the National Guard as a chaplain. He worked very hard for me to get the position. He encountered some resistance! [Laughs.]

There *was* resistance. I think it was because of the whole thing of, "Well, what do we do with a woman chaplain? Do we have to make changes for her to come in?"

There are five women chaplains, all told, in the whole Army structure—National Guard, Reserves, and active. I'm the only woman chaplain, of the five, who is not active duty.

There's still this problem of women not being allowed in the actual combat zone. That has not been tested in terms of women chaplains. Women chaplains are non-combatants.

In essence, I'm kind of hoping there will be a test case. I hope we don't have to go to war! But if we do, I hope there will be a test case because I think that constitutionally we could go into a combat zone because we are non-combatants. I would want to go, because I feel that I would need to be there as much as a male chaplain.

What qualified you to become a chaplain?

To become a chaplain in the military is a long process. You have to have an accredited seminary degree and a bachelor's degree before that. You must have an endorsement by a particular denomination or recognized religious body, *and* you have to have prior pastoral experience. If you meet all these requirements and the slots are available for chaplains, then there is a possibility.

The actual application process took about four months. In February 1976 I applied and was placed in June.

There's an initial commitment to the National Guard of three years. It's the same thing as joining the National Guard. There's no difference really.

Technically, we have one weekend a month of training, but I will be doing more than that. One of the reasons for my getting into the National Guard is that the chief of chaplains of Kentucky wants me to do conferences and counseling in conjunction with his ministry.

How did the army train you?

Chaplaincy training is largely a military indoctrination where we learn Army regulations pertaining to chaplains and get an overview of the military structure. This training is nine weeks at Ft. Wadsworth on Staten Island. All chaplains for the U.S. Army are trained there. The chaplains in training there were about half reserves and Guard, and half active duty.

How many women?

In training at Ft. Wadsworth there were only three women and 110 men chaplains. Because we women are so few, we do stand out. [Laughs.] And that's been good, because I do think we have something to say.

What was the reaction to female chaplains?

There was resistance. Among chaplains, it's kind of subtle. Among other persons it's not quite as subtle. [Laughs.] But I think the resistance is mostly to the unknown. Maybe they think, "Well, Gee! Here's a woman who is a professional and as well-trained as I am or better. What do I do with her?" There's still such a tendency in our culture to see women only in what has been defined in the past as the "womanly role," rather than as professional kinds of persons.

At Ft. Wadsworth there was a lot of stress because we *were* in a man's world. It's especially true there. There were little subtleties which I had to learn to evaluate and not take personally. For a long time I did take comments personally. Now I realize they are sort of blanket statements like we all make. I have to keep my personhood amidst all of that and that's a stress. It's a frustration. My faith helps me in these situations very much.

There was a time when I really came on more strongly. I was on the defensive, which I think gets us nowhere. When we had our chaplaincy training evaluations, my supervisor, who is a Roman Catholic chaplain, said to me, "I want to compliment you on the way that you related here as a person. It seems to me that you've been very comfortable with your femininity. You have related in a way that has been sensitive to the men, and therefore they have opened up more to you than they might have to other women." So that's where I am. That's where I want to be. I wait and I listen, and then when I talk, I come out of a position of strength because I *have* listened. I attempt not to be so aggressive that people are turned off and, therefore, hear nothing.

What theological problems do you face?

There are a lot of theological problems with some people regarding whether or not women should be ministers. That's the eternal debate among clergy people—among clergy*men* I should say! [Laughs.] In our scriptural teachings there are two or three passages that are many times taken out of context which say women should not be doing this or that, or there are specific roles that are assigned to women and men. This can be a source of perpetual debate, so we try not to debate that point. We (women chaplains) simply say that we believe we have been called to be ministers equally with men. We just go on doing our own thing.

I do think that the scripture and its interpretation have been used to keep women in a subservient position. Definitely! That's why it's high time women who know about theology begin saying, "Hey! We have something to say too! We have a different interpretation, and it's just as valid."

Regarding the Bible's account of woman being born from Adam's rib, I learned in studying theology that there are really two creation accounts in Genesis. One is that Adam came first and then Eve, and that gave women a secondary role. But there is also in Genesis One the story that God created male *and* female in his image. That speaks to me of the equality of which we were made and which we should have, instead of the secondary role women have gotten into.

Could your gender be beneficial to your chaplaincy?

As a woman I believe I will have certain advantages as far as my effectiveness is concerned. For example at Ft. Wadsworth, I felt an advantage in a sense because I received a lot of support due to the fact that I am confident in myself and as a chaplain.

I am not in the military for Women's Lib. I am here as a minister. Whatever I can do to further the cause of women—that's fantastic, but that's not my first priority. I think that in being low-key and doing what I do, I have gotten more acceptance and support. I think my approach has been an advantage.

What is your attitude toward men?

I definitely have become much more sensitized about where men are in our culture. I've begun to understand the real burden that I think they've had to carry with their maleness. At times in the past, I have made blanket statements about males being chauvinists. That's not where I am now. I'm coming to see that men have had such a heavy burden to carry with the whole macho influence in our culture. I have to be sensitized to them in order to be a minister, because that's what ministering is all about.

The real important thing to me now in terms of man-woman relationships is the complementarity of the male and female— and that's professionally and every way.

Are chaplains really necessary to the military?

I think there's such a need for creative ministry in the military. It's a very oppressive system.

After one service I held, some women there came up and said, "Wow! A woman really can preach! A woman can really be creative in ministry." I said "Yes! *That's* why we're here." It's just that we have something to say and we say it in a different way.

We really need new theological perspectives from women, I'm convinced. And that's one of the reasons I'm in ministry. Women can bring something to theology, some perspective that men have not thought of.

Women can provide a whole different slant on the scripture which was written by men and has been largely interpreted by men. I think that it's time for women to begin interpreting their own feelings into what they read into the scripture. It's time to say that a woman's interpretation is just as valid as a man's.

One of the things that's going on in the Army right now that's sort of catching on is the PET conferences. That's Personnel Evaluation Training. [Laughs.] We have an abbreviation for everything. Actually, it is just sitting down with a group of people and talking about group dynamics and what happens between people, and raising consciousness and sensitivity to people. This is because sometimes people get swallowed up in the military system which is such an impersonal kind of thing. One of the things we hope to do is to sensitize people to work together as people, rather than as just part of the system.

What is your theological background?

I grew up in a Southern Baptist church. I went to the Southern Baptist Seminary in Louisville, and I also went to the Baptist Seminary in Ruschlikon, Switzerland. I studied for the ministry for three and a half years after college. I have a Masters of Divinity degree.

Women divinity students at Southern Baptist Seminary were kind of a new breed. There were only two or three women in the School of Theology when I was there—out of some 500 people. Only one woman had graduated before my roommate and me. I was among the first women to graduate with an in-depth [Masters of Divinity degree] from Southern. I graduated in 1974. Now I'm so encouraged to see that there are 30 or 40 women in that School of Theology. It's fantastic!

Have Southern Baptists discriminated against you?

The problem is that the Southern Baptists are not hiring women pastors. They do *not* say that you can't take theological courses, but most churches will not hire you. This is my case. I spent probably a year going to thirty-some interviews with Southern Baptist churches. The feeling everywhere was the same: "Your resume is fantastic. You're qualified. However . . . " A great case for discrimination could be brought against the Southern Baptists. [Laughs.] There's no doubt in my mind. So my feeling was that I did not have to continue that trek. I was doing harm to myself and I wasn't able to minister.

I was interviewed, just out of the blue, by an American Baptist Church in Indiana. That's Northern Baptist. I was hired after the first interview, as a pastor.

You must have experienced anger?

I had a lot of angry feelings toward my own church. It was the feeling of being ripped off. I was brought up in a church that said, "You can do whatever you want to do. You relate to God in your own personal way. But we slap your hand when you decide you want to be a minister." So it was really heavy.

I think it's inevitable that women are going to be angry when they realize what's been happening. I had to go through the anger to get on the other side. I still have anger but the anger doesn't control me. It's a healthy kind of feeling that says, "Yes, I know where women have been, because I've been there." I can deal with it better now. There is a feeling of more power, a place from which I can convey my convictions.

Did your attractiveness create difficulties?

If I had been ugly it might have been easier. It's crazy, but in all of the pastoral interviews I had, there was that underlying little feeling of, "If you weren't single . . . If you weren't attractive . . . If you weren't this or that, then *maybe* . . . " The church does not deal with sexuality out in the open. It does not talk about it. My attractiveness has definitely been a handicap to me in the church. I never thought about this as a problem until it started hitting me right in the face.

I have wanted to think of the church as being right up front in dealing with things, but it's not. I'm able to say now, "Okay! Then we need some people who are willing to bring some of these issues to the front, to talk about them."

Several of us women have stuck together and worked it out. Through encouraging each other, I'm thankful to say that I've worked through a lot of that anger. At this point, it's all come out a valuable lesson.

I received the greatest support, while waiting for a ministry appointment, from my mother, primarily, and from a couple of really close friends. I really don't think I would have stuck it out through all the struggle I was having if those people had not said, "Hey, hang in there. You've got something to give."

You were Miss Kentucky?

I was Miss Kentucky in 1972. I was 22. How it came about is actually a long involved story. I got into pageants when I was in college. I went to school at Eastern Kentucky University (Richmond) and my sorority sisters talked me into being in a local pageant which was preliminary to the Miss Kentucky. I said, "Gee! That's not really me. I'm not really stage." But I was into music. I played piano, sang, and played the guitar. So I thought, "Well, why not? It's something new." I entered and won the Miss Richmond title. I went on to the Miss Kentucky and got in the top ten.

The next year when I went on to seminary, a friend suggested I enter the Miss Louisville contest. I said, "I really don't want to do that. That's not really who I am." This guy was one of the sponsors of the Miss Kentucky pageant. He said, "Oh, come on Moore, do it. It's scholarship money."

I had a scholarship to Southern Baptist Seminary but I needed some more money. So I entered the Miss Louisville contest. I thought, "Well, it will be a way to get some more musical performing experience." And I was very amazed to win Miss Louisville. [Laughs.] I thought, "Oh my gosh! What have I done?"

Then I went on to the Miss Kentucky pageant. I came in second, and the girl who won dropped out. So I acquired the title and finished out the year.

It was an interesting year. I probably would not do it again. [Laughs.] I *would not* do it again! Now I'm at such a different place than I was then. The experience *was* a valid part of the learning process for me in seeing who women have been and who they are. But at that time, this really was not that big an issue to me.

What was the reaction to your beauty queen status?

I really was regarded as a beauty queen when I was Miss Kentucky, although the emphasis was actually on both physical appearance and on abilities. I was at the seminary at the time; that's the most significant thing to consider, because the people at seminary had such a difficult time dealing with the idea of my being in the pageants and being Miss Kentucky. These were the same struggles that I dealt with as a woman being a minister.

In Kentucky there's still this nostalgia about ministers. There's still enough of the down-home earthiness so that people say, "Oh, a minister!" But maybe they don't quite know how to relate to me or what to say. As Miss Kentucky, the good part was the traveling I did and the time I was able to spend with the grass roots people. I was invited to a lot of churches to speak. That helped me to see what the ministry was all about, and it gave me some valuable insights.

You were also a model?

To pay my way through the seminary, I did modeling. That was fashion modeling, advertising, catalogs, tv commercials. That was with Louisville Modeling Agency. [She was paid ten to twenty dollars an hour.]

I had problems with modeling and the Miss Kentucky position because those were roles that are seen as so typically female. I still have some struggle with that, but at the same time those were valuable experiences and helped me to integrate my total self.

Have you ever been a member of any women's groups?

I was involved in N.O.W. [National Organization for Women]. I attended meetings in Louisville. I am finding that N.O.W. is so different in different parts of the country. At this point I haven't decided if I'm going to be involved in it or not.

One of the things I do as a minister is start women's groups. I had a women's group in Indiana. They're really consciousness raising groups, where women get together and talk about women in our culture and things that are purely cultural. That's a really important part of my mission.

What abilities are most helpful in the ministry?

Since I was a child I've been interested in reading, researching, thinking through things, evaluating. [Laughs.] I was always one of those "why" people. That has helped me be a minister—to research, to use my brain, to get the facts and then to go from there.

Writing is also a real love of mine, and I hope to do more with it. For example, I enjoy sermon writing very much, and I enjoy giving a sermon. I've always enjoyed public speaking. There's a certain creativity that can be used so much in communicating.

My musical talent is one way in which I am in touch with a deeper part of me, and that helps me be sensitive to people.

Then the other basic tools which I obtained at seminary are really important. That is taking the sensitivity which is there and developing it into skills of pastoral counseling.

Describe your childhood and its influences.

I grew up in the mountains of Eastern Kentucky in Pikeville. It's a very sheltered area in terms of culture and women's roles.

And I am still not accepted as a pastor in the church where I grew up.

My background in Appalachia, more than anything else, gave me strength of character. I can say that now. I couldn't say that while I was growing up there, because there were points at which I wanted to just get out of there. I felt very enclosed and very cut-off. I think that was because of the lack of a lot of cultural advantages, things that are not available to people in Appalachia.

In the very formative years, my family was struggling—I'll put it that way. [Laughs.] We were not poverty-stricken, but we were struggling to make ends meet. Then we had more money as time went along and as my Dad worked harder. He was an engineer with the Chesapeake and Ohio Railroad. He still is after twenty or twenty-five years. My Mom worked also in a local department store. [Moore has one sibling, a brother, one year older than she.]

So we had all the things we needed. And yet, to me, something was missing culturally . . . things that I saw from tv and going to movies. We traveled every year, going different places, and that gave me a look at the outside world.

Both my parents are very strong-willed persons. They came from extremely difficult circumstances in the mountains, and they, in a sense, *made it*. They pulled themselves up and got themselves together. I think I've had that same sort of will from them.

Teachers were most influential for me. I can think of two women specifically who were more than teachers. I look at them now and I can say they were almost prophetesses. They had such a view as to their own pasts and the future. And they were so healthily intelligent about all the oppression they experienced.

I think that religion from a very, very early age made a strong impression on me. It said something to me of deeper things— what really mattered.

My love of nature, almost a oneness with nature, I owe to Appalachia. I've learned a real appreciation of my childhood and almost a thankfulness that I didn't have all the cultural input that the city had. I couldn't say until a couple of years ago that the time I had when I was growing up and the quietness of the mountains, the simple lifestyle which I'm getting back to now, are really important things to me.

The American Dream is sort of that you do what you want. I can't buy that anymore. I've got to be responsible for the way I am and the way I use resources. I think that in our country we've really misused resources so much. I want to learn to live simplistically, and I don't mean that in a trite sort of way.

What is most important to you?

For me the most important things in life are not the tangibles, but definitely the intangibles. The things that someone cannot take away from me.

For instance, in the case of women or any people who feel a need for liberation, there is that need to be in touch with the important intangibles, the things you have that are within you. That's what my faith is to me. It's who I am, apart from what I own or possess, what I look like or don't look like. It's my own personal expression of God and me. It's my purpose for being.

Today there is so much going on in terms of people seeking a deeper understanding of themselves. There's a lot of therapy, meditation. I think we have a definite need to be in touch with ourselves and to know who we are. That's apart from the things that we own. I think *so many times* we identify ourselves by the tangibles.

My mission definitely comes out of being in touch with my inwardness and the expression of God in me. That has given me a whole different kind of outlook in the last couple of years and has given me a great deal of peace. Amid all the struggles by women, I have been given a great sense of hope.

Shirley Muldowney

Drag racing is my life.

The first woman racer voted "All-America" by the American Auto Writers and Broadcasters Association (in 1975), Shirley Muldowney is the only woman licensed to drive "Top Fuel" dragsters in competitive racing. At age 36, she races in fifty events a year, driving her nitro-methane powered dragster some 240 miles per hour on quarter-mile tracks. Her engines sometimes catch fire at those speeds. Men are her only competitors.

One of the top three names in professional drag racing today, Muldowney is the mother of a grown son and lives in Mt. Clemens, Michigan. She is five feet tall and weighs in at 100 pounds. Her nickname "Cha Cha" is heard on loudspeakers across the country. Articles about the diminutive racer or "fighter," as she calls herself, appear in such diverse publications as "Hot Rod Magazine," "The Los Angeles Times," "Playgirl Magazine," and the "Detroit Free Press."

At the time of this interview, Shirley Muldowney has been racing for more than two decades. Her climb through the ranks she describes as a "costly and grueling experience;" nevertheless, her charm and warm personality remain intact.

I'm a professional race car driver on a full-time basis. I perform in what they call a Top Fuel dragster, the fastest accelerating vehicle in the world. It covers the quarter-mile in less than six seconds in speeds up to 250 miles per hour.

By full-time I mean this is all I do for a living. I own my own race car. It's unusual, but I've always owned my own race cars. Most gals just stand around the race tracks and hope that someone will give them a ride—a car to drive.

I am the only woman ever to drive a Top Fuel dragster and the only woman ever licensed. Right now it looks as if I'll be the only woman for a good many years.

I'm one of the top three names. I have been for about three years. I got there by being very persistent, by being a winner.

How did you begin racing?

When I was about fourteen years old I started racing on the streets of Schenectady, New York. That was rather unusual for a young woman. I think I first got interested by just seeing the hot rods go down the street, trying to hitch a ride.

I just had that competitive feeling when I was a kid. I loved cars and I wanted to be good at what I did. I worked hard at it, that's all.

My very first race was in Fonda, New York, a very small raceway. I was fifteen.

Describe your vehicle.

It's approximately a 250-inch wheel base car with little tiny bi-cycle-type tires on the front and big monstrous tires on the back. It stops with a parachute. The car weighs about 1,600 pounds and has approximately 2,000 to 2,500 horsepower. A regular automobile has probably 350 horsepower.

How did you qualify for the Top Fuel license?

Not just anyone can get in a Top Fuel dragster and drive it. You have to take a "blindfold test" in a car and make a series of passes or runs at three different race tracks and three different sessions. The "blindfold test" is given in the car when it's not running, to see if you know where everything is without having to look for it. Then you make passes in front of already licensed drivers at their discretion, along with track officials and tech advisors to determine whether *you* can handle this Top Fuel dragster. The National Hot Rod Association gives these tests.

The only three professional categories are Top Fuel, what they call "Funny Car," and then there is Pro Stock. I'm in Top Fuel, but I also drove Funny Cars for five years. There are about forty amateur classes. We think the amateurs are really the heart of drag racing. They graduate on up over the years.

What is a Funny Car?

A Funny Car is a car that also runs on fuel, what we call nitro-methane. The Funny Car carries a plastic replica of a Detroit-based model car for a body. The Top Fuel dragster on the other hand is just an acceleration vehicle, and has as little body as possible. But the Funny Car carries a body so the crowd can identify with it. The motor sits in front of the driver rather than behind.

I had good success driving Funny Cars, but I *was* burned a couple of times. That's why I decided to get out of them. Top Fuel cars are safer.

I've had those fires at 225 miles an hour. You're on fire, and it's burning the parachute off and a number of things can happen. But I feel very safe now when I get in my car, and I haven't had problems since I've driven Top Fuel. I've never been on my head in 18 years.

Is fire the worst threat?

I was going to say the main hazard of racing is going broke. [Laughs.] It's a sport that's made millionaires moderately wealthy. [Laughs.] But as far as accidents—usually other than the fires—when you pull up to the line, naturally you want to win. You have the car put on what we call "the limit." And the more you push these cars so you can go faster, the more there is a chance of your having an engine explosion. But usually the worst threat is fire. Fires burn the parachutes off. I lost a car in 1972 because of fire.

What do you experience when your car catches fire?

It's hard to describe what it's like to be on fire—to have a nitro fire at 200 [miles per hour]. When you break a motor you've got a hole in the side of the motor and fourteen quarts of nitrated oil coming out on hot exhaust pipes. It's a strange experience. It really is. Hopefully you're not getting burned and you're able to think.

I have the best fire equipment available to the racer today. The only place I got burned was my eyes. It got underneath the goggles. You have on board Freon fire extinguisher systems that are made mandatory by National Hot Rod Association. They've really combatted the fire problem pretty good over the years. When I drove Funny Cars, they were a little more susceptible. You activate these freon systems and 90 percent of the time it puts the fire out. It did a pretty good job in my case, but the fire still came back. The fuel tank exploded, but I got out in time.

What protective clothing do you wear?

When I'm driving I wear a fire suit that costs around 500 dollars. It's made by a very small company, Filler Safety Equipment. I wear their equipment because it's saved me a number of times. I know I'm wearing the best.

I wear a helmet and what they call a nomex sock over my head and then a helmet on top of that. I wear a full-to-the-elbow mitten. And I wear fire boots and fire underwear and then the fire suit. I take advantage of everything.

What is it like—the sensation of driving at speeds over 200 miles per hour?

It's like having a tiger by the tail. That's exactly what it is driving one of these. It's hard to describe . . . the g's . . . I think you pull about three g's coming off the starting line in one of these cars. I don't know how to explain what it's like to drive a Top Fuel dragster. It's something that just takes getting used to. The average person could not get in a car and do even *reasonably* well. It is like controlling a runaway roller coaster. That's the only way I can describe it. The first time I drove a Top Fuel, the first pass I ever made didn't bother me at all. Because I had driven the Funny Cars, I was used to going 225 miles per hour.

The first Funny Car—*that* was a little bit of a trip because they enclose you. They drop this body down around you. The feeling of being all enclosed is quite different. But I was ready for it because I heard so many drivers say, "Wait till they drop that body down on ya!" I made three half-passes in the Funny Car and then one full pass. Then two weeks later I went to a very large race in Lebanon Valley, New York, and I won the whole show! Just *two weeks* after I first drove a Funny Car. They had all the top name drivers there. The *top names!* Every single one of them was there. And I ran 6.82, 219—219 miles an hour! [Laughs.]

What makes a driver successful?

As far as driving the car, it comes very, very easy for me, and I'm very comfortable at what I do. It's just always come natural for me. You're only in the car a short time. You have to have what you call your "act" together. You don't make a mistake in these type of cars because they can bite you very easily.

I just have a system. I usually drive the same way all the time unless I have to make a change on the starting line. Some tracks are different, tires are different. You have to take into consideration the race track itself. Sometimes it isn't easy. I have a crew on the starting line, and we all work together as a team, that makes it quite a bit easier for me.

What I think it takes is experience. It's got to be something somebody really wants to do. Somebody that can listen. A lot of drivers will say to the mechanics, "Well, you do your job and I'll do mine." But in order to run a drag racing car successfully, a driver has got to be able to tell the mechanics what that car did on the run. A lot of the drivers, their heads are so big. You cannot *believe* how big their heads are, and those are the ones who aren't any good!

We've always done it with a team. I'm able to tell the fellows what that car did. I have to know, because I pay the bills. I definitely understand the functions of the cars.

Reflexes are important. And I think that a woman does have better reflexes than a man. Without a doubt!

I think that, because of the starting line procedure in drag racing.

Describe the starting line procedure and critical factors of the race.

They have a series of electronic clocks. When you pull up to a staging light there's a tree—what we call a Christmas tree—that sits in the middle of the race track. You'll pull up to where you see the first light come on. You are what they call "pre-staged." Then you'll creep the car in another inch or two, and you are what they call "staged." Then the other car comes in and does this. And the tension! To watch these lights light up! You know the cars are getting into position. You *can* be late!

I've run a race and I've been beat by one one-thousandth of a second, so you cannot be late on that light. All of a sudden you have the go light, the green light that comes on. It's a yellow-green. And the difference between the yellow and the green coming on is three-tenths of one second. You don't want to wait until you've seen the green, because you've lost. It's as simple as that. Timing is unbelievable. That's it.

It's being able to do this under pressure. You may pull up to the starting line and see something out of the ordinary. You see your crew run back to the car and they may adjust something. That can take your mind off what you're doing.

The cars are so critical. You want to make it back for the next round. You've got the car on what we call instant kill and you don't want to hurt any more parts than you have to. The motors have aluminum components and we have a problem of burning pistons. Too much of a percentage of nitro in the car, or we push it a little bit too hard, and we can burn it up. But you've got to be able to shut that car off right at the lap's time clock.

There are a series of three lights at the end of the race track. The first one is the first mile-per-hour light. So in order to get you miles per hour, they get you between the first light and the last light, running through there. If you run your engine through that last light, the chances of burning a piston are almost 99 percent sure. On a pass where you have it really pumped up—the horsepower—you've got to be able to get that chute out and shut that car off at the time light, the middle one where it counts. That determines the winner. And you don't want to shut it off too early. I've seen many many drivers caught between the first light and the second light and beaten. And that's only thirty feet! Those cars are traveling 245 miles an hour. You *have* to have your act together.

How did you learn to drive?

I'm self-taught, from the time I started driving on the streets of Schenectady. I *have* had people tell me how to drive the car according to how it is set up. Different race tracks have different surfaces. The altitude is different. The length of the race track is different. You have to drive accordingly.

I had just a stock-type, a little hot rod type car. The way I obtained my Top Fuel license was to graduate up through the ranks over a period of eighteen years. I drove every car there was to drive.

Was there resistance to your obtaining the Top Fuel license?

I think that National Hot Rod Association was the first to receive women on an equal basis. And they did not make it easy. They made me earn it. They just didn't give me any breaks, no more than they would give the next guy. I performed and I showed them I could do it, and now those people appreciate the fact that I'm there. They're very good to me.

What is the National Hot Rod Association?

NHRA represents the drivers. They go into a race track and put on a national event, and the people that own the race track don't have much to say about it. NHRA runs a very tight ship.

Very sharp people. They made drag racing what it is today. NHRA owns a number of race tracks also.

I am a member. Dues are a small amount. I think it's $12 a year. It isn't a union. We don't have a union yet. We should, but NHRA puts on the best drag race there is in the United States, an organized drag race. They have the best insurance. They have absolutely the best offer to the racer. If something should happen, NHRA has that insurance on us. You get a lot for your $12.

What is it like to be the only woman competing against men?

A lot of people ask me what it's like to be the only woman Top Fuel driver. Well, you're singled out. Sometimes it isn't easy because people expect so much from you. They expect that you shouldn't have a personal life. But it's an advantage for me. Financially it's an advantage that there aren't any other gals. My personality and my car and my act, or whatever you want to call it, are in demand quite a bit. My phone rings constantly. Because race tracks want *this* race car, and because it is a unique thing to see a woman drive a Top Fuel dragster.

To the public, drag racing is considered to be a male sport. But not to me. That's the way they put it today, that I broke the ice for all of these gals.

It is strange to see a woman drive one of these cars competitively because the cars are a handful. It's like a gal all of sudden playing pro football and all of a sudden outrunning O. J. Simpson. I beat the fellows, I don't just sandbag. I'm in there to win, not just because I'm a woman.

How chauvinistic are the drivers?

Men say women can't do it. That's the easy way, don't give them a chance. That way you keep the gals out of it. Now how does a big strong race car driver impress the girls when he just got his doors blown off by a hundred-pound woman? That's exactly what it is. How do they impress the groupies? They're all my friends now. Now they don't hate me.

Before I proved myself, the fellows were a little hard on me. I'd hear stuff around the pits. They didn't really think a gal could do it. But right from the start I beat the boys. *From the start!* It took me a while to gain their respect, but now the fellows would do anything in the world for me. They're the best friends I've got. They appreciate the fact that I'm in the class, because they feel that it does a lot for the sport.

Naturally, at some tracks, you have officials that believe that a woman doesn't belong there, and I might stay in tech line a little longer. But that was a long, long time ago, and that was at small race tracks.

I had to deal with the male chauvinists. I'm not going to say there were quite a few examples, but there were examples that I do remember. There were no incidents of someone getting physical or trying to cause me accidents.

I like a lot of the fellows. I don't date them even though some of them I would like to date. But I don't because of the situation. I can't because drag racers—they're the best people in the world, but they can be cruel. They're hard on the gals. And I can't take that chance.

How has your climb to the top of the male heap affected you?

I would say it was a costly and grueling experience. It took a lot out of me. I had to sacrifice a lot.

I was a little bit of a hard nose before because I knew I had a fight on my hands. But I got over that. I grew out of that. I was just a hard racer, and I wanted to win. I wanted to be accepted. And I was not the easiest gal in the world to get along with, because I knew what I wanted.

All the bad is behind me, however bad it was. I was a fighter. I've always been a fighter, so I wasn't going to give up. But there was enough discouragement that most people would have.

Who motivated you to be a fighter?

I've always been pretty much a loner. There was never really anyone I can recall who gave me incentive.

My Dad died when he was quite young. He was a prize fighter. He had a state championship. I was a very little girl then.

He was a competitive guy. He liked to hunt and fish, all of those things. And I used to do those things with him when I was a very little girl. But other than that, I can't think of anything else. As far as my parents, they were good working people. My mother worked and still does work in a school system in upstate New York. We weren't poor, but we were just average working people. My father worked for the Teamster Union as a business agent. He was also a musician. He was very, very talented.

Do other women have a chance to get into professional drag racing now?

I think women have a pretty good chance in this field if they work their way on up. I think the gals could do it if they started in the comp-type cars. Those are like little dragsters that run on gasoline.

They don't have to start in the stock-type classes like I started. I started there because that's all the money I had. I'd help a gal if she wanted to do it right. The ones that want to just get in and drive a Top Fuel car and get their name in the paper . . . I don't even want to talk to them because they don't know what they're doing. I don't want a gal getting hurt.

How did you get the name "Cha Cha"?

A spectator wrote "Cha Cha" on my race car a long, long time ago when I was an amateur. And it stuck. The kids love it! They're crazy about it. And it's a lot easier to say than Shirley Muldowney. I don't really like to hear it over the air. But when the racers call me that, it doesn't really bother me.

How do you deal with your success and celebrity status?

I try to accept my position so people can still accept me. I don't want to be so big that people are afraid to come up and talk to me. In the sport of drag racing, the spectator that pays his money can come right over in the pits, talk to me, get an autographed picture, look at the car. That's the difference in drag racing.

You want a nice image, a good image. Those are the people that pay your week's pay.

How costly is your racing?

It's quite a responsibility. My racing is a $100,000 a year program. You could spend that easily. In order for everyone to be paid at the end of the week that car has *got* to run! And that car has got to run good!

The cost of having one of these cars built is probably $25,000. With a motor, between 25 and $30,000. I've had, in my lifetime, probably 10 cars. This car that I'm driving now I've driven for three years.

It costs about $500 to make one pass in my car, to make one run down the quarter mile. We've averaged it out, between the fuel and the parts, the help, the insurance, trucks and everything it takes to go down the road.

By insurance, I'm not just talking about life insurance but the insurance to insure the rig. To insure the rig for, let's say, $80,000 it probably costs you $4,000 a year. My car is worth $30,000. We insure it for $80,000.

Fire and theft is the only thing we carry. But when you lose one, you lose one. [Laughs.]

I have full-time employees, a young man from Seattle and then I have a three-time National winner, retired now, who heads up most of the major decisions on the motor. His name is Connie Kalitta. And then my 19-year-old son, John Muldowney, works for me also.

Over the years I've invested thousands and thousands and thousands of dollars in hopes of getting a return. Some years were good. Some years we went in the red.

How much money do you make?

The money I make varies each year. The biggest purse you could win would be 20 to 25,000 dollars at Indianapolis. Everybody wants to win that. I've been runner-up.

The highest amount I've ever won was $12,000 at the NHRA Spring Nationals at Columbus, Ohio. I was runner-up in 1975, and I won that in 1976.

I was number one qualifier. In other words I had the pole position in qualifying. Like at Indy, the number one qualifier has the pole position and has run the fastest time. I was number one qualifier; I had the fastest time of every round, *and* I set a new track record on the last pass. That was 5.96 seconds, 243.90 miles per hour. That's the fastest on that particular track and for that particular race.

At Indianapolis on Labor Day, 1976, I ran a 5.86. *Brought the house down!* [Laughs.] That's the elapsed time. That's what's most important: how much time it takes you to get from point A to point B, not how fast you're going when you get there. Most of the time you're running between 220 and 250. [Laughs.]

I can book my car for appearance money, and I'm able to keep my car going between the national events.

What is "appearance money"?

A race track will pay me to come in. They'll use me in their advertising. It's not only me. Most of the top names are paid to come in, but not at the national events.

Usually in drag racing there are so many competitors. There are usually 70 some-odd cars hoping to be one of the sixteen fastest. That's the race. A lot of people go home broken-hearted. If you don't win in drag racing, you really haven't made anything.

The fastest sixteen win the money. What they get is a first-round loser. The two go up and they race. The loser gets, say, 500 bucks. That car (the winner) is paired with another winner for the second round, and they come back. Second round loser may get $1,000, but the ultimate winner gets the most.

What is your educational and work background?

I left school when I was a young gal. I wanted to get married and I wanted to go racing—whatever racing was available then. My husband was the one that really got me started. He was a mechanic. He enjoyed working on the cars and seeing me win. So we were a good team. [Laughs.] I got married when I was sixteen, I was married fifteen years. [Muldowney is now divorced.]

I went back and finished high school. I got all of that but I've never really used it. I've never been to college, but I'm hoping to send my son.

I worked for a dentist. I've worked for a newspaper. I did clerical work. I worked in an Italian restaurant. But I've always been really a racer. That's all I've really done as far as being able to promote myself and talk to people.

Patricia Ann Straat

One exciting thing for me has been the evolution of the mind . . . My mind has become a good friend!

Think of the Viking Mars Mission and picture Patricia Ann Straat working seventeen hours a day, six days a week. Consider the more earthly concerns of water pollution. Again, picture Dr. Straat, Ph.D. in biochemistry and biology from Johns Hopkins University, former lecturer who opted to leave academia rather than deal with the discrimination women encountered there.

Since 1970 Straat has been Senior Research Biochemist and Research Coordinator for Biospherics, Inc., a Maryland-based firm. The majority of her time has been spent on the Viking Mars Mission, and she is the only woman scientist who played a key role in Viking. "Although there are many women in other areas of biology, biochemistry, and other sciences," she says, "I am the only woman I know of in space biology." And a scientifically thorough woman she is. Before Straat agreed to publication, she rewrote and edited her interview on several occasions until it represented her as she wished. Her salary and the exact location of Biospherics are withheld at her request.

Outside of her professional life as a scientist involved with history-making Mars investigations and the earth's water pollution crisis, Straat is a woman with "a deep love for horses." When she is at home in Maryland, she rides her horse in weekly fox hunts. In Pasadena—where she worked at the Jet Propulsion Laboratory—Straat spent early mornings at a riding club across the street from the lab. She has a dog, plays the harmonica, and is an accomplished photographer of horses.

Although Straat edited many of the "laughs" sections out of her interview, she laughed a great deal during our original conversation. At that time she was still working on Viking.

Included in her five-page resume is a list of more than 20 articles she has co-authored for scientific publications. With twelve other scientists, she authored "The Viking Biological Investigation: Preliminary Results," published in *Science, 194*, 99 (1976).

Straat's resume includes the following professional recognitions under "Memberships & Honors":

American Association for the Advancement of Science
American Chemical Society
American Institute of Biological Sciences
International Oceanographic Foundation
New York Academy of Sciences
The Society of the Sigma Xi
Selected for Outstanding Young Women of America, 1969
Selected for Who's Who of American Women, 1970
Selected for 2,000 Women of Distinction, 1972

There are few women in high positions in the sciences. There just aren't as many women as men studying these fields. When I was in graduate school, women were a small percentage. Those who finished were an even smaller percentage, because many of them ended up getting married. And they still do.

It wasn't that I was a rebel. I was just too busy to get married. After a while, things changed. I had taken other directions and the cards fell where they did. Once I was older, I preferred my freedom and my profession.

What is your background?

I was born March 28, 1936 and brought up in Rochester, New York. My father is a physicist and directed the scientific bureau at Bausch and Lomb Optical Company until he retired a few years ago. My mother is a housewife. My younger sister also joined that club. She went to college, married immediately, and settled down to raise children. [Laughs.] She has three kids and has been married for twenty years or something like that! [Laughs.]

I went to Oberlin College in Ohio and really liked it. It was a college that let me express myself. I had been to a high school that was a popularity contest! Somehow I never fit. [Laughs.] I *was* my own person from the time I was a kid! Did my own thing. I'm not aware of having pursued anything because of a particular individual's influence.

Anyway, I graduated from Oberlin with a bachelor's degree

in psychology in 1958. After four years, I had *had it* with psychology! [Laughs.] I'd decided that since my professors spent so long convincing me it was a science, I was sure it wasn't! [Laughs.] So I thought I'd find out what a science was.

Because I had had a college course in chemistry and really enjoyed it, I decided to change my field to biochemistry, the chemistry of the living cell. Without really knowing what biochemistry was! I started the Johns Hopkins University one week after graduating from college and earned my doctorate in 1964. It was quite a struggle, because I really had to start from scratch. I hadn't even had organic chemistry before I went to Hopkins!

At Hopkins, I was a National Institutes of Health [NIH] Pre-doctoral Fellow and earned my degree in biochemistry with a doctoral thesis in nitrogen metabolism and electron transport systems. Then I decided I wanted something a little bit more exciting—biochemically, that is! So I took an NIH Post-doctoral Fellowship for four years in the Department of Radiological Sciences at Johns Hopkins, in the field of RNA-DNA enzymology. [National Institutes of Health fellowships are competitive and cover tuition and living expenses.]

I later spent two years as assistant professor in the Department of Radiological Sciences. The field was interesting at first, but it seemed isolated. I wanted to *do* something—I hate to say "something practical"—I don't know that going to Mars is really practical. But I wanted to do something that was timely!

Why did you move from academia to industry?

My first actual job outside of the university was at Biospherics—spelled as in three-dimensional circles—the company I'm still with. It was a major decision to go from university to industry. In my field, there's a lot of prejudice against industry. You were warned not to make that change because it's a one-way move! I justified my change to industry because at that time I did not feel that universities offered equal opportunity and salary to women! Besides, the job I accepted looked fascinating! I haven't regretted it.

My fields became space biology, where you're really going to go to Mars, and water pollution, where you can make a difference! I've been in these areas now since 1970, and I *am* happy with them.

What are your titles? What does your job consist of?

My titles are Senior Research Biochemist and Research Coordinator. I am also Radiation Safety Officer for the company.

Basically what I do is consider scientific problems, design experiments to solve those problems, direct technicians to perform the research, and analyze the data. The process continues until a solution is reached. In general, I direct two to four contracts simultaneously and supervise one or two technicians for each contract I direct.

In space biology, I've been involved in several NASA-sponsored contracts which I've directed for the company. In 1970–71, I participated in the Mariner 9 Mission to Mars and was on the IRIS flight team during the Mariner 9 Mission. But the most exciting contract has been the Labeled Release experiment, one of the three life detection tests on the 1976 Viking Mission to Mars.

[In conjunction with Goddard Space Flight scientists, Dr. Straat worked on the IRIS (Infrared Interferometer Spectrometer) experiment which measured the absorption spectra of the atmosphere of Mars and the reflectance spectra of the surface of Mars. These spectra provided information about atmospheric gases, vertical temperature and pressure profiles, as well as certain physical and chemical properties of the Mars surface.]

Dr. Levin, President of Biospherics, designed the concept of the Labeled Release Life Detection Experiment fifteen or sixteen years ago. The experiment was funded for a Viking Flight Experiment in 1970, when I joined him to implement it and make it compatible with flight constraints and with hardware design and sequences.

What qualified you for your position with Biospherics?

I was well qualified for the position, through my research experience, with many publications, and as assistant professor at Hopkins. Few women made that rank in a major university at that time (1968). My doctoral and post-doctoral training was at one of the leading universities—for my field—in the country.

What is your position in Biospherics' hierarchy?

Biospherics has about 60 employees. I report directly to the president of the company, and I supervise and coordinate the Research Division.

What are your responsibilities with the Viking Mars Mission?

Oh, Lord! You name it! [Laughs.] I work like a Trojan! Both on the Biology Flight Team and during the years prior to the landing. For the first few years on Viking, I directed research in collaboration with Dr. Levin to obtain the scientific background to help design the flight instrument and sequences for automating the Labeled Release Experiment on Mars. Then I began testing flight hardware and obtaining data for the interpretation of flight data.

The flight instrument for the biology experiment was developed at TRW in Redondo Beach. The engineers designed a concept to automate the life detection experiments and built a working prototype called the Test Standards Module (TSM). This is a pretty fancy instrument that has all essential components—test cells, valves, heaters—just like on flight. [See photo.] I've been working with the TSM since December 1972 and, as a result of the testing program, have flagged many problems in the design which were then corrected in the flight instruments.

In November, 1973, I went to California for five weeks to test several new changes in the design. There were *still* so many problems at the time with the TSM and the flight instrument that NASA required all key scientists to remain in residence at TRW and interact with the engineers until an instrument was built which worked properly. So, although I had only gone to California for five weeks, I stayed a *year and eight months!* [Laughs.] Fortunately I'd brought my dog! [Laughs.]

During this period, I attended non-stop meetings to ensure that engineering changes in design would preserve the science. I also directed TSM experiments to trouble-shoot and verify the hardware.

When hardware changes were impossible to correct a problem, you could get very clever in changing the order of performing a sequence of events to make things function properly. It's amazing just how clever you can get when your tools are limited! I worked very closely with the design engineers to produce the final product that now sits on Mars.

Let me tell you that, with all the redesigning, there were many cartoons about people running down to the launch pad and hammering the biology instrument onto Viking at the last minute! [Laughs.] Quite an experience during this time to be rushing that distant deadline with a team of competent, dedicated people. At times I worked fifteen, sixteen, seventeen hours a day, six or seven days a week. It was an experience I, personally, will never forget!

After all this effort, imagine the thrill of being on the Biology Flight Team at the Jet Propulsion Laboratory and seeing these experiments actually perform perfectly on Mars!

How many women hold important positions on the entire flight team?

There are about a thousand members of the entire Viking Flight Team, of which about 225 are scientists. There are two women who rank high in the structure, myself on the Science Team and Carolyn Cooley on the engineering side of the house. You're comparing peaches and bananas, but I guess we're probably of about equal rank in our own areas.

Are women in a minority on the Biology Flight Team?

Of the 20 members on the Biology Flight Team, there are two women: myself and a young lady who assists Oyama on the Gas Exchange experiment. Within the Biology Flight Team, there are nine members on the Biology Science Team. I am the only woman on that team. Other associated women are secretaries and aides.

Have you ever worked with a woman scientist of equal responsibility?

No. I'm the only woman I know of in space biology, although there are many women in other areas of biology, biochemistry, and other sciences.

What is the objective of the Biology Flight Team?

The Biology Flight Team, half of which is engineers, is testing the hypothesis of whether there is life on Mars, by conducting three experiments on Mars, each based on different premises in terms of metabolism and the amount of water required for metabolism. For all three, after an apparent positive life response is obtained from a Mars surface sample, a control cycle is run on a heat sterilized portion of the same surface sample. A significant difference in response confirms a positive response. The responses so far obtained on Mars are positive, but due to possible bizarre chemical reactions on Mars, it has not yet been determined whether the positive response is attributed to biology or chemistry.

What is your specific role on the Biology Flight Team?

Basically, my position on the Biology Flight Team is Co-investigator of the Labeled Release Experiment of which Dr. Levin is Principal Investigator. In general, I analyze the down-link data and develop up-link strategy. Up-link is sending commands *to* the spacecraft. Down-link is receiving data *from* the spacecraft. We have an up-link every other day or so to make changes as necessary to the sequences. I also make sure all experimental sequences are absolutely correct for the strategy desired for the Labeled Release Experiment.

I am also very much involved in preparing papers for publication and in designing a test program to approach the issue of whether Mars responses are due to biology or chemistry.

How do you react to working as many as seventeen hours a day?

I don't consider the long hours a disadvantage. I consider it a privilege to work on something you like. That's worth a lot! Some people claim they would work on Viking for free! [Laughs.] Right now, for example, I have about 400 vacation hours accumulated. It seems I just don't have time for a real vacation. But then, my job is a kind of vacation!

Will you be involved in future Mars missions?

In addition to Viking, I have participated in contracts over the past six years for follow-on Vikings. By "follow-on" I mean another mission to Mars, maybe in the 1980s. All of these contracts are NASA-sponsored, although there are no funded missions at the moment (November, 1976) for follow-on Vikings. But the thing is, you've got to have the science going long before the mission itself is ever funded. Therefore, NASA funds different laboratories to develop different experiments. Maybe two or three will then be selected for the final mission.

At Biospherics, I have participated in the development of experiments proposed for follow-on missions. I've designed new life detection tests and participated in developing plans for the return of a Mars surface sample to Earth.

What work have you done in water pollution?

My other major field is water pollution. Recently, I was Principal Investigator on a contract for the Environmental Protection Agency to assess a variety of aquatic pesticides for environmental impact.

One of the major water pollution problems we have in the United States is that of aquatic weeds. Herbicides developed to alleviate this problem unfortunately affect other organisms, and the standard way of assessing side effects has been by examining fish toxicity. We took a different approach in that we looked at the sensitivity of various species of plankton to assess effects of candidate herbicides. Plankton are tiny floating organisms at the base of all aquatic food chains. Instead of just measuring death, I directed the development of new methods to measure more subtle effects on reproduction, metabolism, and motility or movement. This is because, although a particular herbicide might not kill, if an organism's legs are immobilized so it can't get food or mate, it might as well be dead! On the basis of these studies, we identified herbicides with the least side effects on non-target organisms.

On another contract I was sent to the Caspian Sea in Iran as a consultant for the Smithsonian. We were assessing water pollution problems on the Caspian Sea because the sturgeon numbers were declining. I directed the collection of water and mud samples and brought them back to Biospherics to analyze for pesticides and metal content.

What is Principal Investigator?

Government agencies circulate RFP's, or Request for Proposal for work they want done. I wrote a proposal outlining my approach to the problem and how I would do the job. From the many proposals submitted, mine was considered best, selected, and funded. As Principal Investigator, I was responsible for the design and execution of the entire project and for completion of all work within a given period of time and for a given price. I coordinated two full-time technicians and four other part-time persons, including one woman Ph.D. and one male M.A., to complete the work.

You enjoy your work?

I really do love my work . . . most of the time! [Laughs.] There are always times when you're just so darned harassed and over-worked, and people won't let you get anything done because they're always asking dumb questions so that you'd like to throw them all out the window! But that's normal. You get frustrated.

There's good and bad in every job. As long as the good is sixty or seventy percent, then the job is enjoyable!

What are the occupational hazards?

Occupational hazards are not the kind of thing I'm going to think about. I'm going to do the job. And if there are hazards—and there are minimal hazards working with radioactive materials—I'm not going to dwell on them. These are things you think about, take appropriate precautions, and discard from your mind. If there were serious hazards and I couldn't correct them, of course I'd leave. My health is of prime importance! But I have never encountered such a situation.

How do you account for your success?

I don't know if my "success" has been so much a function of good education as attitude. I'm determined to do the job really well. I'm competing with myself. I think of it in terms that I have a job to do and I'm going to do the best possible job I can, regardless of what the world thinks about it! If my heart weren't in my work, I wouldn't do it! It's enjoyment and self-satisfaction that count.

What discrimination against women have you experienced?

As I said, when I anticipated discrimination in the academic world, I went around the block and joined industry. As a result of going *around* the problem, I have really experienced *no* discrimination. I have experienced no such problems at Biospherics! I feel totally accepted there. And I think I've done pretty well for anyone, male or female!

In today's world, being a well-qualified woman is beginning to be an advantage.

What are the attitudes of male and female co-workers toward you?

I work primarily with men on a professional level. The women I encounter are generally secretaries or technicians. I experience more hostility and difficulties—jealousy, perhaps—with the women at work than I do with the men.

How assertive are you in dealing with peers?

I'm very assertive but not because I'm trying to prove something. I'm trying to get the job done well and quickly. That takes effort! I always exercise authority and pull as much weight as necessary.

How do you maintain your femininity on the job?

Femininity does not belong in business, nor do emotions. Emotionalism certainly does not belong in science. There is plenty of time for emotions *and* femininity in the other 15 hours of the day! [Laughs.]

Your attitude toward women's lib?

I'm not really a women's libber, except in the sense of equal salary for equal work, and equal opportunity for equal education. Most of the rest of it is for the *birds!* But the many women who object to Women's Lib by saying, "But I want to be happily married!" are equally ridiculous. *Let them!* That's their choice. Nobody's telling you "You have to go out and get a job!" [Laughs.]

Biochemistry has made what contribution to *you*?

One exciting thing for me has been the evolution of the mind. I wasn't as sharp intellectually when I was in my twenties. Oh, I got good grades and all that sort of thing. But my mind wasn't as sharp in creative thought. Research forces one to become creative and quick. And contrary to physical abilities, which unfortunately decline after the twenties, the mental capabilities seem to improve with age!

My mind has become a good friend! [Laughs.] I know I'll never be bored. I'm not afraid of the unknown because I know I can go out and do whatever I want to do.

Consequently, I don't really worry about job security. I know damned well that I can change professions and I guarantee you, within a brief time, I'll be doing just fine! I'd like to think I know a formula for success—intelligence and hard work! I don't see any reason why a person can't change fields and be competent within a reasonably short time. You learn how to learn!

Outside of work, what do you do for pleasure?

In my personal life, I've always had a deep love for horses. I bought my first horse in college and kept the horse for seventeen years. Three years ago I bought a hunter and joined a fox hunting group. When I'm home I try to ride at least every other day. I love to fox hunt which is more fun than a barrel of monkeys—the best sport in the world! [Laughs.] But, although I'm totally involved in my sport, part of maturity is recognizing the role things play in your life. For instance, I really would not be happy with horsemanship as a career. You know, no matter how much you like something, you have to recognize how many hours per day you can put up with it. This also includes people! [Laughs.]

What is your attitude toward your life as a single career woman?

My personal goal is to get as much out of life as I possibly can. You only go around once. The unifying thread throughout my life has been my career and horsemanship. Beyond that, I pursue other interests—for example, photography—as I have time.

Frankly, I wouldn't trade this life for a married life for all the tea in China. To me the opportunities are so great if you're single. If I want to spend a weekend in Hawaii, I spend it! If I want to go skiing in Europe, I go!

I feel so fortunate to be in this country at this particular time in history and to have these opportunities. I'm just delighted with where I am! But there's a hell of a lot more I want to do!

Pesticides Inspector

Judith Ann Swenson

FIFRA is what I live by.

"Only five of the 68 pesticide inspectors in the country are women," according to Judy Swenson, one-fifth of this federally employed minority. Working with one percent women and 99 percent men, Swenson is the butt of crude jokes aimed at her gender. She is the only female enforcing the Federal Insecticide, Fungicide, and Rodenticide Act (FIFRA) in Region Nine which includes Arizona, California, Hawaii, Nevada, and Guam. Swenson constantly insists that she knows "how to deal with men."

Born in 1943, Swenson was the oldest of eleven children. When she was told, at age sixteen, to go out and get a job, she left home. She learned responsibility, she says, from an early age. In 1971, Swenson found a niche in the federal government, beginning as a clerk-typist for the Environmental Protection Agency.

The objective of my job is to carry out FIFRA. FIFRA is the Federal Insecticide, Fungicide, and Rodenticide Act. It was passed in 1972 and amended three times. It is the law that gives us authority to inspect a place.

I go out to companies who produce pesticides for consumers. I check labelling to make sure the companies are in compliance with our national regulations, mainly making sure that a label includes all the ingredients which are actually in a product.

These are companies like Chevron, Standard Oil, and lots of small companies which produce certain pesticides such as chlordan/heptachlor and malthine.

When a directive comes down from Washington that something has to be recalled, we have the authority to make these

215

companies do it. This involves public relations and characterizations on the inspector's part and someone who can deal with people and make them do what you want them to do.

I've been on this job since January, 1976. It's called an Upward Mobility Position, where you go from a non-technical position to a technical position.

How did you begin your Civil Service career?

I first worked for EPA as a clerk-typist GS-3. [General Service-3, the federal employee classification system]. I started in November, 1974. There were five federal agencies I wanted to work for. EPA offered me a position first. I worked in the Permits Branch of EPA issuing permits which give authorization to discharge pollution into the waters. The regulations state how pollution must be disposed of properly.

In a three-month period, I issued something like 77 water permits. Nobody had ever done that many before.

Then I became a GS-5 branch secretary and held a more administrative position. My superior respected me and I was given a lot of responsibility.

When Upward Mobility jobs came along, I applied for all of them. They're mostly for women. It's a federal opportunity program for women. You have to be with the government, in good standing, for one year, and you have to have the ability to advance through training.

The training program was six months concentrating basically on FIFRA. Every three months I met with my supervisor to discuss my progress. I finished the training program in June 1976.

What are you "inspecting" and what are your procedures?

There are three types of inspection: the Producer Establishment Inspection, Market Surveillance, and Use Investigations Inspection which is done by a higher GS level. They go out and actually watch pesticides being applied.

I do PEIs [Producer Establishment Inspections]. I get the background on the company, find out if they have been in violation, and check our labels against theirs. I look at directions for use, EPA registration number, and the establishment registration number. We have a national emergency phone number 24 hours a day, so people can find out exactly what is in a product. This is one of the purposes of registration numbers.

I go into the company and present a Notice of Inspection which states the law, gives my name, who I want to see, what the reason—if any—is for the inspection. I usually do suspect a violation.

I meet with the company president, plant manager, or records keeper. I sit down and talk to them about our law, FIFRA.

The people want to show you their plant, so you act like you're really interested. It's interesting to meet all kinds of people, and most of them really want to help me. I get to handle, manipulate, deal with particularly men.

We women inspectors are more hard-nosed and very leery of these companies when we're out in the field, and I am experienced with men. My bosses have usually been men.

I try to be a liaison officer between the federal government and private industry, which is very hard to do.

A label is what I review when I go to a company. Certain things have to be on the label: the product name, the active ingredient statement, and how much is in the product. It has to have who makes the product, their address, *and* the EPA registration number, "Caution: Keep out of reach of children" or "Warning: Keep out of reach of children." Directions for use and warnings—if it's toxic—and antidotes must also be on the label. These are the things we look for. A small company might have from one to seven labels. If the label doesn't list everything it should, then I pick it up and usually collect a sample.

If a company is selling a product that is not registered with us, they have to come into compliance. It's regulated. Information on a container must be accurate. This protects the consumer.

In order to pick up a sample, I have to use an inverted polyethylene bag. I write the sample number on the seal. It's a long procedural operation which I must follow, otherwise it could be thrown out of court. I send the samples to the lab to be analyzed.

Most of the time, companies *are* deceiving the public. They don't put the right ingredients in the product.

Define "pesticide."

A pesticide is anything that kills or repels pests, insects, molds, et cetera. Deodorant is a pesticide—anything that controls the growth of bacteria.

You deal with toxic materials. What risks do you run?

The hazards in this job aren't that great unless you're clumsy.

There is some danger that I could spill a chemical and lose my life pretty fast! [Laughs.] The consequences could be *quite* serious if I did something stupid. I must follow procedures about how I put my gloves on, how I wear the respirator. If I took a whiff of dust out of a sample, it could be very harmful to me. All of the materials I take samples of are toxic to some degree.

If I'm taking particularly toxic samples, I wear a full body suit. It's a white plastic suit. I usually wear plastic gloves, a respirator, eye goggles, sometimes a hardhat, always a scarf to protect my hair, and safety shoes with steel toes in them. If I'm involved with paraquat—the very toxic chemical that will go right through your skin—I wear big, black, ugly, thick, plastic gloves.

What are your tools?

I have a sampling kit. It has plastic bags that I have to wrap the samples in. There's glass containers for my samples—plastic and glass tubing to get the samples out. There are the big rubber gloves that nothing should go through, plastic gloves. There's a respirator, goggles, paper towels. And there's a camera and film—I take photographs. It's all in a black kit a little bigger than a brief case.

What is market surveillance?

Market Surveillance Inspection entails going into Walgreens, for example, and picking up an unregistered Black Flag can.

What has been your most interesting inspection?

I have collected samples and accumulated 45,000 dollars worth of fines on this one company. They are going to be *very* hard up. The only problem is that our policy is *not* to put anybody out of business. A letter came down through EPA stating that, "We are not in business to put people out of business. We are in business to protect the environment." I *personally* think some companies should be put out of business. We have a lot of problems.

Your inspections cannot result in a company closing?

We are *not* in business to close down companies. We can only regulate them with fines. If I go into a company and the product is not registered with us and it is a pesticide, right away that's a count against the company. It's based on how much the company makes, if they are previous violators, what their intent is to improve the condition.

For each thing that is not listed on the label, the company can be fined 5,000 dollars.

What steps lead to action against a company?

When I come back to the office, I make two reports. The Collection Report talks about the sample itself. And I write up an Inspection Report about the company.

First the sample goes to the lab and it's analyzed for the active ingredients on the label, to make certain that the percentages listed on the label are in the product. Then the lab analysis and all of my reports go to the registration man in the office. He reviews it. He knows what every label is supposed to be like. He recommends actions. Then he sends the information to the lawyers in the Enforcement Division. They review it and decide if it's going to be a warning letter, a no-action letter—which means doing nothing at all—or a civil penalty which means the company is told they will be fined a certain amount of money. The company can either pay the fine, ask for a pre-conference hearing, or go for an actual suit hearing. Most companies settle. They come into our office and talk about it and settle right here. We have very few court hearings. It takes from a few weeks to four or five months to do this.

I deal with our lawyers daily. There are four pesticide inspectors in our office and three lawyers. [Her office is in San Francisco.]

What discrimination have you experienced?

In Arizona, primarily, most people don't think I can do the job. It's mostly awe. I have to show them that I know what I'm doing.

One man told me I was the best looking man he'd ever seen from EPA. [Laughs.] Another man at a conference said I had the nicest looking rear-end of any man at EPA. [Laughs.] I have comments like this *all the time!* But being the kind of person I am—with the people I've had to deal with in my life both socially and career-wise—I just kind of laugh it off. It just doesn't bother me. I feel that if I get very uptight about it, they're going to, too. If I kind of ignore the situation, maybe they're going to think, "Well maybe she's not really so bad."

What women's groups have you worked with?

I have never been a member of NOW or of any similar groups, mainly because they're too liberal for me. I'm a woman in my own right, and I don't feel I need the type of women who want to be like men. I *don't* want to be like a man! I *know* I can carry my own weight.

I started the Women's Committee at EPA, mainly because of the discrimination when I worked in the Enforcement Division. There was a training course which I felt I should be sent to, and I *wasn't*. Someone's secretary was sent instead. So I went to our Equal Employment Opportunity office and complained. I decided I couldn't get anywhere that way. I started talking to a lot of people at EPA; I found I wasn't the only woman who was being discriminated against, so I asked women if they'd be interested. Sure enough, about 50 women showed up for the first meeting. We do a lot of interesting things. We had the Board Chairwoman of the first women's bank of San Francisco come in to talk with us.

What is the Equal Employment Opportunity Office?

These Equal Employment Opportunity people are what we call our EEO officers. If you really feel you're being discriminated against, you can go and talk with them. But they don't really work. It's a long involved process.

What do you like best about pesticides inspecting?

No matter what their attitude is when I go into a company, it's usually very good when I leave. I make it a point to establish good rapport. I achieve rapport through my personality, understanding, and through my having worked with people for many years. And I know how to deal with men. I think that we leave a good impression with people we encounter in the field. We're *not* all bad guys! I feel like I'm making a contribution. I have the authority to do inspections, and I'm respected for what I say. If I say that a particular company needs to be inspected by the Office of Safety and Hazardous Materials, it is done.

How does this compare to former jobs?

It's more challenging and interesting, and I have the feeling that I can make a very good career out of it.

I studied geology in school because I enjoy nature, rocks, the ocean, and I like to be outside a lot. In this job I am outside or in warehouses 50 percent of the time. I do about ten inspections a month.

I had one outdoor job before where I worked with Fish and

Wildlife. I took water samples, but it was nothing like this job as far as working with people.

Most of my jobs have been administrative but on a higher keel than just doing what the boss said. Usually they've carried quite a bit of responsibility.

What other work have you done?

During high school, I car-hopped for A & W. I baby-sat. I was on my own from the time I was about sixteen. I left home at that age.

I worked in the Registrar's Office of New Mexico State in Las Cruces for a 70-year-old old maid who did not like women *at all!* I reviewed transcripts and decided that wasn't what I wanted to do. [Laughs.] I worked there while I was going to New Mexico State, then I worked part-time for Metropolitan Life Insurance Company and adjusted claims. I hated that job. What a *horrible* way to spend your time! Because it was such a large company, you were just a number.

What aspects of pesticides inspection do you dislike?

On this job, the traveling is pretty lonely. It's tiring. You're always staying in strange places and meeting strange people. [Laughs.] The paper work is quite involved. I have to write up two reports for every place I visit. It takes a whole week in the office to cover one week out in the field.

What are the salary expectations?

Promotion opportunities in my work are very good! I can go probably to a GS-9. Now I'm a 5. It usually goes 5, 7, 9, 11 and on up like that.

Right now I make $9,800 a year. A seven makes $11,000, and a nine makes about $13,500.

I do plan to stay with EPA indefinitely. I want to become a really good Pesticide Inspector and go on up the ladder.

Have you had to change to be more effective in your career?

I would say no. I'm basically me. I feel that my personality and mental capabilities do fit in well with my work without changing.

What are your attitudes toward males and females?

My attitudes toward men and women, as a whole, have not changed since I've had this job. Basically I feel that men are very narrow-minded and very stereotyped. I feel very strongly about that, because I've worked with a lot of men in different jobs. Women are also stereotyped and narrow-minded. People are pretty much the same in federal government as they are in other walks of life. Men in *industry* may be a little worse, but I've handled businessmen before, so it's no big struggle for me.

You deal almost exclusively with men?

In the field and in the office, I deal with probably one percent women and 99 percent men. That's one percent professional women and about ten percent non-professional. By professional women I would mean chemists, company presidents, general managers of quality control. I've run into one woman general manager out of about fifty. I've never encountered a company president who is a woman. I've always had a good rapport with the women I've encountered.

How *do* you deal with men?

The main thing is to be knowledgeable in my field, which usually freaks them out. Because I *do* know the law and I'm courteous. A lot of women who go out into the world carry a chip on their shoulder. I don't carry a chip on my shoulder at all. I just accept everybody for what they are.

Over the years, I've also learned to deal with men through *knowing* what I'm walking into. When I go into a company I'll have background material, but I've found that I can almost tell instantly whether I'm going to have trouble or not. It's by intuition. I can almost tell just by shaking their hands what kind of reception I'm going to get. They might let me know that I'm not welcome just by being very crass, sarcastic and egotistical.

In this case, I'm more than courteous. I do everything the way it's supposed to be done. I try to be pleasant. Even if they get upset, I maintain my pleasantness.

I've worked with men for so many years, usually in a non-technical level. I've been a secretary. I've slept in the same tents without really being a sex symbol. And I just think I've worked with them and gained a lot of experience.

How do other women respond to this work?

Only five of the 68 inspectors in the country are women. Most women can't really handle it. The men frustrate them. I love it. With the travel, I have lots of freedom.

Do you feel like a number in Civil Service?

No, I don't feel that way working for the federal government, but I think this is largely due to my particular job.

Inspectors and supervisors are about the only people in EPA who meet the people. Also, because of my consciousness of the public, I'm not the typical bureaucrat. I *am* related to the bureaucracy, but I am also related to the public and the people who actually have to fulfill FIFRA. I'm more in the world than I would be if I were only involved in policy.

Is the federal government a good employer for women?

A lot of women will disagree with me, but I think the federal government is a good employer. If you've got the get-up-and-go, you can get ahead. I've had very good luck in the federal government. I'm happy, and that's my first priority as far as personal goals. And I think I have a good chance to get ahead in the Pesticides Division.

Personally I feel that it's a benefit for a woman to be in the federal government. It depends on her attitude and where she thinks she's going, of course, but it's very secure. After you're in the government for about three years, it's next to impossible to get fired. Once you reach permanent status, it's just the policy. You *could* be let go, but that's very, very rare.

Working for the federal government is just what each individual makes out of it. For me it's a very worthwhile endeavor. A lot of people don't like it, but I like my particular job.

Being fired is highly unlikely?

It's very difficult to get fired from the federal government for *anything*. A rapist probably wouldn't even get fired! [Laughs.]

The Peter Principle has a living example in the federal government. It's a perfect illustration. [Laughs.] And there *is* a lot of deadwood. It's stuck to the chairs usually. I'm serious! [Laughs.]

Is EPA a political animal?

Our regional administrator is politically appointed and the deputy administrators are politically appointed. I think it's a political animal.

What is the hierarchy?

We have a section chief, who is my boss. Then we have a

branch chief, and then we have a division director, then the deputy administrator. Then the R.A., the Regional Administrator.

My section is the Pesticides Section. I'm in the Air and Hazardous Materials Branch. The division is Surveillance and Analysis. Most of the people in Surveillance and Analysis are some type of inspector.

There are four inspectors in my division. [The other three inspectors in Swenson's division of Region 9 are men.] There are five divisions in my region, and there are ten regions.

You really believe EPA can clean up the environment?

I find that, with all its problems, EPA is still a good organization. It's accomplished a lot since it was founded in 1970. Messing up the environment took almost 200 years and you can't expect to clean it up in ten. I do feel that it can be cleaned up.

Has your formal education been helpful in your occupation?

No, not in this one. Not at *all!* I do *not* feel that there was enough counseling about job possibilities when I was in school. I'd like to see high school counselors actually council students on a very personal basis, not just as a number.

I went to a very large high school in Las Cruces. There were 600 in my graduating class in 1961. And I don't think any of us were really counseled about whether we should go to college or what we should do.

Why did you quit school?

I quit school because it was so hard to support myself and go to school. This has been my basic problem—supporting myself. I *will* finish my degree, but I really don't feel that it's so important anymore.

What is your background?

I was born in Rochester, New York in 1943. When I was five, my parents moved to Las Cruces, New Mexico, and then back to New York. My Dad is like a self-made electrician. Whenever he could get a job, he did. That's why we moved so much. I've lived in Florida, Mississippi, Georgia, Missouri.

Your mother?

My mother is a very *dominated* housewife, but that's what she wants. I have six brothers and four sisters. I'm the oldest.

How did being the oldest of eleven children affect you?

It made me very responsible at a very early age. My parents held me responsible for a lot. I learned to be a good cook. I learned all about housekeeping. I watched my younger brothers and sisters at a very early age. I learned to be reliable. If I needed to go to the grocery and buy 100 dollars worth of groceries, I could do it.

This taught me a sense of survival and gave me an awareness even in high school that there must be a better life. I had no social life during all my years in high school, because I had so many responsibilities at home.

My family never encouraged me to do anything professionally. Mainly, my siblings have no education beyond high school. They're mainly workers. I have one brother who's in a supervisory position. I'm not very close to my family. My family's socio-economic level? Low. Lower middle class, if anything.

What did your parents want for you?

My parents probably wanted me to get married and raise a family. I didn't respond very well to that idea! [Laughs.] But I have been married. After a certain point, I just got tired of being on my own. The opportunity arose to marry and I took it. It was too bad! I've been sorry. [Laughs.] [Swenson is now divorced.]

I left home because my parents said I had to go out and get a job. My Dad and I have never gotten along. It's not that he's a bad person or anything. I'm a lot like him! I'm very strong-willed. When they told me to go out to work I said, "Well then, I might as well leave home too!" They never really fought it!

I knew that I had to get out of the socio-economic position my parents were in, and I knew I had the potential. That's what I've been striving for and what I'll continue to strive for.

Bank President

Doris Tarrant

Shoot for the top. There's nothing *in between!*

In the United States, according to the American Bankers Association, there are 14,700 commercial and savings banks. (Savings and loan institutions are not recognized.) Of the 14,700 bank presidents, a mere fifty are women. Doris Tarrant has presided over United Jersey Bank/Ridgewood since December 1973.

Tarrant's banking career, less than a decade old at the time of this interview, has been marked by rapid success. She entered banking in 1967 virtually as a traveling saleswoman, "an untitled person." In 1971 she was named the first female vice president of People's Trust, the lead bank in United Jersey Banks, a thirteen-bank holding company. In 1973, after less than three years as vice president in charge of correspondent banking, Tarrant became president of United Jersey Bank/Ridgewood.

Because of her meteoric rise, Doris Tarrant stands out among all bankers. Even among female bank presidents, she is exceptionally noteworthy because she does not have a college degree.

When I spoke with Tarrant in her New Jersey home one Sunday, she was sewing a vest to wear for one of her many television appearances on behalf of the banking industry. She was extremely cordial. Her sense of humor and frank style are delightful—hardly what one would expect from a bank president, but then Doris Tarrant *is* no ordinary banker.

I have been president/C.E.O. (Chief Executive Officer) of United Jersey Bank/Ridgewood since December of 1973.

United Jersey Bank/Ridgewood is one of the banks in a thirteen-bank, multi-bank holding company, and I first did correspondent work for the lead bank in the holding company. As a correspondent banker, I called on small banks who need the services of a bank that clears with the Federal Reserve System. My job was talking to the presidents of non-member, mostly smaller banks.

While doing that, the thought occurred to me [laughs] that I was as smart as most of those *men!* I was calling on them for two or three years, and after a while you think, "Hell, I know as much as they know! Why couldn't *I* do that kind of job?" I have to say that now, three years later, they knew a *lot* of things I never even heard of! [Laughs.]

All I ever called on were other banks. As a result of being with a large corporate banking structure, you work in *one area*. If you're a commercial credit man, you work in commercial credit; if you're a correspondent person, you're out making calls. It's not very diversified.

I started to want more forward movement, and *where* could I go? I really didn't have *banking experience*. I had sales experience in selling correspondent banking. I sold bank services, computer services, clearing services.

What was your title?

I started off as a non-titled person and ended up as a vice president, the first vice president that corporation had. I was in charge of correspondent banking.

I became restless. Management talked to me a little bit about it and I said, "Well, really, all I want to do is be president of a small bank." I really never thought they'd let me go on. But my thought was that it never hurts to *say*. [Laughs.] That was maybe two years prior to my move [to president]. I don't know whether they had thought about it first or I planted the seed . . .

How long were you vice president?

Two years. I was with the lead bank in the holding company for six years, plus these three. And that's all I've been in banking.

What chain of events took you from vice president to president?

From my side of it, I started to take courses that would prepare me.

I went to the out-student Harvard Business School. Several people in the lead bank went to Harvard Business School.

You actually went to Harvard?

No, but I took their books when they came back. I thought,

well, I can start with that. Then I went to AIB [American Institute of Banking] where I had taken courses that would help my correspondent banking.

I had never taken any courses, for example, in platform and teller, that type of operation. I wanted to find out what these people do, because I had never been exposed to any retail banking. I did that for about a year and a half and then, fortunately for me, the man that was president of the bank in Ridgewood decided to move to Vermont and leave banking completely.

Ridgewood is a very attractive community. It is in Bergen County where I lived all my life. The bank in Ridgewood caters to the community. I fit into the community because I grew up in the same area, ten minutes away.

It's 90 percent a corporate executive type of community. It was written up in *McCall's* as being one of the *ideal* communities in the United States to live. It is a *fine* community.

I could relate to the customers they had. I think that's why I've had more success than my predecessors. They were *not* local people.

You have been more successful than your predecessors?

Yes, the bank's making money. That's the criterion. [Laughs.]

The bank has made money during the last two years. It's not that I'm a miracle worker—the bank is six years old. It takes the bank a few years, obviously, to work off the expenses of opening. [The population of Ridgewood, a bedroom community for New York City, is 28,000. The average home sells for $100,000.]

There were other persons who had positions comparable to yours as vice-president? How do you account for the fact that you were chosen over them?

I hate to give credit to them, but I do think part of it was the local women's movement. I really do. I think they made corporations more aware. You know, so much of business is playing a political game, and I think that's one of the places where women kind of fail. If you're politically oriented—I don't mean Democrat-Republican, but corporate politics—I do think in today's world most corporations *will* take the woman. I do think so. I don't think we're discriminated against. Maybe as a *whole* women have some complaints. But on an individual basis, I think, in today's climate, they'll take a woman.

For example, headquarters of UJB [United Jersey Bank], our parent bank, are in Princeton, New Jersey. They're very pleased about the fact that ABA [American Bankers Association] has chosen me as Consumer Representative and I'm traveling on the eastern seaboard for ABA. They feel this is tremendous corporate image type of public relations. They can't *buy* it.

I am interviewed on television, radio, and they have call-in programs. There are questions, everyday questions, lay-people questions: "How do I get a loan?" "How do I establish credit?" That sort of thing. Women call in more than men.

What exactly is the process when a bank elects or appoints a new president?

I can only speak for this one. When they knew the president was going to resign they usually give quite a bit of time on it. In this *particular* case they went to the lead bank and said, "Do you have any people?" and several resumes were submitted. Usually a committee of the board, appointed by the board and similar to a nominating committee, will meet with the various people and sort of narrow it down. In my case I don't know that there was too much narrowing down. I *don't know*.

I met with the committee appointed by the board. There were four members on the committee.

All men?

All men. And subsequent to that, I had a cocktail with another few members of the board. At that point there were twelve members. So by the time the board voted, I had met all but one.

Who are the board members?

They are *mostly* local business people. [They are not major stockholders in the bank.] Our shares of stock are owned by the parent in Princeton which is called United Jersey Bank and which is traded on the New Jersey Exchange.

A director's responsibility, in addition to being responsible for the bank being run properly, is to help develop business for the bank. Obviously if you have local people and local structure, they can help.

What was your reaction to being named president?

Oh, I was thrilled! [Laughs.]

Were you nervous?

Yes, I was nervous on *many* sides of it. I gave up what I felt was a nice job that I enjoyed. As an outside sales person your hours are always *much* more your *own*. You can work like mad one day and sort of goof the next, as long as you produce. The bank that I was with had very fine profit-sharing and pension. I have neither of those now.

What is your salary?

It's over 30 [thousand]. When I took the job as president, it was in the low 20s.

I came in at the salary my predecessor had when he left. I was pleased about that. I didn't know it at the time.

Do you work long hours?

Yes I do. I'm usually in the bank before 8 o'clock and I do not leave until after 6.

And I work on Saturdays; I'm around. During the summer I try to take Wednesday mornings off to play golf, and in the winter, I take Wednesday afternoons off to go to a matinee.

What are your responsibilities?

Well, it seems to me [laughs] that they're *everything*, and I talk to *everyone* who has a complaint! It seems they all end up on my desk. [Laughs.]

You are very accessible to the public?

Yes, the bank is a two-story building. Upstairs is the operations area. I have an office from which, by rearranging the furniture, I can see the banking platform. I did that so I could see what was going on. I wasn't so experienced that I could isolate myself. On the side from the customer, there is no way of hiding. My secretary can't say, "She's not in," because they can see. [Laughs.] Unless I go into the john, I *can't* hide! [Laughs.] On the day-to-day, I am really the commercial lending officer of the bank.

Commercial lending officer?

The commercial lending officer handles any business-oriented loans. Loans that I don't usually handle myself are the automobile loans or the personal loans for your vacation. We have more than ample staff for that. If there is a turn-down on a loan, then I see it. If there is an acceptance of a loan, I don't become involved with it. The loans I work on particularly are the unsecured loans where people want to start businesses, have started businesses, that type of thing.

In overseeing the other banking operations, what do you do?

I coordinate with the other officers of the bank. We have a

once-a-week staff meeting, early morning, so I can become absolutely aware of a problem, be they personnel or operational,
handling the customer who feels they have not been treated
properly. And, as I say, the good customers I have little or no
occasion to see. [Laughs.] [United Jersey Bank/Ridgewood,
with its two branches, employs 36 people.]

Your bank *is* part of a huge banking operation?

Yes, but we don't become *involved* with the large one except on
policy matters.

People's Trust, the lead bank, is a large bank, the largest
bank in New Jersey. There you would do one job. You specialize. The difference is that in a small operation we have to do
everything.

Once a month, the thirteen bank presidents go to a meeting in
Princeton. We get direction from the parent. We have discussion sessions on investment policies where they might have an
outsider come in and talk about the economy and how we
should invest funds, their recommendations, whether interest
rates are going up. Economics is all guesswork, but they're a lot
better qualified to guess than I am, on an everyday basis. And
they may have our advertising agency, which is the holding
company level, come in and talk about a new promotion program that would be a *statewide* program.

For example, we have just gone into the check-guarantee
card and that is a check guarantee for every bank in the holding
company—every branch.

What are the bank's assets?

The bank has $32 million in assets. When I took over three
years ago it was a little over 20. It was *not* making money then.

My feeling is that to have a strong banking community, the
banks must make money because we must pay our employees.
We don't have shareholders because we're a wholly-owned subsidiary. The parent company is United Jersey Bank. The stock
sells for a little over eleven dollars a share, and it has almost a
ten percent return in dividends. There are thirteen banking corporations and three non-banking. [United Jersey Bank/
Ridgewood is one of the thirteen banking corporations. The
three non-banking corporations are a finance company, an insurance company, and a leasing company.]

How do you conduct your public relations to be particularly effective?

I have to say I get a great deal of P.R. [public relations], a lot of it by purpose, of course. I'm active in the community and with the volunteers for the large, well-established hospital in Ridgewood, called Valley Hospital. Each year there are several fund-raising activities related to the hospital. I am active in them. [In 1975 she chaired a committee selling advertising in the *Journal* distributed at the hospital's annual fund-raising fair; she contacted corporations. A total of $16,000 was raised by her committee.]

This gives you a lot of P.R. You meet all these ladies under *nice* circumstances. Maybe they'll go home and talk about it. And maybe in the next month or the next year, they'll open an account with the bank. As a result of these activities, your name is constantly in the news.

How do people respond to you, the "woman" bank president?

I think there are two types of response. I think the older ladies would prefer to talk to a man. For example, we have a great many widows. I have a man that recently retired from Chase working with me—43 years with Chase [Manhattan Bank]. He hadn't, for many years, dealt at a retail level; he was part of the corporate structure at Chase.

I think part of it is due to the loss of a husband who they *leaned* on, but the widow ladies would *prefer* to talk to my associate, rather than one of the [bank's] ladies on the platform who deal with what they're interested in. Maybe it's just investing in a U.S. Treasury Bond, something simple, but they would prefer to talk with the man, even though he hasn't been doing this type of work recently.

Older women's preference is based strictly on gender?

That's right. I find that this is true of older ladies *particularly*, or recent widows who have leaned on sons and/or husbands.

The younger women seem to be *delighted* to talk to me because I think they all are quite pleased to see a lady as president.

To the men, I don't think it makes a *bit* of difference.

Younger women have a more open attitude toward women's abilities?

Absolutely yes. I really do think so.

How do you account for men's acceptance of your authority as a banker?

Maybe the difference is that I don't notice it here.

When I first took my job at People's Trust in correspondent banking, a female had never been on the road in New Jersey selling bank services. I think maybe I got over most of my feelings and some of the men I dealt with got over it at that level, so I don't notice it any more.

There were four men and myself selling correspondent services, and I ended up in charge of the *department*.

So many women in business say, "Lunch is such a *hassle*. How do you pay the check?" Well, all you can do is offer to pay it. I said to one man—a very nice man, not belittling me at all—I said, "Look! If one of the fellows from my bank came down and took you to lunch, would you plan to *pay?*" He said, "No!" I said, "Well, you know, you're discrediting my *job*." And he said, "You know, I'd never really thought about it like that."

You just put it on the line, "I'm trying to do a job." So by the time I got to Ridgewood, if the men felt this way, I didn't notice it.

I really do think you have to prove you know what you're talking about. If you're *bluffing*, people will find out.

One of the things I have found that I think helps women, *really*, is that we're much more inclined to say, "I don't *know*. I'll find out." Maybe women can do this easier, because people never expect us to know everything. But a man is hard-pressed to admit he doesn't know something, because we *expect* him to know everything! [Laughs.] What a burden to go through life with! [Laughs.]

Have you always had a sense of equality with men?

It never occurred to me that I wasn't [equal]. I grew up as an only child. I think an only child under normal circumstances has to become a *lot* more self-reliant. They don't *have* anyone else but themselves. Parents can't spend all their time entertaining you, so you have to be someone that builds up a source of resources and activities within your*self*. And I think that helps you in business. You don't *expect* anyone to help you. When I was a child, I couldn't have my brother or sister help me complete a project. I either did it myself or it didn't get done. I think this goes on through life—if you want a project done, you do it yourself. It never occurred to me that I had less chance of going ahead than a man might have.

Who most influenced you as a child?

My father did. He owned his own trucking business. His attitude is always "Shoot for the top. There's *nothing* in between!" He instilled that in me when I was a child, a *little* child. "Shoot for the stars," was his expression. "Shoot for the *stars!*" Maybe this was why it never occurred to me that there was any reason that I couldn't do anything I wanted. It wasn't always easy! [Laughs.] [Her mother was a housewife who did not work outside of the home.]

How did public schooling influence you?

I wasn't a good student! Maybe that's why I tried much harder when I went to work. In school I had to work like *mad*. Then when I went to work, working turned out to be *easier* than going to school [laughs], which was *fantastic* for me!

I went to Katherine Gibbs. You work *very hard* there. When you finish, you go out and do a good job as a secretary. At Gibbs I worked like a demon, but Gibbs was the first place where I realized that I only had to work hard at certain things. There were other things that come *easier*. So when I started out in secretarial work, I tried to get a job geared to that. For example, I was always good in accounting. When I took a job after Gibbs, I worked with the *treasurer* of a company, thinking that there might be more for me than just sitting and doing shorthand and typing every day.

What was your first job?

I worked for the Army Air Force at the end of World War II. It was six months, so it really doesn't count. Then I went to work for the treasurer of a company in New York City, United Board and Carton. I found that I could really understand the accounting and the treasury more than I understood other things.

From there I went to work for the treasurer of U.S. Steel Corporation. I was working as a secretary, but *always* in the area of accounting or finance. My interest in this area was growing *all the time*. I decided to get out of secretarial work and do something else. This was in 1963. I had a friend who owned a computer company, and he said, "I need a new secretary." I said "That's *not* for me! I'm going to do something *different* with *my* life!" He said, "Well, I'll make a deal with you. I'm going to open an office in Florida. If you want to go to Florida to open the office, I'll be back and forth and help you on it. You can hire the people and get the office set up. And then when I come down, you can go on the road with me calling on the customers. If it doesn't work out, you can come back to

New Jersey and be an office manager/secretary." And we agreed.

I took a chance. And I *loved* being out on the road. I was fortunate enough that he sent me to some IBM schools, and I went on the road selling computer services to *banks*. Our office was in Miami. And when that office was open and running well, I came back to New Jersey and worked out of the New Jersey office.

After two years there, I got the idea that I really didn't want to work for a service bureau because it's small factory-type of work. It's not the kind of atmosphere I like working in. But I now had a product that I could apply at a bank with. Now I could go out and sell the banks computers. I knew how to *call* on people. And this goes back to about 1967 when I went to the bank.

Most banks in the country at that time [1967] were just getting into computers, being behind industry. They were saying, "We have extra time, let's sell that time to someone." Actually I was someone already trained in that kind of selling. The only *problem* was, of course, they'd *never* had a woman on the road! I think there are still very few traveling saleswomen. I was replaced by a girl who didn't work out, and they have a man in the job now.

Why did they hire you?

Just because I was the only person applying for the job who had experience. And I had just come from a service bureau that they *knew* of, one of their competitors. Here I was, already trained to do the job. But they took a *long time* to make up their minds!

I didn't realize it at the time, but I would not regularly have been interviewed by as high management as I was. The man who I would work for *had* interviewed me, but I guess that there was a hangup about hiring a *woman*, so then I was interviewed by a little bit *higher* management. He said to me, "Well, don't you find being a woman a terrible handicap?" There was not much I could say except, "Well, you know there *isn't* anything I can do about *that!*" The job was out the window as far as I was concerned. I was qualified for it, but I thought that was *it*. [Laughs.] It hadn't occurred to me that it was a handicap. I thought that people I'd be calling on would be as happy to see me as someone else!

As a traveling saleswoman, what sexist behavior did you observe?

I don't think any more than if I wasn't working for a bank. *Sure*, I went to a convention and got a couple of propositions. But you'd get that whether you were working for a bank or you were someone's wife. I'm not someone's wife, but I understand that people *are* pushy enough to make suggestions to wives. I don't think the job had anything to do with it. I think it's just sort of the nature of the world.

On the road, I stayed at the hotels with the fellows. I'd be the only female at a convention. Maybe I'm wrong, but I think a lot of it has to do with how the woman conducts herself.

Was tokenism part of your rise to bank president?

Yes. Not tokenism per se. Not tokenism to the extent of putting me in and not giving me any authority. But let's say tokenism to the extent that, "We really *should* have some women in high spots."

I don't belong to the N.O.W. [National Organization for Women] but I do think they're so vocal that they make corporations *aware*, and they have pushed these quota systems. I don't agree with their policies, but I do think they make people aware.

When were you born?

The honest truth? I *say* I was born in 1927. That makes me 49. October first is my birthday.

You have never married; has this affected your sense of career?

Yes. It's *had* to, because I have to earn a living. And also I haven't taken time off to raise a family. There are lots of women who are more than capable. They take time off to raise a family; then they go back into the market and they're five or ten years behind.

What qualified you for bank president?

It was part track record. I had come in [to the correspondent banking operation] and turned the department around from a losing operation to profit-making. I just don't believe in working hard and not making a profit. If a bank is losing money, why not put someone in there with a proven record? I worked hard.

One thing that women short-change themselves on is that, like men, we can move from industry to industry. Executive ability is not confined just to banking, steel making, or merchandising. If you're a good executive, you *can* move around. But I think that women are more inclined to stay in one spot, usually in the same structure.

How do you account for women's lack of mobility?

I think that we've been intimidated for *years*. When you hear of men changing jobs, it's always, "Well isn't that great!! When you hear of a woman changing, people ask, "Why?" They never think that she's moved on up.

At the time when I decided not to do secretarial work anymore, I went to some employment agencies in New York, prior to taking the job in Florida. The agencies didn't even want to talk with you *unless* you wanted to stay with what you already knew how to do, which, for me was *secretarial* work.

These people at the employment agencies were women. And they just couldn't understand this idea of changing from one type of work to another.

The attitudes of women, themselves, need to change?

Yes. One of the female officers who was at the bank when I first came in as president told me that her first reaction was to make up a resume and send it out because, she said, "I'm *not* working for a woman!" She laughs and tells this story, today. She was not going to work for a woman; she was going to go *somewhere else* and work! Now she is one of my greatest supporters. She does an excellent job for the bank. It was just that she had never thought of a woman being in *charge* of a bank! [Laughs.]

How many of your bank's employees are women?

We have four men and 32 women. In most banks our size, you would find the four men as the four officers. We have two men as officers and two as tellers.

On the officer side, it's a pretty even breakdown. Teller-wise, it's very difficult to find young men who are willing to start at the bottom. Most young men have degrees by the time they're ready to go to work, and they don't want to start at the level of a teller. [Weekly salaries for tellers at her bank range from 95 to 170 dollars.]

What are your attitudes toward men and women?

I don't know about my attitudes, I *like* them! [Laughs.] I have several *friends*—men friends. I've always had some men friends. I *still* have some.

I will say that I think, because of my job, you end up with a different group of male friends and married couple friends. You don't end up with too many married couple friends where the wife is only involved with household and children, because we have nothing in common. I talk with the men, instead of with the ladies. If I go to a function where the wives work, then *we* have something in common.

I never want to appear to be an overly aggressive female in mixed company. It's one thing how I operate the bank. But then when I go out in the evening, I don't want to be the person running the show.

Does your status as bank president create social problems?

One thing that I think makes businesswomen become unattractive is that they're always on the taking side socially. Just because I'm unmarried and live alone, I do not always accept the invitations of others without having dinner parties in my own home. In my case, one of my men friends does the bartending. If he didn't, I would have to hire someone. You've *got* to do it.

[Tarrant is a member of a country club which had no regular membership provisions for single women—women neither widowed by nor divorced from club members. Tarrant applied for regular membership; she was *not* turned down—she *was* "approved as a lady." A year later she was *invited* to become a regular member, paying "men's dues" but golfing only when women are allowed. "If you're going to do these things," she says, "you can't make a fuss."]

How do you cope with pressure from your job?

This isn't how I deal with it, but how it's dealt with *me*. I took the job in December, and in about March I broke out with bumps on my face. I went to the doctor and he said that I must be allergic to something. Finally he decided it was the pressure of my job.

Each time I have *terrible* pressures, I seem to break out with sores on my gums. Usually nothing shows on the outside.

How do I cope with it? I really don't know. I don't precisely "cope" with pressure. I sew for relaxation, maybe that's part of it. I make a good many of my own clothes.

I don't have a problem sleeping and I don't take pills. I *don't* believe in pills. I have a little dog which gives me a lot of joy, a little black poodle named "Touché."

But *again* I'm fortunate *not* to be someone who gets depressed.

You do not have a college degree?

I went to Gibbs for two years. Then I took night extension courses at Columbia University, but I did not get a degree. I took the AIB [American Institute of Banking] courses which are geared just for banking.

Are you the only bank president in the United States who does not have a college degree?

No. The president of our lead bank in the holding company does not have one. He went to Harvard Business School, but he does not have a college degree.

Did this affect the attitude toward you?

I think so. One of the things in our own holding company, which I'm sure had a lot to do with it, is the age of the chairman. He is now 59 years old. So you don't have a lot of *old* thinking. Management is that *young*. You're not taking someone 70 years old—who is accustomed to women staying at home all their lives—and trying to change their ideas.

Bank presidents without college degrees *are* uncommon?

Yes, it is rare. I think any young men I was competing with all have degrees.

Among some 50 women presidents of the 14,700 banks in the United States, your level of formal education must also be uncommon?

Yes. I think they would all have degrees. And not to pat myself on the back, but I was on a panel in Florida with one lady who was a president. And the bank had been her father's. He *owned* the bank. He died and she took over. You wonder how many are doing it *that* way. There are a *great many* women in charge of savings and loans, but we bankers don't acknowledge savings and loans as banks.

What is your attitude toward women's banks?

Of course, I'm not sympathetic to the whole concept. I go back to my original philosophy: you *have* to make money. You *can't* just gear your operation to minorities. I think the concept is wrong. You can't gear a bank to a little segment. In order to make money, you have to offer all services.

True, lots of women have money today by virtue of inheritance. The women have money. But what about the young people? We can't just give a bank to one group. It's just like a bank saying, "I'm only going to deal with men," or "I'm only going to deal with senior citizens." It doesn't make any sense!

Are you a member of any women's banking organizations?

I'm not a member of the National Association of Bank Women. It is made up of female bank officers who want to improve the position of women in banking and help to move women forward. They have this educational fund. They have a conference around the nation, and they have an annual convention.

They are never happy with *me*. I've spoken before the group in New Jersey, before the one in New York State. Each time I go, I say they should disband, because I don't think that women who want to get ahead in banking should have a group of *women*. I should be a *bank* officer, not a *female* bank officer.

Most banks belong to American Bankers Association. Our dues support the schools that are provided for by American Bankers. Now the National Association of Bank Women wants to start a commercial lending school of their *own*. Instead of *that*, why not push to have their female bank officers accepted at the established, accredited schools that are in existence?

I attended the Graduate School of Commercial Credit in Oklahoma several years ago, and there were maybe 600 bank officers enrolled and only *three* of them were women. *Three women!*

Grace Smith Whatley

> *If a competitor can't out-think or out-maneuver a woman, there is one classic approach a man will always fall back on: he questions her morals. The sons of bitches will do it 99 times out of 100!*

Gracie Smith Whatley in 1966, at age 27, began a modest scrap business in Benton, Arkansas; seven years later she was "worth over a million."

As chatty as your next-door neighbor, the amiable Whatley describes the trials, tribulations and triumphs of jockeying junk batteries and radiators into a multi-million dollar complex of corporate holdings. Whatley has done "battle" with and routed myriad foes, ranging from banking industry prejudice to sexist rumor-mongering of disgruntled (outwitted) competitors. Miraculously she won a life-death struggle with uterine cancer in 1975. Also a veteran of the political arena, Whatley contended for the prestigious and powerful office of county judge in El Dorado, Arkansas in 1974.

At the time of this interview Whatley, 38, is chairperson of Universal Investments, Inc. and several other firms including Vista International Productions (a motion picture company), Whatley Oil Corporation (oil treatment and reclamation), A & A Leasing (industrial equipment), and Bonded Investments, Inc., which "buys properties, develops, and resells them." This woman is to be believed when she makes the no-bones statement, "I *am* business!"

I am chairman of the board of Universal Investments, Incorporated. Universal Investments is a company that's basically interested in industry. We seek out new industry, ways of helping them, ways of financing for them, with the intention of enticing them to locate in our industrial complex in El Dorado. We have industrial sites which we encourage industry to locate

241

on, and we have a fuel storage terminal. We lease storage to companies that have chemicals and fuels. This is in El Dorado, Arkansas.

How did you get started?

I really started from scratch. I started a small scrap processing operation in Benton, Arkansas (population 25,000). That was how I originally began my business career, with the Benton Iron and Metal Company in 1966. It was such a *small* operation to begin with. My cash assets were a total of $3.65 when I started.

I worked so hard and put so much effort into my business, it was just kind of like a snowball, coming off a mountain. It just grew and grew and *grew.*

I was engaged in a type of reclamation. I didn't realize it until the ecologists started crying out for reclamation. I took contaminated materials and materials that no one else had any need for and reprocessed and resmelted them. That's what Benton Iron and Metal Works did.

Now all of the yards that I have are under lease, and I'm more in the investment end. I hold stock in individual companies and I vote stock. I'm really not too much involved in the actual day-to-day operation any longer.

Now I'm working on building apartment complexes, office complexes and that sort of thing, *and* overseeing the industrial complex. It's kind of like having a tiger by the *tail!* [Laughs.] Most of my days are sixteen hours long!

How do you account for your success?

To get where I am I've worked beyond belief. Most people want to be successful, but the majority of the people do not understand the terminology of being successful.

Anyone can be a success if they have plenty of money, ambition, et cetera. But when you start *from the ground up,* it's a completely different story; you not only have to have determination, you have to have stickability. If things go wrong, you *have* to persevere and keep your initial goal in mind. You have to *keep working.*

I always set my goals *nigh!* When I started, I wanted to make $100,000. I worked and *worked* until my assets grew and exceeded $100,000. When I was 34 years old, I was worth over a million.

I started this small scrap steel processing operation. I got out and convinced customers that I could give them better service than the larger companies.

What was the reaction to a female scrap dealer?

Because mine was such a small company, everyone just laughed at it. The bigger dealers thought it was so amusing that a woman would try to build a business that was strictly a *man's game.*

The scrap business is a different entity all unto itself. You're either born into it or you marry into it. My mother and father had been in it, but they didn't want me to get into the business on my own. It's so highly competitive. My parents knew what I would be facing. If I challenged the established scrap dealers, they thought I would be *in trouble.*

What was your first step in entering the scrap business?

The first thing I did was rent a piece of land for $120 per year from the railroad company. I had no office, no labor, no financing. All I had was me. I was 27 years old.

I just worked at my business day and night. I would not allow myself to quit and go home until I had reached my goal for the day. I set a $200 daily goal for myself, and until I had bought or processed $200 worth of materials, I would *not* go home. I was processing the materials myself.

How did it grow so rapidly?

It was a real rough operation—very basic. I sold almost on a daily basis at first until I got my capital built up so I could hold scrap for a week, and then for as long as a month. You can turn your money very rapidly in the scrap business.

The accounts kept pouring in. People saw that I was very determined to make this business work, and they liked the way I did things.

As the business grew, so did my world of business. I was able to hire labor, and I began to bid on larger contracts, to call on larger and larger accounts. I started bidding on stock liquidation sales. A company would fall into bankruptcy and all machinery and scrap would be offered up for sale. I went in there to *buy.* I would keep what materials I needed for my particular company, and I would scrap the rest. That enabled me to bid on a bigger plant the next time. Eventually I was bidding against the nation's number one contenders in the scrap business. It was a long *hard* battle.

Scrap copper, scrap brass, junk batteries, old car radiators—these are what started my business. It was not an attractive job in the beginning, I'll have to say that!

The scrap began to literally pour in. If I bought a radiator, it would have a steel strap around it. That steel strap would have to come off before the radiator could go into the foundry. I separated all the metals then sold it to a broker who shipped it to steel mills and non-ferrous foundries.

Is this a difficult business?

This is a very difficult business, and it's not attractive to most people. That's why the profit potential is so great in the salvage business. I don't mind working in any type of labor provided it's *honest* and *honorable.* I like to work where the profit potential is the greatest!

What was your profit margin?

Some of the things I would buy for $5 and sell for $500. You are *not* limited in the scrap business.

What was the worst discrimination you experienced in the beginning?

The banks would *not* help me! This is what other women need to know. It really was quite discouraging. When I hear women complaining now, I think of how hard it was for a woman to secure financing back in 1966.

We women would go to banks, and they allowed that our incomes counted for *naught* because we were subject to bear children! When I would go in to borrow money, they would listen to my story very politely. But if they would loan me any money at all, it was usually a *tenth* of what I needed.

It was a hell of a note! That was before the advent of the birth control pill. The pill has been one of the most liberating forces in history for women.

You must have helped break down these barriers?

I feel like I *have* done a lot in the state of Arkansas to change banking attitudes toward women in business. It's much easier for a woman on her own to secure financing now than it was ten years ago. Women need to take advantage of this and get out and build their businesses!

If I had wanted to start a dress shop or a beauty shop, perhaps the lending institutions would have been more sympathetic. The fact that I was building a heavy industrial operation really blew their *minds!* [Laughs.]

People doubt a woman's ability. She has to prove herself over and over and over again! A woman *cannot* rest! She *has* to be *better.* She has to be the *best!*

How did you get into the investment business?

The nicest thing that's happened to me was in 1972. American Oil Company [Amoco] announced that they were going to close a 45,000 [barrel] per day gasoline refinery in El Dorado. Every major scrap dealer in the United States began to look at the project and began to send their engineers to bid on it. I read about it in the newspaper. I called them and told them I wanted to bid on it. They were very nice, but it was quite clear that they didn't figure me as being much in the competition.

But I would *not* rest! I kept on pursuing it. I wanted to make them recognize me and that I was serious about the project. As luck would have it, I came up as one of the top competitors. My bid was the highest.

As a result of my winning the bid on American Oil Company, I ended up with $50,000,000 worth of assets. That's original cost on assets. But at that time oil refineries and gasoline refineries were really ten cents a dozen! No one wanted to mess with them. Scrap processors had bought these facilities before and some of them had lost over a million dollars *on one job!*

Why did you want the refinery?

I had looked at the refinery from the standpoint of scrap. I bought it for scrap, but, almost simultaneous with my purchase, the energy crisis hit.

The refinery could have been the *biggest fiasco* of my life! But I am a gambler—a *cinch* gambler! I only bid on things that I know I can control. When I bid on this refinery, I knew I couldn't go wrong.

Everyone thought I was *crazy!* My mother was very distressed. My father said, "Well, leave her alone, and let's see what she does!" But he's also the one who told me when I went into the scrap business, *"Gracie!* I'd rather see you stand on a street corner and sell 20 dollar bills for ten dollars each. You'll get rich *faster!"*

I bought the machinery and equipment, but I did not buy the

land. The land had been donated to the county. The energy crisis had hit. Everyone was desperately in need of fuel storage tanks. They were trying to buy up enough gasoline and fuel to assure that they could operate their plants through the winter. People were having to build storage tanks. They couldn't get steel. The steel mills couldn't run. I had 500,000—a half a million—barrels of fuel storage which I had planned to tear down. But that storage was needed! Things changed and I changed my plans, accordingly.

I decided that I needed to negotiate for the piece of property and keep the fuel storage intact. I bought the 200 acres for $880,000.

I began attracting industry on the basis that I had storage for the fuel to run their plants. Then I attracted many of those companies into the industrial park.

Overnight I went from negotiating for $100,000 contracts to negotiating for million dollar contracts.

[Whatley leased fuel storage to such companies as Dow Chemical, Great Lakes Chemical, Ethyl Corporation, and Michigan Chemical. *The National Observer,* January 3, 1976, reports that the American Industrial [Park] Complex—created by Whatley from the American Oil Company Refinery—has "45 oil storage tanks," all of which "are full now—with 500 million barrels of the fuel and chemicals of the 15 new companies Gracie persuaded to move there."]

Grayco Chemical Company was established. Pollution Controls, Inc., out of Minnesota, was in a poor capital position so that they could not buy the machinery and equipment they needed for their chemical plant. They needed a plant. So they looked at my oil refinery site where I had so much equipment. I traded them machinery and equipment for stock in their company, with the stipulation that they locate a new company in the industrial complex.

This chemical plant was an enticement to other companies to locate in the industrial park, because Grayco, a subsidiary of Pollution Controls, disposed of hazardous and toxic industrial chemicals. Their plant was built in El Dorado to handle industrial wastes. Then other companies like Haliburton, one of the largest chemical companies in the United States, came into the industrial complex.

Describe Universal Investments and your other holdings.

In August of 1976, I sold my additional holdings in the Industrial Complex into Universal Investments which came into existence at that time.

I own the major portion of Universal Investments, Inc. I started the company in cooperation with three other individuals. I set up every business deal for the industrial complex. I negotiated the leases, secured the tenants. At a certain point, however, the American Industrial Complex outgrew my financial resources. I wanted an arrangement that would enhance and expedite the growth of the industrial complex. Two other investors and I pooled our resources. This brought in new money, new ideas, new property, and we formed the corporation of Universal Investments, Inc. Only Universal will be doing business internationally. It's handling my international investments now.

Bonded Investments, Inc., another company where I'm Chairman of the Board and majority stockholder, is an investment company that buys properties, develops them, and resells them. It's an Arkansas corporation.

I have recently sold other properties and companies that I own into the investment companies. In 1976 I started in the investment business.

I have one other investment company, A & A Investments, Inc., which is involved in business and commercial investments.

I have just started a new pipe and mill supply business, A & A Leasing. We'll be leasing industrial machinery and selling pipe and mill supplies.

Universal, Bonded, and A & A Investments have swallowed up all my other companies. The four scrap metal operations, which I had owned and worked, have been sold to these investment companies; I get income from them.

Whatley Oil Corporation, of which I am also chairman, has its own oil treating and reclamation company. For so *many* years, oil was wasted in the United States. It was put in old fuel storage tanks. It was contaminated with other things. Now we are reclaiming this oil. [Whatley Oil Corporation, she hopes, will "process and reclaim a major portion" of one million barrels of contaminated oil located in the three counties in and around El Dorado.]

Vista International Productions is another new corporation

which I own. It's a motion picture company. [The movie *Wheeler* is the company's first film venture.]

You *are* quite a gambler!

Sometimes when people ask me what I do, I tell them I'm a gambler. I will always gamble a little money if the returns and the odds are great enough.

My story has been likened to that of the bumblebee. No one ever *told* the bumblebee that it was impossible—because of the way he's built—for him to fly. But everyone *except the bumblebee* knows this. And *because* the bumblebee doesn't know that it's impossible for him to fly, he *flies!*

I never believed that it was impossible for a woman to build a business empire. I just built it *regardless* of the obstacles and the odds!

Business is becoming like a gigantic game of chess. Right now I'm making mergers with other companies to try to build my buying power and my control. I'm using my wealth as leverage to secure control over other companies. [Whatley's "business investments are around ten million" dollars, she says, and about 500 persons are employed by her various enterprises.]

What is your most important tool?

I have only one tool and that's my *brain.* I keep my mind active and alert. I read the newspapers, listen to newscasts. I try to know what's going on in the community, in the nation, and in the world. Events that take place might relate directly to my business, so I have to be well-versed.

Twice I have been to Arabia. One of the members of the President's court of the United Arab Emirates invited me. I worked very hard with the officials and businessmen. That is strictly no-*woman's* land, so I felt like I made some inroads on behalf of women.

A reporter from the Abu Dhabi Gulf Times interviewed me and called me "Woman of Action from the United States." The article described my will as being "stronger than the will of men." Now *that's* a pretty strong statement for an Arab! [Whatley was "negotiating to build one of the largest oil refineries," anticipated to be a "500,000 barrel per day refinery."]

What do you advise women who want to be successful in business?

My advice to other women who would like to have their own

business enterprises is, "Determine your goals early, and work toward those goals. Be prepared to battle for your business to a greater degree than you have ever had to fight for anything in your *life!*"

Being a woman in business is *not* easy! You have to be certain that you really *want* to be in business, because the sacrifices are *tremendous* along the way.

How old were your children when you opened the scrap business?

When I started my business, my children were age three and seven.

I was in school until I married. Then I needed a supplemental income. My husband and I divorced, and I tried to build the business and take care of the children at the same time.

Do you encounter many women in your business dealings?

More and more I am encountering women in the companies I might call on. They're so much more *efficient* than men! These are usually executive secretaries.

I have encountered only one woman who is the president of a business. She is president of the Savings and Loan in Morristown, Tennessee. She really impressed me, because she stood a toe higher than any of the men at that conference.

How do business*men* react to you?

Men have ceased to think of me as a woman. When businessmen in other communities first meet me, they're very courteous and very complimentary. This lasts for about an hour, until they find out that I am *all business, and* that I am their business equal. Then they very quickly drop their gentlemanly attitude! [Laughs.] They get right down to serious business and we start negotiating.

When I sit down at the business table, I sit down as an *equal.* I ask no quarter and I give none. I *am* business!

If I were masculine and maybe had a few tattoos on my arm, I think people could accept me more. But I'm a very feminine woman.

Men from all over the United States come to El Dorado to do battle. They open the door to my office and here sits this fluffy little woman. They are *stunned!* And while they're getting over their amazement, I lay down the ground rules.

Over the years I have learned to be more on the alert when I am dealing with businessmen. Over the years I have been educated to their ways.

Have male competitors ever tried to take unfair advantage of you?

If a competitor really can't out-think or out-maneuver a woman, there is one classic approach a man will *always* fall back on: he questions her *morals*. The sons of bitches will do it 99 times out of 100!

For a long time I let derogatory remarks upset me, but not any more. The newspaper *The Memphis Commercial Appeal* said that "Gracie Smith Whatley has one of the most shrewd business minds in America today."

I understand that you once ran for an elective office?

In the state of Arkansas, the office of County Judge is very important. I am the only woman in the state ever to actively campaign for that office. In 1974 I ran against six men and made a very, very good showing. I *love politics!* I would have continued my political activities even more if I had not become ill.

Were you seriously ill?

I had the world by the tail when I came down with cancer in October of 1975. I had just married. I was semi-conscious for a month. I went through operation after operation. I had uterine cancer. I don't know how in the world I fought it off. But I was so damned determined. It was a medical miracle.

Did competitors try to take advantage of you during your bout with cancer?

It became even more clear to me, when I was ill, that a woman can *never* feel secure in her position, because men are constantly fighting to gain advantage over her. This was evidenced to me when I had cancer. When I recovered, I had to fight *very hard* to gain back the ground that was taken from me during my illness. [Whatley would not go into detail, but I gathered that she regarded her competition as using extremely underhanded tactics during this critical illness.]

What is your attitude toward your accomplishments?

For the advances I've made, I know that I have worked hard. I respect myself for that. I know that I have put out far more effort than a man would have put out to accomplish the same goals. As a result, I never take my accomplishments lightly. My business career just shows what one woman's determination *can* do!

Isn't this a lonely existence?

It *is* a lonely position. When it comes down to the final decision, it's mine *alone* to make. When you put yourself in a position of responsibility, you *must* be willing to accept all of the characteristics of that position. One of those characteristics is that you are alone when you make major decisions. It's *not* a lot of fun.

When you attain a top rung of the ladder in business, there's *always* someone that will try to bring you down. If they can't bring you down on their own merits, they will often times try to dig a hole beneath you.

Do you enjoy your work?

Business is my *life!* It's just the essence of my being. I can't be happy if I'm not what I am. And I *am* a businesswoman.

Attitude is the primary thing for me. I just never believed I *couldn't* accomplish any goals I set for myself.

Has business interfered with your personal life?

Businesswomen and happy marriages don't usually mix. It takes a rare individual to be able to combine the talents of a business executive and a devoted wife and mother.

I married again in 1975. My husband, Billy Ray Whatley, wildcats for oil all over the world; he is with the Penrod Division of Hunt International Oil Company. He *exudes* personality and happiness. He's so *alive!* [Laughs.] He is like a breath of fresh air in my life. I'm around so many business people who just operate their businesses and vegetate. My husband is more alive than anyone I've ever *seen!*

How exactly were you educated in business matters by your parents?

I learned from my parents. My father had a rather different attitude toward my upbringing than most families have toward a girl.

My father thought that, along with the things that make young ladies young ladies, they also should have some business sense. I was required to sit in on his business conferences and business deals, even at the age of three years old! My father's *quite* a person. And so is my *mother!* They are both business people. My father is in heavy railroad salvaging. My mother is president of Malvern Salvage Company in Malvern, Arkansas. [Whatley has one sibling, a younger sister.]

What is your business background?

I have been in business for myself, off and on, ever since I was eight years old when my father put me in a produce stand. My father would buy a truckload of produce and I would sell it. It was then I learned that I had to get up early and stay up late in order to show a profit!

[Whatley's first business venture as an adult was a barbecue stand which she owned and ran. She next managed a small motel operation. Then, for six years, she was a buyer for her parents' scrap and salvage companies, sometimes working "20 hours out of 24." She worked on commission and before long was buying on her own and selling to her parents. She made about $800 a month and provided for her two children. By 1966, Whatley, who was beginning to buy "little junky pieces of real estate," was knowledgeable enough to start her own scrap business.]

What is your formal education?

I was educated in Arkadelphia and at University of Arkansas in Fayetteville. I also attended Henderson State Teachers College. I was a pre-med student.

After I started the scrap business, I went back to school to study interior decoration and design. It has nothing to do with my work, but I love to study and *learn!* I am so hungry for knowledge.

How do you wear so many hats?

I am a wife, a mother, and a businesswoman. My husband sums my situation up in a little story he tells. He says, "How in the world can you watch the metal market fluctuate up and down, make or lose thousands of dollars in a day's time without batting an eyelash? But you break down and cry a heap of tears because it's the night of a P.T.A. meeting and you have a runner in your nylon *hose!*" That is my life in a nutshell.

Doris Williams

People don't want to believe and accept that a woman can be a healer. They believe that it is a man's right to do healing . . .

Shaman, bush pilot, ordained minister, abused child/concubine prisoner during World War II, Samoan-German hypnotist: all of these describe Doris Williams, the many-faceted, complex woman who functions officially as a healer in the state of Alaska.

As coordinator of village health aides for the Alaska Public Health Service, Dr. Williams—often receiving pleas for help through dreams and ESP—flies her experimental plane through the continent's most forboding weather to minister to the needs of Eskimos and Indians in remote villages. Within the framework of native Alaskans' ritual and myth, Williams applies her "Touch for Healing," employing knowledge of herbal medicine, acupuncture, and acupressure.

The unusual has long been commonplace for Doris Williams, but the fact that she has been accepted as a shaman by isolated Indians and Eskimos is, she agrees, a phenomenon. "To have a white woman accepted as a shaman," she says, "is extremely rare."

To Alaska's conservative "Anglo" population, Williams is "a freak," but to thousands of native Alaskans, she is clearly a woman of strength and vision.

I operate as a psychologist and as a naturopathic physician. The federal government defines "naturopathic physicians" as those who do not use chemicals, synthetic drugs, x-ray or mechanical type treatment. We use a combination of herbs and natural products, manipulation and utilization of muscle structure. I'm an herbologist, also a hypnotist. I'm a nurse, an R.N., and a master acupuncturist.

253

Women are unusual as naturopathic physicians?

At a national meeting of naturopathic physicians recently, there were only two other women out of 170.

Do you find it an advantage to have so many professions?

In order to actually survive in the state of Alaska, you need more than one profession. You tend to go out of your mind; it's like cabin fever. At least that's my problem. In order to have a variety, I do a number of things.

I'm also an adjunct professor for Chapman College and I teach in remote military sites where the men are put for a year—very remote places like Tent City, Point Lisbon. This extension program [of five or six week semesters] helps the military men obtain their degrees. Usually one or two semesters I teach psychology, usually "psychology of adjustment," some self-analysis and a little bit of meditation.

In addition I have a private practice which has to do with naturopathic medicine or keeping your body well. It is preventive medicine.

And I am contracted by the Native Corporations. I've been in this capacity for the last five years. We have twelve Native Corporations in Alaska. After the native people came into their own money, they began to take back their own power. In 1975 the state-operated schools were dissolved, and the native regions are now responsible for their own schools. In this package, with each region having its own money and knowing that more money will be coming because of the oil and the land rights, non-profit corporations within each region are highly motivated to produce for their people a culture—an environmental culture—that returns to that which they had originally, before the Anglo came in.

Teenagers who have gone outside for training are so ambivalent. They don't know whether they want to work outside or whether they want to return to the tribe. They're pulled because, for many of the young men, once they start fishing with their father or relative, it becomes a very strong pull to the man and to the water; it has something to do with the mythology in their religion. These young fellows return to their villages and then they realize they can make more money outside. They go back and forth. It's a totally destructive program. So they have felt that if they have their own mental health and their own, at least partial, medical facilities within the tribal concept they could do a lot better for themselves, especially if they gave status to their own health aids and credence to the older women who were doing the birthing, rather than going clear into Anchorage to the hospital. So that meant a training program and reeducation as far as the village council is concerned, so that they also would be able to accept the old ways as being as valid as the new. That has been primarily the program, and we've gotten it off the ground. It's a teetery situation.

I have been a coordinator under the Alaska Public Health Service for the village health aides. The health aides are village natives. In 1975 I had 190-some women that were health aides. That takes in four regions: Cook Inlet, the Aleuts which is the whole Aleutian Chain almost to Russia, Copper Center over by Valdez, and a portion of the Tanana Chiefs' Area—including Tetlin, Metlakatla, McGrath and Nikolai.

What is your daily job?

Right now I'm the only coordinator for the Public Health Services training village health aides. I fly all over the state.

On my daily job, I fly about 220 days out of the year to remote villages. It's very comme-ci comme-ca as to whether I can get in and out. If I schedule myself for a twenty-four hour day in a village, it's kind of laughable, because you usually get weathered in. I can't be in a hurry, because I fly a small plane.

You are a licensed pilot?

I have a twin rating and also have a single-engine rating. My oldest son, who is a mechanical engineer, built an experimental plane recently and I'm flying it as a single-engine. I started flying when I was seventeen.

I was the first person in Alaska to get a pilot's license through the "grandfather clause." It specifies that I had flown for such a long time that I did not have to take all the written examinations. There *was* a practical.

Why were you chosen as the coordinator?

I was chosen for the position because I had lived in the state a long time. I know a number of the languages. I speak Yuik and Inuk. I've lived in Alaska for thirteen years.

Why did you originally come to Alaska?

My husband and I came from Ecuador to do linguistics work in the villages. At that time I was first accepted as a shaman. The village people are very leery of a woman with any authority.

The societies within the Eskimo tribes are matriarchal, but to have a white woman accepted as a shaman is extremely rare.

What powers qualified you for shaman?

From very early childhood, I have been very well aquainted and indoctrinated with—I suppose you would call it—witchcraft. It's parapsychological aspects of the phenomenon of controlling mass—people, mass media, whatever you want to call it—by way of hypnosis, so that they are willing to walk along with you depending on their beliefs and how you go.

In Ecuador one of the things I had learned to do was to "shake the tent." If somebody has been ill and they feel they have been enveloped by an evil spirit and that nothing else can be done for them, the shaman is called. They call the witch doctor, because they feel they have gone as far as they could with their own medicine.

One of the ways of helping the whole group, so that energies of each one of them will help with healing, is the shaking of the tent.

What is the shaking of the tent?

They sit in a circle. You sit in the middle and turn rhythmically, very slowly, so you face each one of them. You begin talking about the tent that you are erecting over you, and they help you erect the energy tent. It's a psychological phenomenon. Outsiders who have watched it say they can actually see the tent. You, as the witch doctor, lay down in the tent. You put yourself into a trance. Then you begin to emit the sounds of animals that you know are respected within that tribe. The wolf is a highly respected animal. They also use him for a symbol of power. So you howl like the wolf. This is a psychological energy field that is working. Then all of a sudden, the people in the circle will see the wolf rise up out of the shaman's body. The wolf rises up and walks out of the tent; then they feel that the fever is broken. If they feel that the fever is not broken, they will not break the circle and let the wolf through.

Sometimes they know that they can do nothing, but they want a good traveling situation for the spirit leaving the body. Then, instead of leaving the circle, the wolf will go around the circle; all of a sudden they will part, and the wolf will look like he's crawling out on his belly. And the spirit has gone with him.

Why were you accepted as a shaman in Alaska?

We had been working in one village far north. We were working on the languages, and we'd been there for maybe a month. We'd gotten to know a number of the people and were very friendly with them.

A mother was very ill. She had never recovered from childbirth. They had asked for their own shaman to come from another village, but the weather did not permit, and he didn't come. So finally, my husband suggested that they allow me to do it. The chief came in and he touched my hand and he felt a positive energy flow which was complementary to him. He didn't feel any opposition. He asked me if I felt that I could do it. I said I did. That was the beginning of my notoriety as a shamaness. They have accepted me in the villages. Along with that, I have been able to minister medically to them.

Your acceptance as a shaman and your public health work must dovetail nicely?

When I come into a village as a public health officer, I'm usually totally on my own. The curriculum which I have written is being administered adequately, and it is in conjunction with what I'm doing as a shaman in helping the tribespeople. I live with the village people during my stays, rather than live in a separated place. I am accepted as part of the tribe. I'm fed like I am one of the tribespeople. And I'm never talked to like I am separate from them.

The acceptance I have received has a lot to do with my reputation as a shaman, and a lot of it has to do with the fact that I have never criticized or put down any of their beliefs. And I have traveled with them on hallucinatory travels, so they have felt that I am part of them. The fact that I was not born as an Anglo in this country helps a lot with them, too. I am half Samoan. I was born in Samoa.

What is the population of the villages?

These villages range in population from 10 to 500. There are about 680 villages now. I don't think there's a one I haven't been to. There are villages above the Arctic Circle. Mostly above the Arctic, it's Eskimo. And of the Indian tribes, we have the Ainu, the Tlingit, the Aleut, and Tanana Chiefs. The total population of native Alaskans I serve is between 7,000 and 10,000.

What is your procedure from the time you arrive in a village?

If I get a call from a village, the first thing I do is check in with the village council or a councilmember. There usually is a host and hostess within the village—either Eskimo or Indian—that have been designated to serve as a house. That means you have water, and they see that the honey bucket is emptied. There will be a bed for me in that house. I usually go there, and some of the villagers will come and get me for a specific reason.

If there is an individual that is very ill, they've usually been brought to a dispensary. A dispensary can be a village home where the woman just has a closet with first aid equipment in it, stethescope and other things.

If they're too ill to be moved, then you travel either by snowmobile or by dogsled to the individual's home.

Ritual is very important?

Each thing has to be done in a certain ritualistic way. You cannot push them. Even though an individual is very desperately ill, you must first go to the council and go through the chain of control. When you get off the plane, someone meets you, takes your luggage, maybe puts it on a snowmobile, and takes you to the council.

After you arrive at the council home, they'll offer you tea, coffee, or whatever they have hot, and you must drink it with them and discuss the illness and how the illness arrived and the point it's at now. Then there is a general discussion as to how the treatment is going to proceed, how many people we'll need and if a drummer is needed.

The drummer is a storyteller—somebody that comes with a big ring, almost like a bicycle wheel—and the skin, like the oogaluk ("the bearded seal," a walrus), is stretched across it. They brush the drum skin with their hand and tell the story. The story can be of the individual's life. He's reminding everyone of how this person has acted in the village and that they are responsible for his continuing life, to some extent. Whatever is determined necessary is brought with me to the patient's bedside. That might include a drummer.

In every village there are health aides who are trained in the basics. The Public Health Service has been the originating trainer. This is what we know as Western medicine. My part has been to help erase much of that Western medicine and return to their original Eskimo medicine, to the earth part of things. So I go into the villages for training, regular visits and emergency situations.

What are your healing techniques?

I use a very unconventional type of healing. It's called "Touch for Healing." It's the use of your own energy to get the energy of the individual moving. When you lay on your hands, you're using the meridians which are Chinese medicine. You're helping them flow faster. Meridians are what we call the life flow within the body. They run from your feet to the top of your head.

What other Oriental techniques do you use?

In what would be the Western evaluation of the patient, I take breathing and heart-tones, then I begin with the pulses. Pulses are part of Oriental medicine. That's the acupuncture system of diagnosis which uses the twelve pulses.

Then I do an akabani. Akabani is Oriental diagnosis where you're checking to see what meridians are not balanced in the body, using a five-element system. You balance the meridians. For example, if the right and left meridians are not in balance, you balance them either by using acupressure, or you use the needles themselves, or you use the moxa. The moxa is an herb which you use to heat the meridian. You make it like a little pyramid, and you put it right on the meridian point. It can be the horary point, which has to do with the peak. All the organs have a certain two-hour period out of every 24 when they are flowing more than at any other time. If the individual is being treated when he is at his peak, you use that horary point. If it's not that peak time, then you are sedating it. When you've gotten that balance, you know that the organs—or the officials within the body—can begin to pick up and correct the problem.

How does the Health Department respond to your healing techniques?

The response from the Health Department of Alaska, my employer, has always been that since I have the legal right to treat the individual I can use whatever treatment I see fit, as long as the patient accepts it.

I use medicine that is well-known to the Eskimos, like acupuncture. They're Asian. Acupuncture has been used by Eskimos for centuries. They use a bone needle and stones for the pressure point.

If the patient feels that he can be helped in a traditional system of herbs day after day and the specific exercises, then we'll use that program. If he feels that he can't recover, but the villagers feel that he has more time to spend on this earth, then we go to a conventional style of some of the antibiotics to get him back on his feet. That type of drug is just covering it up. We're not getting to the problem of what caused the debilitating situation.

The native Alaskans have what attitude toward Western medicine?

The problem has always been that the Eskimos and Indians have so much faith in Western medicine that they have made the doctors their big daddys. So their traditional approach to medicine went by the wayside. Children would be born in a village and, unless their ears ran, the adults thought something was wrong with them, because every time the doctors would come in, the running ears would be treated. They figured that if the child's ear didn't run there was something *wrong* with him.

They really came to regard the doctor as a god. Because the doctor would come in every three months, line them up 300 strong, run them through in two days, give them a shot, give them a pill, whatever they needed. And they would retain the illness until he came. Many of our children in the villages have become deaf because of that.

Now the health aides teach the people that running ears are caused by a deficiency of iron. Dr. Helen Burn, who is with the state legislature, had a grant and did a great deal with children's books for the villages. They were written by Eskimo and Indian people and were well done. She also had a film strip made. The health aides have that in the villages.

How did you learn "Touch for Healing?"

Being raised as a Samoan, acupressure was taught me from the time I was a child, within the culture. You fall and hurt your knee or something, and each child helps one another. If your nose is bleeding, you use a certain point.

The fact that Western medicine began to say, "Maybe there's something *more* to this kind of medicine" led me to become interested in the idea that maybe I could be licensed in the United States.

In some states, you can obtain a license as an acupuncturist. Nevada now has a law where you can take your exams if you have at least ten years experience. You need to have at least two years of anatomy and at least a year of chemistry, plus ten years of practice. Some people practice under another umbrella, as a pharmacist, for example. The state of California will recognize that, and if you pass the written exam, then you get your license.

Alaska is different. Alaska says you have to be an M.D. before you can have your acupuncture license.

How are you able to practice acupuncture?

I am able to practice because I have a pastoral coverage and a village coverage. The church by which I was ordained is Christ Church, a universal church which incorporates many ideas. For instance, I am a Zen master which would normally be objectionable as far as fundamental religions are concerned.

This sect has actual churches throughout the country?

Christ Church is not an organized religion in regard to having churches. Our headquarters is in Delavan, Wisconsin; from there, the ordinations and schooling and so forth are administered. We report back there quarterly, as far as what we're doing to help mankind and to help the progress of people getting back to understanding themselves rather than being so mechanized. I have a degree in theology.

The fact that I am an ordained minister has been very complementary to my work in healing. Many people in Alaska are very conservative. If you mention to someone, "Maybe you ought to go see a psychologist," they turn it off. But if you say, "*Christian* psychologist," people's response is much more positive.

What is your education?

There have been a lot of things in my education that are "different." A lot of it came as a result of challenging courses, because of the experience I have.

When my husband died, I found that the marketable abilities that I had were rather negligible, due to the fact that they were integrated mostly in the religious area. The religious order I was with at that time felt that women, as a whole, had no significance unless they had a man with them. My husband and I had been joint directors in Alaska for an evangelistic organization, but when he died, I was not regarded as an equal director. I felt very bitter about that. The injustice was very difficult. Plus I had three children to raise. [Doris Williams' children are now in their twenties. Her sons are engineers and "excellent healers" who use the laying on of hands and ESP within their family.]

I have an R.N. from Emmanuel Hospital in Portland. I had done that many years earlier. I had worked as a nurse/teacher in the bush when we were in Ecuador from 1948 to 1950. So after my husband died, I went back to school at the University of Alaska in 1967.

What led you to Ecuador?

I had been taken captive by the Japanese during the Second World War. My father felt that—coming from Samoa—we should move out when the war began. He took us up on the Malaysian peninsula, which was the wrong move. We were taken captive. I was twelve at that time. I never saw my mother and father again. I had no brothers or sisters.

How were you affected by being a prisoner of war?

The hard part was that I spent my puberty in a prison camp, which was a learning process and was destructive in very many ways. Physicially and mentally, both.

I was used as a concubine. I belonged to some of the higher officials in the Japanese government. Many times I would sit just like a child that has been thoroughly abused, in a cocoon. I was a captive for four and a half years. We were released when the United States government came in. We were in the Philippine Islands at that time. When I say "we," I mean everybody that was there and alive.

The only reason that I wanted to live was that I met a man who was about twenty years older than I. He felt there was something in that little ragged existence that wanted to live. He had been in the Bataan Death March. He really did keep his will to live. Being older, I think he could rationalize some of the things that were going on a little easier. He kind of mothered me and fathered me. When I came into California to the hospital at Alameda, I weighed 65 pounds and I was 5 foot 6 inches tall. I was almost 17.

He felt that there were a lot of things that I needed to get straight in my own head. He was not my husband then, but we contracted to be a married couple. We went to Ecuador where he felt I could be restored a lot easier. He was a key figure in the church work in Ecuador. That's how I became part of it.

My husband felt that I should go on to school. He sent me to the University of Mexico to study. I have an M.D. degree from the University of Mexico which is not recognized in the United States. Later I went to Emmanuel to take my R.N. because I thought that, at least, would be a legal aspect. I didn't have to do it so long because I could challenge a lot of courses, based on the fact that I had the background. I just had to do my internship there.

I also have 203 hours in psychology from the University of Alaska.

I took a degree in hypnosis from the Family Institute in New Orleans. The laying on of hands was part of my theology training. You begin to learn that there is a great deal of power there. I took that from Crossroads Graduate School in Farmland, Indiana. Both of these schools are accredited.

I have been teaching with the Humanistic Psychological Institute in San Francisco for two years. I am in Alaska and the students are in San Francisco, and they have to try to pick up the energies and the utilization of healing through extrasensory powers. One of the things they learn is the power of seeing auras around people.

You see auras?

I see auras. I have always seen auras. They help me with my diagnosis of an individual's ailment.

Do you use ESP?

We used ESP a great deal within our family when I was a child, and I use ESP in my work. I work with a native Alaskan we call "Doctor" because it gives her more clout with the tribe and also with the Public Health Services. Dr. Della is an older Eskimo woman. She and I agreed eight or nine years ago to communicate with each other by ESP when there were problems, because many times radio or telephone were not available when she would need help in healing or delivering a baby or when somebody had fallen into the water. She does many things that I am not proficient at and vice versa, so we complement each other. Many times she will come in a dream—a daytime dream or a nighttime dream—and I will see her visually just like she's standing in front of me. She will indicate that she wants me to come, or I will get an idea that Della needs me.

What emergencies might trigger this contact?

One of the biggest things is when men fall out of their boats when they're fishing or seal hunting. They'll fall into the water and then the body, because of the temperature of the water and the air, immediately begins to freeze and the skin begins to bubble like you've blown air into a balloon. They suffer hypothermia where the body no longer gets enough heat, and they die very rapidly unless somebody can get to them and help them. Sometimes we're successful and sometimes we're not.

If Della is already working with the person and feels that there is hope and she wants help, then I will go. Psychically I can sometimes help her retain life in that body until I can get there. Again, this is the use of extrasensory power. You're sending extra energy.

You fly a great deal. Isn't this dangerous?

When you fly in a small plane, you always take emergency gear. You have to be equipped to put down anywhere. Your plane can ice up due to the fact that the weather changes within a very short distance. We do not have radar control. We fly by the seat of our pants. You always must report where you're going and when you expect to return, so the military can hunt for you. But it's very questionable whether you would be alive if they found you, because usually you're going through a pass and, due to the weather conditions, you would hit a mountain. *Or* you would be on a glacier, and there's no way to get you off. Or you would freeze to death. So you take emergency gear.

So far, it has not been my time yet. I have had some emergency landings and had to walk out on snowshoes.

What was the worst emergency?

Probably the worst experience I ever had was when I went through Rainy Pass. It was closed at the other end; I mean the fog comes in so that you cannot detect where to come out. You have certain landmarks to watch as you go through the pass. It began to ice up. I had my de-icer on but it didn't work. I had to set the plane down, and when I set it down, I tore one of the landing gear.

I had taken with me some canned heat, and I used a lot of brush that I found around. I usually use moose brush—like hazel brush—if I have something to start it.

It was probably about 30 below zero. I had my heavy down sleeping bag, and I also wear down pants and down jacket and thermal underwear. You just keep yourself warm by not expending too much energy. That's very important.

I had radio, but there was no way to get out with it at all. We have a landing piece of equipment on the airplane that, when it's down, puts out a signal. That was working until the second day when it quit. I decided I'd have to leave the plane, because nobody had been able to come through the pass at all. I put on my snowshoes and took my skis—I have short skis—put my pack on my back and started to walk out. I knew that I had to go about 30 miles to find help.

I had a small nylon tent—just a one-man kind of thing you crawl into. I also had dry provisions with me, little packages of liquid protein; a small amount will carry you through for a day. I was on snowshoes for two days before I was spotted by a helicopter and rescued.

What is your annual income?

My income runs anywhere from $30,000 to $50,000 a year. It depends on how many private clients I have. My salary with the Public Health Services is $22,000 a year.

Exactly what service do you offer private clients?

My private clients vary. I'll do family counseling. A family will come in and say, "We would like to have a natural process of healing within our family, because we feel that we can no longer remain married like it is." Rather than take them in for counseling for an hour a day, which is kind of a sterile situation, I usually set up a yearly program with them. I will go to their home for maybe an hour or two hours twice a week. And then, I usually leave a tape recorder and I'll say, "All right, I want two or three days monitored." Sometimes I'll take the video in and have them do a video for me. Then we play it back and have the whole family look at it.

Usually it is not that there is a psychological problem but that they have a dietary problem. That's where many of the nervous and sexual problems come from. They're not eating sufficiently to have a good balance in their own bodies. Nutrition is *very, very* important.

What was the procedure when you were hired by Public Health Services?

I had to send in a resume and I was screened by the Public Health Services in Anchorage. Then I was sent over to the Native Corporation, the Cook Inlet Native Corporation which did the original hiring. When I finally received the position, I had to write letters to the other eight final applicants and six of them were men.

One of the requirements for the job was that I have a pilot's license. I have been flying close to thirty years. I started when I was seventeen in Ecuador.

Pilot's licenses are common in Alaska?

It's figured that one out of three people in Alaska owns an airplane. I would say that probably a third of those are woman pilots.

Are you well-received by caucasian Alaskans?

As far as the caucasian Alaskan population is concerned, they regard me as a freak. It really is disgusting, because if you do not fit a particular mold, you are regarded as a freak by the majority of the conservative Anglo population.

I have felt my relationships with the Anglo population to be very difficult at times, because they have been so insensitive to their abilities and to their own psychic powers, powers that *everybody* has. They were told in childhood by their parents, "That's just *not* so!" This is primarily the reason for their unreceptive attitudes.

People don't want to believe and accept that a woman can be a healer. They believe that it is a man's right to do healing; they will throw scripture at you. These people are usually the conservative element of Alaska that have to do with the churches.

There is also the feeling that ordination of a woman is wrong. Now there are three women, of which I am one, who are ordained ministers in the state of Alaska. That is all—only three.

The only reason that my job position with the Public Health Services has not been threatened is because of my *age*, I'm sure. Some people are afraid that the older woman might have a little more power.

But I have never had any problem with being accepted by the native Alaskans [Eskimos and Indians].

What is the attitude of Anglos toward Eskimos and Indians?

Those Anglos in Alaska that don't understand feel that the native Alaskans are lazy and without motivation. They don't want to listen to the truth. The only way that I can communicate the truth to them is to try to relate some of the things that have happened to me in the villages where I have been so totally accepted.

One example I use is a young girl who was married to a native man in a village. She is an Eskimo girl who had learned to read and write because she was in a type of foundling home—her mother had left her. Her husband didn't read and write, so she became the administrator in a little community store out at Platinum, which is a village. His folks primarily owned the village and were the main people in the village.

When Martha had her first baby, she had like a poisoning. She was kind of out of her mind at times during her pregnancy. Because the family didn't understand that condition, they thought she was mad and she was chained with the dogs. The Public Health worker came in and tried to explain that Martha was only temporarily ill. They didn't understand that. Martha was taken to the Public Health Hospital in Anchorage. Then, because of lack of communication between the Anglos and the Eskimos, Martha was moved, after her baby was born, to the Psychiatric Hospital, and her baby was put up for adoption.

At that point, I met Martha. Martha wanted to keep her baby. Because of some of the things that are done with people that are retarded or that they think are not adequate to reproduce again, Martha was given a paper to sign and she was sterilized. She believed they wanted to help her, and so she signed the form.

In the meantime, they were ready to take her baby away. I went to court with Martha so that she could keep her baby. Her last name is the same as mine. And when we went to court, the judge asked, "Are you sisters?" Martha said, "*Yes!*" And when she said that, the judge said, "You may *keep* your baby." The judge recognized the fact that Martha felt that we had a relationship that would be educational and helpful for both of us.

The baby was returned to Martha, and she was turned over to a social worker. The social worker condemned Martha's method of rearing her child which was the native way of spoiling the child totally.

I received a great deal of criticism because of my role with Martha and the child. I experienced *intense* criticism from the Public Health Service, too, due to the fact that I raised a big stink about the process of sterilization. Not only is it automatic, but the individual's rights are taken away because the native woman is not really told, not informed of what's being done. The native is often treated like an ignorant animal that has *absolutely* no use. And the Anglo population really is not interested.

The village that probably had the most interesting case was Tatpileikta where there was a woman who had a number of abdominal tumors that began to grow. The tumors were created by a psychological attitude that became a physiological problem, so the correction had to be first physiological and then psychological. The tumors were created because of her attitude toward her husband and his family. She had a lot of aggravation which caused a lot of acid. She didn't want to get pregnant, and every time she conceived a child, she would spew it out in an abortive type thing. Each time she did that, another little polyp grew in her uterus. The more times she became pregnant and aborted by thinking, "I don't want the child," the meaner and more ornery she became with her family. Her husband kept asking me to come, by extrasensory powers. I went.

The first thing the women did when she saw me was run into the bushes. She kept saying, "I don't want to see you. I know what you're going to do!" She didn't want help, although she knew she needed it.

Her husband and I talked and held a type of council. Finally the woman came out. She had begun to bleed vaginally and was very frightened at the profuse amount of blood. I said, "Well, let me help you." She didn't know whether she wanted to be helped or not. We discussed the fact that if she were going to kill herself, she might have to return and do the whole process over again. They believe in reincarnation. We talked about how she might have to return as something other than herself, and she wasn't very happy about *that*. So we decided I would help her.

They had killed some caribou in the village, and they had kept the entrails. I had some bladders brought to me. I split a clean bladder and laid it over the top of her abdomen, and I began to work with her, with just the energy of my hands, moving them so that the polyps or tumors began to separate within the uterus and began to come down one at a time. I continued to move my hands, and then all of a sudden she coughed. When she coughed, she expelled a big clot of blood, probably as big as my fist. Seven of those benign lumps that she had helped build came out. She accepted the responsibility for those growths, too, and she was cured.

Using the bladder of a particular animal also establishes the relationship with the animal—the caribou—which is the sustainer of life. She'll remember that bladder the next time she harbors those feelings again. She also takes that bladder and hangs it up to dry, and it's a symbol for her.

Understanding the mythology is instrumental in your work?

I have to work within their myths. And many of their myths are almost parallel with the Christian religion, with some of the Buddhist thought, with the Bhagavad-Gita. There really is a tie in between them all. The classic example, of course, is the Flood.

A Celtic Legend, related by David Guard and illustrat-
en Guard, is a beautiful retelling of a 2,000 year old
ing love, jealousy, courage and subterfuge. The lyric
 prose and the expressive drawings are outstanding.
ft cover, $4.95

LK TALES by Louise and Yuan Hsi Kuo is a fresh
 translation of traditional stories from the Chinese
ealing new and fascinating aspects of their culture
sons for much of the conflict occurring during their
 years of history. 176 pages, soft cover, $4.95

stoms and Culture by Duane Rubin is not a travel
 introduction to the exotic customs which make
 exciting country to foreigners. Rubin describes
eir customs, traditions and culture. 128 pages,
.95

 by Randolph Falk depicts the efforts of a unique
nily to seek out, research and recreate the art,
tuals of the "People of the Salmon and Cedar," the
dian of the northwest. Illustrated with more than
aphs. 144 pages, soft cover, $7.95

 Randolph Falk is an intimate portrait of one of
ost controversial artists, Beniamino Bufano. Su-
aphs in this comprehensive view of the man some
 and others called charlatan. This is a unique work,
llery. 144 pages, soft cover, $7.95

your local book or department store or directly from
r. To order by mail, send check or money order to:

s
Road
 94030

e $1.00 for postage and handling. California residents

EVERYWOMAN'S GUIDE SERIES

The immediate success of EVERYWOMAN'S GUIDE TO COLLEGE clearly illustrated the demand for information by women who are re-entering society at every level. We are attempting to meet that need with a major, continuing series of books modeled on the GUIDE TO COLLEGE format. These are books on

SUBJECTS THAT ARE TIMELY, of particular concern to women, about which information is not readily available elsewhere, that provide
COMPREHENSIVE COVERAGE, with emphasis on practical, useful, widely applicable or adaptable information, with
SOURCES OF ADDITIONAL INFORMATION in a separate chapter listing relevant publications, courses, organizations and knowledgeable people, and they are
REASONABLY PRICED so that every woman can afford them.

EVERYWOMAN'S GUIDE T
Eileen Gray
176 pages

A logical, no-nonsense study
realities of the returning wor
on how to finance yourself i
outlook for the woman colle

EVERYWOMAN'S GUIDE T
Phyllis Butler and Dorothy
128 pages

This is a fact-filled handbook
introduction to institutional
itical structure, types of activ
how to get involved, basic do
paign, and much much more.

EVERYWOMAN'S GUIDE T
Mavis Arthur Groza
144 pages

Rich or poor, single or marrie
to handle finances are answere
It covers investing, budgeting,
saving and security, as well as
programs affecting the monet

EVERYWOMAN'S GUIDE TO
Peggy Granger
128 pages

This practical guide presents a
analysis to I Ching to humanis
interviews with women who h
into practical and meaningful

EVERYWOMAN'S GUIDE TO
Donna Goldfein
128 pages

A back-to-basics, step-by-step
housewife or profession—who
tine and wants to take charge